Phyllis Chesler is an associate professor of psychology, a lecturer, a custody consultant and psychotherapist in New York. Well-known feminist and activist, she is the author of several books including the much-acclaimed *Women and Madness*; *About Men*; *With Child*; and *Mothers on Trial: The Battle for Children and Custody*. She lives in New York.

In *Sacred Bond* Phyllis Chesler uses the celebrated 'Baby M' case to take an incisive look at contemporary attitudes to the family. Surrogacy is seen as a potent symbol of broader social problems of economic inequality and the denigration of motherhood. This polemical text demands a radical rethinking of the attitudes of a society which will allow the idea of fatherhood to overcome the fact of motherhood.

'A powerful critique of the way many of us were inclined to think'
– *The New York Times Book Review*

Some people believe that contracts are sacred; others believe that family ties constitute sacred bonds. Still others believe that mother–infant bonding in utero and/or immediately after birth are sacred bonds. The title refers to all of these beliefs.

SACRED BOND

THE LEGACY OF BABY M

Phyllis Chesler

Introduction by Ann Oakley

VIRAGO

Published by VIRAGO PRESS Limited 1990
20–23 Mandela Street, Camden Town, London NW1 0HQ

First published in USA by Times Books, New York 1988

*A CIP Catalogue record for this book is available from the
British Library*

Printed in Great Britain by Cox & Wyman Ltd, Reading, Berkshire

To Ariel Chesler

CONTENTS

Acknowledgments   viii

Introduction by Ann Oakley   ix

CHAPTER 1
The Creation Assignment   3

CHAPTER 2
On Civilization and its Discontents:
A Meditation   19

CHAPTER 3
Industrialized Pregnancy:
A Decade of Surrogacy   51

CHAPTER 4
Journal of a Brief Campaign, 1987   71

CHAPTER 5
A Pound of Flesh:
Surrogacy, Adoption, and Contracts   109

CHAPTER 6
The Verdict, 1988   147

Epilogue   165

Appendices   167

Notes   205

ACKNOWLEDGMENTS

The author would like to acknowledge the following people for their invaluable assistance: Sim Ariel, Mary Marshall Clarke, Patricia DeRosa, Peter Kimball, Judith Kuppersmith, Elaine Markson, Ruby Rohrlich, Ilana Rubenfeld, Elisabeth Scharlatt, Alison Ward, Bill Weinberg.

INTRODUCTION

The issues raised by Phyllis Chesler in this thoughtful and passionate book are among the most fundamental and urgent of our time. They also remain largely unresolved. As Chesler ably demonstrates here, the efforts so far made by governmental, legal and medical agencies to achieve a resolution constitute part of the problem itself. Whatever the essential meanings of motherhood are, they cannot be spelt out by male-dominated professional agencies claiming technical and legal power as the basis of their jurisdiction, and maintaining a critical social distance from those they judge: mothers – women – themselves.

The social study of gender has long told us that women are a problem for any male-dominated social order. The main reason for this is the uneven balance of social relations deriving from the biology of parenthood. Worldwide, and throughout history, motherhood has involved far more than fatherhood in terms of risk and commitment, more in terms of physical labour, energy and endurance. Fatherhood can be incidental – even unknown – in the life of a man, but motherhood is virtually never so for a woman. This remains true even within the newly-technological scenarios surrounding reproduction in modern industrial societies. But to speak of women's relationship to reproduction as inherently different from men's is at the same time fraught with dangers of its own. Another lesson we have learnt from the study of gender in different social systems is the need to avoid anything that resembles an appeal to biology as an unchangeable imperative driving human behaviour. 'Women mother', as Nancy Chodorow puts it.[1] But how they do so, with what consequences to themselves and others, and within what counterpointing framework of paternal rights and obligations, can vary a great deal from one culture to another.

The case of Baby M presented in this book can be read as one attempt to force the meaning of motherhood out of this context of cultural flexibility, and into one in which it is defined in a highly specific and limiting way. At the heart of the Baby M case are questions about women's rights as the biological mothers of children. The central problem the case illustrates is that these rights cannot be defined without a position being taken on what motherhood itself *is*. In a patriarchal society, the conclusion is then foregone: motherhood will be something that it suits men to say it is.

Among the recent social processes without which the case of Baby M would not have arisen as it did are the following: increasing social recognition of men not only as breadwinning, but as participatory fathers on the level of everyday domestic care; the colonization of parenthood, and especially of motherhood, by professionals; the definition of pregnancy, childbirth and, indeed, womanhood as disease processes; the increasing arbitration by the legal profession of delicate and troublesome human issues; the deficiency of the modern State in limiting professional power generally; the proliferation of uncontrolled and unevaluated technology at all levels of society; and, last but most fundamental of all, the continuation of socially structured inequality between genders, classes and ethnic groups, according to which women remain second-class citizens.

If women are a problem for society, then men are a problem for women. Somewhat paradoxically, it seems that men become more, not less, problematic whenever the political impetus of feminism plots a less gender-divided world. As Chesler observes in this book, twentieth-century feminism can now be seen as in some sense hoist with its own petard in regarding increased male participation in childrearing as a gain for women. Those of us who were involved in women's liberation consciousness-raising groups in the late sixties and early seventies remember how men's attitudes to the domestic division of labour dominated the dialogue: Pat Mainardi's paper on the 'Politics of Housework' ('The measure of your oppression is his resistance') described for many of us the most painful of private facts.[2] As a result of the anger unleashed some fathers began to understand, for a time, that parenthood is not just a title on a birth certificate. But by and large no long-term shift in parenting practices occurred: there's no evidence that fathers in the late 1980s are really doing more for their children than their own did for them.[3]

Why should men change? Children and childcare work are only valued as ideals. Bringing up children is relentless, socially and financially unrewarded work, and the status of childrearer (mother/'just a housewife') not one any man 'in his right (i.e. patriarchal) mind' wishes to emulate.

None of this is to say, of course, that there was anything intrinsically wrong with the feminist aspiration to encourage more active fathering. The problem lies in the invalid assumption on which equal parenthood rests, namely that men and women are able to live in harmony with one another. Much evidence shows that such conflicts remain endemic. Divorce rates continue to increase, male violence against women is almost an institution in its own right,[4] heterosexual relationships are painfully described as reservoirs of emotional inadequacy.[5]

The twentieth-century ethic of intimacy between man and woman is hard to realize in practice. The sole exception is probably the stage of falling in love, but the prototype here is not heterosexual domestic stability; significantly for the issues discussed by Chesler in this book, it is, rather, the highly charged and powerfully nascent state existing between a mother and her newly born child.[6] The description in *Sacred Bond* of baby Sara/Melissa's enforced removal from the breast at the instigation of her genetic father by judge, lawyers and police is not only a dramatically distressing instance of patriarchal power, but an episode serving to highlight the emotionally intense image of the biological unit of mother-and-child – enclosed, self-sufficient, mutually gratifying, a happy sanctuary where we would all like to be. The capacity of this unit to evoke envy and hostility has been seriously underestimated. How many women, for example, enraptured by the early bond with a newborn baby, have personally experienced veiled – or unveiled – hostility from the fathers of their children? As Adrienne Rich has shown, insofar as the experience of motherhood can be reduced to simple formulae at all, it may be summed up as resistance to male power on the one hand, and expression of human feeling on the other.[7] Fatherhood is about power, not about the loss of power, and this is another aspect of parenthood that is demonstrated acutely in the Baby M case. Threatened with separation from 'his' child, Baby M's genetic father, William Stern, is not able to relinquish the power he wields by virtue of his male, professional, class position in the interests of the child, which are here enmeshed with those of her birth mother.

It is significant that one of the experts who offered to give evidence for the birth mother in the Baby M case was paediatrician Marshall Klaus, widely regarded as the world expert on mother–infant bonding. The invention and technical labelling since the 1960s of the postnatal relationship of birth mothers with their babies[8] is one manifestation of the need for a patriarchal social order to get motherhood under control. Recognition of the existence and intensity of mothers' attachment to their babies isn't enough: the emotion must be named and organized, become the subject of experimentation and of bureaucratic rules.[9] Significantly its inventors are men, figures in a long line of male experts on women, some of whom have been motivated by genuinely humanitarian impulses that have benefited women, while others have had frankly misogynist attitudes, and have been concerned to perpetrate an ideology of women's incompetence and essential opposition to children's interests.[10]

Patriarchal ideology, it seems, can relate women and children only in two ways. Either women are seen as the same as children: vulnerable, in need of protection, naive, innocent and incapable of the same standards of adult behaviour as men; or women are seen as antagonistic to children, and particularly as unable to act in their best interests. Over the last thirty years this latter view has increasingly prevailed, to the extent that legal injunctions are now served on pregnant women who do not readily consent to medical or surgical procedures being imposed on them, or who deviate from medical advice in not seeking prenatal care at the requisite intervals, take non-prescription drugs, smoke, drink, have sexual intercourse, or otherwise demonstrate their competence to choose their own individual life-styles. If men can sue their wives for taking drugs in pregnancy that discolour their son's teeth, it seems there is no limit to maternal culpability (or paternal vindictiveness). Indeed, it has already been established that pregnant women can be jailed and criminally prosecuted for failing to follow doctors' orders.[11] Needless to say, the same is not true for doctors who fail to follow women's.[12]

The implication of these attempts to construct the fetus as a person whose interests can be better represented by fathers, lawyers and doctors than by the woman giving it life are enormous, profound and totally abhorrent to anyone with any concern for the promotion of a society organized around caring human relations, let alone the pursuit of one which values more than a notional form of women's entitlement to self-determination. 'Fetalist' and 'feminist' are not necessarily conflicting terms, though as Janice Raymond has argued, one critical difference inheres in the relationship perceived between the female self and the female body.[13] Fetalists see the woman's body as 'owned' (usually by others), feminists note an equivalence between body and identity: 'Our Bodies Ourselves', as the Boston Women's Health Collective put it.

The legal enforcement of professionally arbitrated standards for motherhood becomes an even more bizarre phenomenon when considered in the light of the status of professional 'knowledge'. The contractual agreement signed by Mary Beth Whitehead, Baby M's mother, for instance, commits her to a schedule for medical prenatal care which has never been shown to have any scientific basis whatsoever. That is, it has never been established that visits to a physician/hospital/midwife at monthly intervals to the twenty-eighth week, then fortnightly until thirty-six weeks and weekly thereafter, is the safest and most effective way of organizing prenatal professionalized health care. Indeed, the whole edifice of routine medical surveillance of pregnant women rests on an untested assumption that this form of health care is the best way to promote maternal and infant wellbeing. On the contrary, evidence has long suggested that the eradication of poverty and material disadvantage and the provision of social support for women, together with better education, employment and out-of-home childcare opportunities, would much better tackle the large residuum that exists, even in the affluent capitalist nations, of preventable death, disease, discomfort and distress.[14] To the extent that issues of the kind raised by the Baby M case concern reproductive technology *per se*, they are not seen to be about the need to subject such technology to proper scientific evaluation. We are, rather, in the midst of a moral panic which by its very nature countermands women's wishes for recognition as women.

Social and economic parameters of women's position as mothers are underlined with a particular cogency in 'surrogate' mother cases, and language itself is, as always, inherently judgmental. Stanworth has pointed out that a woman who gestates a child which she will hand over to someone else can only be considered 'surrogate' if pregnancy itself is not an act of mothering,[15] which most women would consider it to be. But the view of women as ambulant uteri has the weight of history on its side.

Many women who undertake 'surrogacy' do so because of the money involved, despite the fact that it isn't particularly well-paid. Chesler points out that, on the assumption that a surrogate mother is paid for her gestational and delivery labours rather than for the child (which *would* be illegal) then her rate of pay contravenes legal minimum pay agreements. In the Baby M case, even the lawyer, who needed to do rather little, was to receive 75 per cent of the fee paid to the mother.

Prior to the question of surrogate mothers' rate of pay is an earlier question about the commercialization of surrogacy itself. Here the argument resonates with other debates about the commercialization of sex and housework. Within marriage, women provide both in return for financial support. The wages for housework campaign of the early seventies drew attention to this contradiction in the most conventional of all formulae for womanhood. Whether or not women's rights include the right to treat their bodies as commodities to be exchanged for money, any such practice will reflect the low value attached to women. Surrogate mothers aren't paid much; neither are housewives. Even 'professional working' women can expect the operation of the double standard to prevent them reaching a position where equal pay with men is possible.

Beyond that, the Baby M case is about the ways in which the human body under capitalism can become just another commodity. Blood can be sold, and semen, or breastmilk; organs can be donated for money. The moral and medical dangers of such commercially based transfer systems have been known for a long time.[16] Where the fetus itself becomes a commodity fetish the implications are more, not less, far-reaching, for the subject of the commercial transaction becomes potentially a human being.

William Stern and his wife Betsy were desperate to have a child of their own. Such desperation is traded on by pioneers of in vitro fertilization (IVF) programmes, who are able to enhance their moral status by appearing as saviours. This preoccupation with procreation as an end in itself conceals the causes of the problem of this 'desperation' to 'have' children, two of which are involuntary medically-caused infertility and the enormous, destructive social pressure which still exists to become something which does not exist – a 'normal family'.

Because infertility is a difficult subject to study – there are, for example, no national statistics on it – it is impossible to say whether or not its incidence has increased. We do know, however, that all the major contraceptive innovations of the twentieth century have caused as well as solved reproductive problems. Post-pill sterility is a recognized phenomenon: so is sterility caused by intra-uterine contraceptive devices (IUCD). Diethystilboestrol as a form of hormonal contraceptive has known generational effects on both female and male fertility. The decline in use of barrier methods of contraception also makes transmission of infections which cause sterility more likely. While the contribution of environmental and other hazards to loss of reproductive potential is probably substantial, the effects of these cannot as yet be quantified. Research on the causes of infertility and the provision of medical services for infertile individuals are hardly top of the health care agenda; the glamour and the money attach themselves instead to hazardous, high cost, low effectiveness IVF programmes.

Such programmes do not exist to help women to become mothers but rather to aid couples to achieve the goal of becoming and being a family. Surrogacy cases are embedded in traditional family life morality – something which this book demonstrates over and over again. The same observation can be made about the official books and reports in various countries which have considered the implications of new reproductive arrangements. The Warnock report in the UK, for instance, which stood as a model for many others, is deeply heterosexist and committed to a view of children and marriage as morally necessary to one another.[17] Such metaphors crop up in the most unlikely places; in the Baby M case Mary Beth, the birth mother, criticizes Betsy, the adoptive mother, for not being a proper mother because she employs a nanny to look after the baby. But despite this ideological deviation, William and Betsy together with baby Sara/Melissa are seen to constitute a family in a way that Mary Beth, her husband and other children, and baby Sara/Melissa are not. The contrast deserves thought. It's not an argument about genetics, for the putative 'real' family, the Sterns, contains the same amount of the baby's genetic material – half – as the disenfranchised family. What is it an argument about, then? Betsy Stern is a different kind of woman from Mary Beth Whitehead. She hasn't done anything as independent and/or as degrading as Mary Beth. Even where Mary Beth does fall into line – she bonded with her baby, which ought to be a mark in her favour – she's told she shouldn't have done, because she wasn't supposed to let her feelings get the better of her. Betsy Stern conformed and Mary Beth Whitehead didn't: that's one difference. The other one is that not everyone's genes are equal: some genes are more equal than others. Particularly men's.

Margaret Mead once observed that the recurrent problem of civilization is to define the male role satisfactorily enough for men.[18] A prominent British male gynaecologist was once shocked to discover that 30 per cent of babies in a sample population whose blood groups he was studying couldn't have been the children of their mothers' husbands – though this biological fact was not apparently recognized by any of the families themselves.[19] Artificial insemination is one way of knowing what's going on. In vitro fertilization is an even better way. We come back, in short, to the point made at the beginning. The drawing up by men of contracts arbitrating women's behaviour during the reproductive process belongs to the same category of attempts to control what it is feared is out of control – women. Chesler's contrasting of the fact of motherhood with the idea of fatherhood expresses it well. Patriarchy needs somehow to institute fatherhood as indisputable fact, and in complementary fashion to render motherhood a matter of ideas – about what children really need, about who mothers are, about which women can be considered 'fit' mothers and which unfit, about the secret, raw and therefore antisocial interior of the sacred *and* profane bond between mother and child.

'Where were you the day we decided to put biological motherhood on the line?' interrogates Chesler. In the Baby M case, feminist opposition to the primacy of paternal custody and support for the rights of the birth mother succeeded in changing the final decision. But there will be many more such cases, and it will take much concerted thought and action before women's interests as mothers achieve proper representation in child custody cases. The overarching threat to women is, 'If they take reproduction from us what do they want next?' And the realization that this is what it's about enables us unimaginative Britons, as Jalna Hanmer has said, finally to understand the real meaning of the worst swear word in the American lexicon – 'motherfucker'.[20]

Ann Oakley, London, 1989

NOTES

1. Nancy Chodorow, *The Reproduction of Mothering*, University of California Press, Berkeley, California, 1978.

2. Pat Mainardi, 'The Politics of Housework' in Robin Morgan (ed.), *Sisterhood is Powerful*, Vintage Books, New York, 1970.

3. See Charles Lewis and Margaret O'Brien (eds.), *Reassessing Fatherhood*, Sage Publications, London, 1987.

4. See Jalna Hanmer and Mary Maynard (eds.), *Women, Violence and Social Control*, Macmillan, London, 1987.

5. See Lillian B. Rubin, *Worlds of Pain*, Basic Books, New York, 1976.

6. Francesco Alberoni, *Falling in Love*, Random House, New York, 1983.

7. Adrienne Rich, *Of Woman Born*, Virago, London, 1977.

8. See Marshall H. Klaus and John H. Kennell, *Mother–Infant Bonding*, C. V. Mosby, St Louis, 1976.

9. This argument is developed further in Ann Oakley, 'Feminism, Motherhood and Medicine – who cares?' in Juliet Mitchell and Ann Oakley (eds.), *What is Feminism?*, Blackwells, Oxford, 1986.

10. See Frederic Leboyer, *Birth Without Violence*, Fontana, London, 1977, for the violence in Leboyer's images of women.

11. Janet Gallagher, 'The Fetus and the Law – whose life is it anyway?' in *MS Magazine*, September 1984.

12. Raymond DeVries in *Regulating Birth*, Temple University Press Philadelphia, 1985, discusses the highly significant differences between doctors and midwives in this respect.

13. Janice Raymond, 'Fetalists vs Feminists: they are not the same', conference paper *Liberation or Loss? Women act on the new reproductive technologies*, Canberra, Australia, May 1986.

14. See Ann Oakley, *The Captured Womb*, Blackwells, Oxford, 1984.

15. Michelle Stanworth, 'The Deconstruction of Motherhood' in Michelle Stanworth (ed.), *Reproductive Technologies*, Polity Press, Cambridge, 1987.

16. Richard M. Titmuss, *The Gift Relationship*, Allen and Unwin, London, 1970.

17. Department of Health and Social Security, *Report of the Committee of Inquiry into Human Fertilisation and Embryology* (Warnock Report), H.M.S.O., London, 1984.

18. Margaret Mead, *Male and Female*, Penguin, Harmondsworth, 1962.

19. Elliot Phillipp, *Ciba Foundation Symposium 17* (new series), Elsevier, Amsterdam, 1973.

20. Jalna Hanmer, 'Reproduction Trends and the Emergence of Moral Panic', *Social Science and Medicine*, vol. 25, no. 6 (1987) pp. 697–704.

SACRED
BOND

CHAPTER 1

THE
CREATION
ASSIGNMENT

On February 6, 1985, Mary Beth Whitehead, a twenty-eight-year-old housewife and the mother of an eleven-year-old boy and a nine-year-old girl, signed a pre-conception or surrogate-parenting contract with lawyer Noel Keane's Infertility Center of New York (ICNY).

The Agreement provided that she (the "Surrogate") would not smoke, drink, or take any drugs during pregnancy; that she would assume any and all medical risks—including death—and that she would submit to amniocentesis and/or abortion upon the demand of thirty-eight-year-old biochemist Bill Stern (the "Natural Father") and his wife, thirty-eight-year-old physician Betsy Stern.

Mary Beth was to receive no compensation if, after trying, she failed to conceive; one thousand dollars if she miscarried or gave birth to a stillborn; and ten thousand dollars if she gave birth to Bill's healthy baby—and legally surrendered custody to him, i.e., if she signed the adoption papers. Noel Keane was to receive seven thousand five hundred dollars for his services. Thus, the Sterns were to pay a minimum of seventeen thousand five hundred dollars, "plus all medical expenses not covered by [Mary Beth's] present health insurance," so that Betsy could legally adopt Bill's genetic child.

On April 26, 1984, ten months before the Sterns selected Mary Beth from a photograph, ICNY's own psychologist, Dr. Joan Ein-

3

wohner, had written that she was concerned about Mary Beth's "tendency to deny feelings." Dr. Einwohner "thought it would be important to explore with [Mary Beth] in somewhat more depth whether [Mary Beth] will be able to relinquish the child at the end. [Mary Beth's] husband Rick [a Vietnam Veteran and sanitation worker] has had a vasectomy. [Mary Beth] may have more needs to have another child than she is admitting." The Sterns were not informed about Dr. Einwohner's concerns.

Inseminations began the same day in February that the Sterns and the Whiteheads signed the contract. Bill drove Mary Beth in to ICNY from New Jersey. Mary Beth was inseminated. They repeated this procedure nine times until, in July 1985, Mary Beth became pregnant. Betsy decorated the Stern bathroom with pink and blue party streamers. In August, the Sterns bequeathed the bulk of their estate to the six-week-old fetus.

In November 1985, Bill and Betsy wanted Mary Beth to undergo an amniocentesis test. The Sterns did not want a defective child. Mary Beth did not want amniocentesis but felt she had to allow it because of her contractual obligations. In addition, she developed phlebitis and was bedridden for three weeks. Having to take the test made her angry and she refused to disclose the child's sex to the Sterns. Now, Mary Beth also changed her mind about allowing the Sterns to be present at the birth.

On March 27, 1986, accompanied by her husband, Mary Beth gave birth to a daughter—whom she thought looked just like herself. Instantly Mary Beth knew that she'd made a mistake, that she couldn't abandon or sell her own flesh and blood, that she must keep and raise her child. Mary Beth and Richard named the baby Sara Elizabeth Whitehead and, as required by law, filed the birth certificate in their own names. (A husband is automatically the legal father of all his wife's children whether she becomes pregnant by him, by artificial insemination, or by adulterous intercourse.)

According to Mary Beth, she called Noel Keane from the hospital and informed him of her change of heart. He reportedly assured her that "the Sterns might want visitation rights, at the very least." Mary Beth said she would not object to this. She began breast-feeding Baby Sara.

Mary Beth refused to take the ten thousand dollars or to sign the adoption papers. She took Sara home and baptized her in the Catholic Church.

On March 30, Easter Sunday, three days after she delivered, the by-now distraught Sterns pressured Mary Beth into letting them have the baby. After a sleepless and agitated night, Mary Beth implored the Sterns to give her baby back to her. Moved by her suffering, they did so. From that day on, Mary Beth refused to part from Sara. On April 12, 1986, after many phone conversations, Mary Beth finally informed the Sterns that she could not surrender Sara to them.

The Sterns hired a lawyer, Gary Skoloff, who sought court intervention. On May 5, 1986, when Sara had already been breast-feeding for forty days, Judge Harvey Sorkow issued an ex parte order granting the Sterns sole custody immediately, on the grounds that Mary Beth was allegedly "mentally unstable," i.e., *she couldn't give Sara up!* The Sterns believed that Mary Beth was so "mentally unstable" that she might even exercise her constitutional right to move elsewhere. Sorkow issued his custody order without interviewing Mary Beth and without giving her a chance to hire a lawyer.

On the evening of May 5, the Sterns, accompanied by the police, arrived at the Whitehead home with an order for "Melissa Elizabeth Stern" (the name the Sterns had picked for Bill's genetic child). The Whiteheads showed them the birth certificate, which identified Mary Beth's biological and her husband Rick's legal child as "Sara Elizabeth Whitehead." Then Mary Beth went into the bedroom and passed the baby out the window to Rick. When the police discovered that the baby was gone, they handcuffed Mary Beth and led her into the back seat of the squad car. The police, with no legal basis for arresting her, released her. Within twenty-four hours, Mary Beth and her family fled to Florida and took refuge with her parents, Catherine and Joseph Messer.

Bill knew that Mary Beth was hiding somewhere in Florida. She kept calling him in distress. Judge Sorkow had frozen the Whitehead bank account. Rick and Mary Beth had run out of money; the bank was about to foreclose on the mortgage to their New Jersey home. On July 15, Bill taped the following conversation:

> *MARY BETH: Bill, you think you got all the cards. You think you could do this to people. You took my house. I mean, we don't even have a car anymore. I can't even afford the car payments. You took everything away from me. Because I*

couldn't give up my child? Because I couldn't give up my flesh and blood, you have the right to do what you did?

BILL: I didn't freeze your assets. The judge froze your assets. He wants you in court. I want my daughter back.

MARY BETH: And I want her, too, so what do we do, cut her in half?

BILL: No, no, we don't cut her in half.

MARY BETH: You want me, you want me to kill myself and the baby?

BILL: No, that's why I gave her to you in the first place, because I didn't want you to kill yourself.

MARY BETH: I didn't anticipate any of this. You know that. I'm telling you from the bottom of my heart. I never anticipated any of it. Bill, please, stop it. Please do something to stop this.

BILL: What can I do to stop it, Mary Beth?

MARY BETH: Bill, I'll let you see her. You can have her on weekends. Please stop this.

BILL: Oh, God. I can live with you visiting. I can live with that, but I can't live with her having a split identity between us. That'll hurt her.

MARY BETH: What's the difference if I visit or you visit? I've been breast-feeding her for four months. Don't you think she's bonded to me?

BILL: I don't know what she's done, Mary Beth.

MARY BETH: She's bonded to me, Bill. I sleep in the same bed with her. She won't even sleep by herself. What are you going to do when you get this kid that's screaming and carrying on for her mother?

BILL: I'll be her father. I'll be a father to her. I am her father.

MARY BETH: Bill, she knows my smell, she knows who I am. You cannot deny that. Don't I count for anything? Nine months I gave life to this baby. If it wasn't for me, Bill, she wouldn't even be here.

BILL: That's true. She wouldn't be here if it weren't for me either.

MARY BETH: Oh, come on, Bill, it's a little bit different.

BILL: No. I want my daughter back.

MARY BETH: Well, Bill, how about if there's no daughter to get back?

BILL: *What do you mean by "no daughter to get back"?*

MARY BETH: *I took care of myself the whole nine months. I didn't take any drugs. I didn't drink alcohol. I ate good. And that's the only reason that she's healthy, Bill. I gave her life. I did. I had the right during the whole pregnancy to terminate it, didn't I Bill?*

BILL: *It was your body.*

MARY BETH: *That's right. It was my body, and now you're telling me that I have no right.*

BILL: *Because you made an agreement. You signed an agreement.*

MARY BETH: *Forget it, Bill. I'll tell you right now I'd rather see me and her dead before you get her.*

BILL: *Don't, Mary Beth, please don't do—*

MARY BETH: *I'm going to do it, Bill. You've pushed me to it. I gave her life. I can take her life away. If that's what you want, that's what I'll do.*

BILL: *No, Mary Beth, no, Mary Beth, wait, wait. Please.*

MARY BETH: *You've pushed me.*

BILL: *Please don't—I don't want to see you hurt. I don't want to see my daughter hurt.*

MARY BETH: *My daughter too. Why don't you quit doing that, Bill, okay? It's our daughter. Why don't you say it, "our daughter"?*

BILL: *All right, our daughter. Okay, Mary Beth, our daughter.*

MARY BETH: *That's right. Bill, I can't live like this anymore.*

BILL: *Please, Mary Beth, please.*

MARY BETH: *Please forgive me. Tell Betsy to please forgive me. Tell Betsy that I always really cared about you two.*

BILL: *Where are you Mary Beth? Please, Mary Beth, don't hang up.*

MARY BETH: *I'm sorry, I'm sorry. Good-bye Bill.*

On July 28, 1986, when Mary Beth was hospitalized in Florida with a severe infection, Sara had already been breast-feeding for four months or 123 days. On July 31, while the Sterns waited at the police station, detectives armed with an order for Melissa entered Catherine Messer's home. They allegedly knocked the grandmother down, took

Sara from her crib, and pushed away her older sister, Tuesday, who was screaming and hitting an officer on the leg with a hairbrush.

Judge Sorkow did not permit Sara and Mary Beth to see each other for five and a half weeks. Sara was weaned that day by the police, per Judge Sorkow's order. Then, in mid-September, he allowed Sara to see her mother twice a week, for an hour each time. He forbade Sara to breast-feed. The visits took place in a state institution, in a room approximately twelve-by-fourteen feet with an armed guard and a nurse matron in constant attendance. Sara was not permitted to see her half-sister Tuesday, her half-brother Ryan, or her legal father, Rick, except for two hours at Christmas and for three hours on March 29, 1987.

A year after Mary Beth gave birth, ten and one-half months after Sorkow first awarded temporary custody to the Sterns, eight months after his order went into effect, and seven months after a stressful public trial, the judge upheld his own ex parte order of May 5, 1986. On March 31, 1987, Sorkow terminated Mary Beth's parental rights, not because she was in any way unfit but in the "best interests" of the child. He legalized the surrogacy contract, gave permanent custody to the Sterns, and allowed Betsy Stern to legally adopt Baby M, "Melissa Elizabeth Stern."

Who is a child's true mother? The woman who gives birth to her? Or the woman married to the child's father? The woman who actually takes care of her? Or the woman who can offer her the most money?

Is a child's true mother really her father? Does a child need a biological mother, if her father wants to take exclusive care of her—without involving any women?

Are most biological mothers "unfit" or are they less fit than genetic fathers or adoptive mothers? Should biological motherhood be abolished in the "best interests" of the child? What is a "fit" mother? Who should decide?

Would each child be better off served by a minimum of four "mothers": she who donates the egg, she who incubates the fetus and gives birth, she who legally adopts the newborn, and she who is the child's primary caregiver?

What if compartmentalizing "mother" into specific functions actually enlarges and enhances our experience of both motherhood and childhood? What if such vivisection allows both men and women, the infertile and the fertile, the single and the married, to "mother" children? Would it be civilized—or barbaric—if everyone were to take nurturing and economic responsibility for children, even if they're not bound by blood or suited by temperament to do so?

What would replace the mother-infant bond—the oldest and strongest bond known to man (and obviously to woman)? Would the absence of this very specific blood bond ultimately weaken and destroy us as a species? Or is the ability to "let go" of this bond precisely what will free us to control our destiny more scientifically?

We must decide: Is a biological mother a human being with a heart, a mind, and an eternal soul—or is she only a surrogate uterus? Is a biological mother the best possible person to mother her baby? If she *is* a fit mother, what entitles a sperm donor or even a legal husband to *sole* custody of her child? Must every woman become a mother? Is every biological mother who is fit to do so obliged to raise her child?

We must decide: Is a father only an income-generating sperm donor? Or is he as "maternal" as any biological mother? If he is, then should biological mothers and genetic fathers "parent," that is, should they both mother and generate income in equal or identical ways? If a custody battle erupts, which "parent" is presumed entitled to custody?

Must every man become a father? Is every genetic father who is fit to do so obliged to raise his child?

Should any blood relative: a grandparent, sibling, aunt, uncle, even a distant cousin, be entitled to sole custody of a child "for its own good," e.g., if they have more money or a less troubled relationship with the child (or with the state) than a biological or genetic parent does?

Is a child a "thing" that blood relatives are entitled to fight over? Does a biological mother or a genetic father "own" a child? Perhaps all biological families are unfit, i.e., too possessive, too invested in owning each other.

Should we abolish the biological family in the "best interests" of the human race? Should we more readily honor the custodial claims of any adult or group not related to the child by blood, for instance, a foster, adoptive, step- or co-parent? On what grounds should we do this?

Should the male-dominated state replace the father-dominated biological family entirely? Should we have baby-breeding farms and children's houses staffed by trained and paid employees chosen for their "fitness"? Would children be better off if those who took care of them had decent working conditions and had to meet certain standards?

Should parenting become a blue- or a white-collar occupation? If so, should poor or otherwise disadvantaged women be paid to "incubate" babies for higher-income women who are sterile, have chosen careers, or wish to avoid the risks of pregnancy?

Should male-dominated science clean up the imperfect "mess" of human reproduction and traditional family-style child-rearing? Should each child of the future be born at scientifically timed intervals with its sex, personality, skin-and-eye color all carefully pre-selected?

This scenario has its advantages. For example, if people were *produced* technologically and impersonally instead of *reproduced* biologically and personally, then neither abortion nor involuntary motherhood would have to exist. No human being would have to get pregnant, stay pregnant, or have an abortion.

No one would have to suffer from sterility. How could one? No human being would be personally engaged in biological reproduction; no one gene pool would be used for technological production of the next generation. (Docility might come from one gene pool, the shape of a smile from another, hand size from a third.)

No one would have to marry in order to reproduce. Families as we know them would probably become as extinct as the dinosaur. Racism and sexism could be eliminated. We could all be identical: biologically (male) and racially (white).

Am I describing Paradise or Purgatory, a Golden Age or a Brave New Nightmare? We aren't there yet, but on our way to the future, there are some immediate questions to answer.

If a woman has a legal and moral right to her own body, isn't she free to exercise that right in any way she deems fit? Doesn't she have the legal right to rent her vagina or her uterus, or to sell her one-of-a-kind and irreplaceable heart—or unborn child?

If a woman has the legal right to terminate a pregnancy *because she and no one else has a right to her body,* then at what point does her (pregnant) body cease to be hers alone? When does a sperm donor, an unwed boyfriend, a legal husband or the state, on behalf of the fetus, have the right to prevent a woman from having an abortion on the grounds of their future right to custody? One minute after conception?

Or does a pregnant woman retain the right to her own body until she is five months pregnant? After this, does a sperm donor or legal husband have the right to force her into an amniocentesis test or an abortion?

Does the state have the right to try a woman for murder if her child is born dead—and it is viewed as her fault because she drank alcohol, smoked tobacco, thought "bad thoughts"? Will the state start imprisoning pregnant women for "fetal abuse"? Will the state automatically take custody of these children at birth, wall them up in institutions, sell them to the highest bidder?

The Baby M case raises all these questions—and more. The case is about the reproductive rights of women and men; about biology, human bonding, parental rights and parental obligations; about surrogacy, legal contracts, indentured servitude, and slavery; about mother-blaming among psychiatrists—particularly those involved in custody battles; about the increase in sterility in North America and the consequent increase in custody battles, adoptions, and new reproductive technologies; about the role of the media and legislation in our daily lives—the list is a long one indeed.

The Baby M case is also the story of two women and one man, all united by their passion for the same child. The story has no heroes and no heroines: only monstrously flawed—i.e., ordinary—human beings.

Which makes the issues even more important.

All over the country, people argued and took sides. We tended to "like" and "feel sorry for" Bill and Betsy, and to "hate" Mary Beth. Everyone felt very strongly about who should "get" Baby M—as if we really knew or were entitled to decide; as if this rather public spectacle was, in essence, a family affair. And it was.

We were all "voting" on the future of motherhood and on the future of the human family.

Most of us wanted our future mothers and families to be educated, solidly middle class, and in scientific control of their lives. According to two separate polls, between 74 percent and 92 percent of Americans agreed with the decision to place Baby M with her biochemist father (Bill is employed by the Unigene Corporation) and his pediatrician wife (Betsy's Ph.D. is in human genetics) where, as the child of scientists, she would have the kind of life that would innoculate her against the bad teeth, bad grades, bad health, and bad luck that characterizes life among the hard-working, working-class poor.

We were also "voting" on the past collective performance of mothers. We blamed them (not our fathers or presidents or even Our Father Who Art in Heaven) for failing to love us completely enough and for failing to save us from unhappiness. We were Americans. We believed we had a constitutional right to happiness and prosperity.

We were all so angry at mothers (they were the ones, after all, who'd birthed us) that any media "fact" that couldn't be used to condemn Mary Beth didn't register. Other "facts" canceled it out. We heard it—but we promptly forgot it. ("Oh, she refused the ten thousand dollars? But she did sign the contract, didn't she?" "Oh, she really was breast-feeding? But didn't she want to kill the baby?" "Oh, no one ever proved that she was an unfit mother? But the Sterns can offer the child so much more.")

Add to this the "fact" that the media, like everyone else, was also biased in favor of the educated middle class and had more sympathy for the problem of middle-class sterility than for the problem of either working-class *fertility* or sterility.

Sterility has increased—probably due to the combined effects of birth-control technology, delayed childbearing, and an increase in environmental toxicity. Simultaneously, abortion and birth control have led to a "shortage" of adoptable white babies. Many of the journalists, as well as the lawyers, judges, psychiatrists, and social workers involved in the case either themselves were or knew other middle-class people who were sterile, or adoptive parents, or who had experienced great difficulty in trying to adopt a "desirable" baby. The infertile had our "sympathy vote"—at least superficially.

At a deeper level, most people refused to question their own genetic narcissism. For example, no one demanded that *fertile* people adopt a child-in-need before they'd be allowed to reproduce themselves. We were quick to blame the infertile for not wanting to adopt "flawed" children, but we, the fertile, were not about to overturn either adoption procedures or the definition of what constitutes a family.

We (or the entrepreneurs among us) preferred to profit from the suffering of the newly sterile by strip-mining the fertility of the poor, i.e., by industrializing polygamy or surrogacy.

Everyone in America focused on *one* custody battle (Baby M's) as a way of denying (or as the unacknowledged symbol for) the *millions* of custody battles and legal kidnappings that raged all around us. Men (and higher-income couples) were fighting women (and lower-income couples) for custody of the children birthed by unwed or impoverished Third-World mothers—and also by marriage-contract mothers.

The Baby M case is what a custody battle is really like. Marriage constitutes the most common reproductive contract between a woman and a man; a wife may have as much (or as little) right to contested custody of her child as Mary Beth Whitehead—or any other "surrogate uterus" does. Marriage contracts don't exist, but are enforced anyway. Ask any divorced woman about the covenant she so eagerly signed with all of patriarchy, but never read or understood.

According to most Americans, not all contracts are created equal. A football or movie star's employment contract may be amended or broken, but a woman's contract with a man about his sperm may not be overturned—at least not without threatening our "procreative liberties," the "joys of parenthood," and our "loving homes."*

Ultimately, the Baby M case is important for what it teaches us about ourselves.

Where were you the day we decided to put biological motherhood on trial? The day a judge in New Jersey ruled that a man's contract with a woman about his sperm is sacred and that pregnancy and childbirth are not? The day the psychiatrists decided that a biological mother's desire to keep her breast-feeding infant was proof of mental illness and that her flight "underground" was proof, not of heroism, but of an evil so great that the state had no choice but to publicly torture

*These phrases are lawyer Gary Skoloff's, from his appeal brief for the Sterns.

her for a period of at least two years, to ensure that no other woman would ever again try to break a contract with a man about his sperm?

I was in bed with a bad cold. I turned on the TV in time to catch Dr. Lee Salk on the evening news. He was explaining that Mary Beth Whitehead wasn't even a "surrogate mother," that she was merely a "surrogate uterus." He said:

> There was no intent on Mrs. Whitehead's part to be a functional mother or to care for and raise a child. In both structural and functional terms, Mr. and Mrs. Stern's role as parents to Baby M was achieved by a surrogate uterus and not a surrogate mother. . . . The Sterns are far and away more capable of meeting the baby's needs than the Whiteheads. I recommend the complete termination of contact between Mrs. Whitehead and the baby.

Dr. Salk has had my attention ever since his ex-wife, Kersten, came to see me early in 1976, after she lost custody of their two children to him. I telephone Kersten.

"I am sooo upsyet," Kersten says in her Swedish accent. "I think he's gone too far. That poor mother!"

I remember Kersten's descriptions, both in her trial transcript and in person, of how Lee verbally humiliated her.

On October 28, 1975, New York Judge Guy Ribaudo awarded sole custody of Pia and Eric Salk to their father, Lee, giving their mother visitation. The judge used an "affirmative standard" to decide which parent was "better fit"—neither had accused the other of being unfit—to guide the "development of the children and their future." To me, it's appalling that Kersten's full-time mothering and home-making were given less weight than Dr. Salk's professional expertise. The judge granted both parties a divorce on the grounds of cruel and inhuman treatment on both their parts.

Later, Kersten said she had not told the whole story in court. At a speakout on custody, she said: "Continual attempts were made to break me down emotionally. . . . He engaged in fact-twisting and clever manipulation to show me in a bad light."

I remember how shocked I was by Kersten's story. How could feminists hail Salk's victory as if he were really Dustin Hoffman in *Kramer vs. Kramer*?

Over the next ten years I was to discover that you don't have to be a stay-at-home (or an unfit) mother in order to lose custody. I could find no explanation other than that mothers were *women*—and therefore were both impoverished and vulnerable to charges of any kind.

Employed mothers who were custodially challenged lost because they were "working" and still couldn't earn as much as a man. "Career" mothers lost because they were viewed as selfish women who cared more about their careers than about their children.

Although mothers still received no wages for their work at home and far less than equal pay outside the home, although most fathers had yet to assume an equal—or even a significant—share of housekeeping and childcare, divorced fathers launched a highly successful media and legislative campaign for equal rights to sole custody, alimony, and child support, and for mandatory joint custody and mediation.

Since the early seventies, divorce has increased. Custodial mothers and their children are increasingly poor. Between 10 and 15 percent of all divorces now involve a major custody battle; the remaining are dominated by threats of a custodial war if a mother demands substantial child support or alimony, the family home, and other material assets.

In the spring of 1986, the New York State Task Force on Women and the Courts published a study on sex bias in the courtroom. It concluded that "mothers are losing custody on grounds unrelated to the child's best interests." The study notes the existence of a gender double standard in custodial determinations that "holds that a woman's behavior must be blameless but a man's indiscretions are to be ignored"; the study also acknowledges the existence of a judicial prejudice against mothers who work full time.

The study states that—contrary to popular myth—children often remain with their mothers upon divorce not because judges are biased against men but by "parental choice," and that "substantial evidence exists that when fathers do litigate custody, they win at least as often as mothers do."

According to a study published in the *Family Law Quarterly* in 1984 and according to my own 1986 study, fathers win custody at the trial level 62–70 percent of the time, respectively, when custody is contested.

How can this happen? Very easily—in a culture that overvalues men, fathers, and money and undervalues women, mothers, and mother-child bonding.

We also have a double standard for "good enough" mothering and fathering. An ideal father is expected to legally acknowledge and economically support his children. Fathers who do *anything* (more) for their children are often seen as "better" than mothers—who are, after all, supposed to do everything.

The ideal of fatherhood is sacred. As such, it usually protects each father from the consequences of his actions. The ideal of motherhood is sacred, too. It exposes all mothers as imperfect. No human mother can embody the maternal ideal perfectly enough.

Therefore, *all* mothers are custodially vulnerable because they are women; *all* fathers, including incestuous, violent, absent, passive, or "helper" fathers can win custody, not because mothers are "unfit" or because fathers are truly "equal" parents, but because fathers are men.

The equal treatment of "unequals" is unjust. The paternal demand for "equal" custodial rights; the law that values legal paternity or male economic superiority over biological motherhood and/or over maternal primary childcare, degrades and violates both mothers and children.

Oh, the mothers! Their collective message is a chilling one: that children belong to men (sperm donors, boyfriends, legal husbands)—when men want them, but not when men don't. Judges say they can't force a father to see his children. On the other hand, women (birth mothers or primary caregivers) are obliged to mother children—whether they want to or not and under only very harsh and specific conditions.

No birth mother has a right to her child if she's poor or unwed, lives in an impoverished country, signs a surrogacy or adoption contract, or has less money than her child's genetic or legal father.

People think that a child is entitled to maternal care—but not necessarily from her birth mother. Any woman—an adoptive mother or stepmother, a paternal grandmother, a housekeeper—will do, as long as, like Betsy Stern, she is obedient to the child's father.

What mother freely chooses to lose her child at birth or later, to the plagues of war, disease, and accident? What slave mother freely hands her child over to his genetic father and master? What mother freely hands her child over to blood strangers to be legally adopted by her "superiors," to be taught to forget her, to be punished for who she is—small hostage of her misfortune, bone of her bone, apple of her eye?

Baby M is every child who has ever been physically, legally, or psychologically separated from her birth mother "for her own good" in the mistaken belief that a child needs a father, a father-dominated family, and/or money far more than she needs her birth mother, love, and freedom.

CHAPTER 2

ON CIVILIZATION AND ITS DISCONTENTS: A MEDITATION

This is a picture of America in the late twentieth century, a family photo of Mary Beth Whitehead and Bill-and-Betsy Stern with their baby, Sara Elizabeth Whitehead, a.k.a. Melissa Elizabeth Stern, a.k.a. Baby M.

Here we are, we the people, caught up in another "trial of the century," a case as mesmerizing as the Lindbergh child kidnapping or Vanderbilt custody cases were; as much about the triumph of Civilization over Nature as any missionary or scientific expedition ever was; as much about freedom versus slavery as our Revolutionary and Civil wars were; and about class antagonism and the war between the sexes, for which there is no military precedent on American soil.

We hold this truth to be self-evident: that if we pull ourselves up by our own roots, and plunge ourselves into the American melting pot, that we'll rise to the top—all alike and all entitled to own property (land, slaves, women, children) and to worship the white male god of our choice. This is our immigrant heritage.

Why should the Sterns have thought that a child would suffer if they uprooted her at birth? What memory of her previous existence—that cramped and sunless place—could she have? It would be un-American to prevent any child from leaving her country of

19

(maternal) origin. We'd be condemning her to repeat her mother's life. She'd never be able to better herself. (Better not to be born if you can't be re-born.)

Last year, a white, midwestern couple I know adopted an infant child from Mexico. The boy needed extensive surgery. Without it, he would have grown up to be a blind man on crutches. Should this boy have remained with his impoverished birth mother and embraced his "destiny" as a beggar? Or should my friends, the monied North Americans, be forced to share their wealth with him and his mother?

Is the lifelong pain this Mexican birth mother might feel for having surrendered her son more important than the pain her son would have experienced had he stayed by her side? Who is to judge?

Am I more sympathetic to Mary Beth's plight as a biological mother because I am also a biological mother? Or because I have written about pregnancy and childbirth as rites of heroic passage? Vowing to hear the other side of the adoption story, I interview my friend Rita, an infertile adoptive mother.

Rita's husband, Leonard, kisses me hello at the door, then leaves the room.

"I'm furious that Betsy Stern has to go through this," begins Rita, before I've shrugged off my coat. "I tried so hard, for so long, to get pregnant. Nothing worked. If I had to face a public trial after all that agony, I think I'd just die."

"I don't think Betsy Stern ever tried to get pregnant or to adopt a child," I tell her.

"How do you know that?" Rita is sharp with suspicion and surprise.

"The information is contained in the mental-health reports," I tell her. "It's also buried in the transcripts of the trial."

Rita is silent for a minute. When she speaks it is with more sadness than anger.

"You know, I really despise society's romance with its own genes. What narcissism! I think biological and genetic narcissism, not racism, is the true reason people don't want to adopt already homeless children."

"You have a point," I say.

"I think the human race will feel a sense of responsibility to all children only when and if they lay this biological narcissism to rest.

But I don't think this will ever happen. Technology is only catering
to it and reinforcing it."

We sit in silence for a while. Then Rita says:

"I'll tell you something that most adoptive mothers won't admit.
I'm guilty. I know I got my daughter away from her birth mother only
because that mother didn't have any money.

"What if my daughter turns on me someday and accuses me of
separating her from her birth mother and from her country? What
will I tell her? That I cared more about my need to have a child than
about her need to stay with her birth mother?

"It's not fair that I have to pass muster with the small, mean minds
of adoption-agency bureaucrats when any woman who can get pregnant is automatically entitled to her child. Even if she's totally unfit
to be a mother."

"You're right," I say. "Should we license motherhood? Should we
get rid of biological reproduction entirely?"

"But why should I be punished because I'm infertile?" Rita asks,
weeping.

"You shouldn't be," I say, holding her.

"**S**he *knew* what she was doing when she signed that contract." My student's voice is husky with contempt.

"She's after Mr. Stern's money. That sneaky bitch finally figured out a way of sinking her hook into a rich
man."

These voices almost come to a growl. A lynch mob must
sound like this. My students are mostly Catholic working-class
women (like Mary Beth), yet they have no sympathy for her. They
speak as if they'd like to stone her to death.

"What would happen if we all reneged on our half of the bargain?"
This speaker is sneering, practically snarling. "What if we all did
that?"

*Did what? Turned our backs, for example, on heartless arrangements
with our employers for money? We'd have a revolution on our hands,
that's what, and then where would we be? We'd better police Mary Beth
right back into line.*

Ah, so that's it. Mary Beth has failed to show her so-called class "superiors" the proper respect. How dare an uneducated girl run off with the family jewels and refuse to return them? She'll ruin it for the other girls. The Masters will import foreign girls or invent machines to replace their domestically unreliable handmaids. My students are unable to see themselves in Mary Beth. They are driven to disassociate themselves from her (and/or from her fate).

The women say that she holds herself too cheaply; that she is driving the definition of Woman downward from "Mother of God" to "incubator of a made-to-order product." The women say that she agreed to abandon a child for money. Punish *her*, not us. In fact, just give her to us, we'll punish her for you.

The women also say: "We don't like Mary Beth"—as if that somehow justifies what was done to her; as if any woman so disliked by those more powerful than herself deserves to be punished and publicly humiliated.

Ah, sisters: do we personally have to "like" every slave before we'll take a stand against slavery? Does each prisoner have to please us before we'll fight for her right not to be tortured? Aren't there certain inalienable human rights that, when denied, diminish us all? Are we or aren't we endangered along with Mary Beth Whitehead?

Some feminists say: "It's a woman's right to sell her vagina, her uterus, her brain power. It's *her* body." Perhaps, but don't women also have the right to simply "be or not to be?" Are we entitled to control our bodies only by treating them as marketable commodities?

Some feminists say: "If women can't do what they want with their bodies, then we'll lose our right to abortion and pay equity." I hope not, but must women give up the right to keep our children—a right we don't yet have—for the right not to bear children?

Some feminists say: "Patriarchal motherhood has enslaved and destroyed women—who in turn have emotionally wounded their own children. There's nothing sacred about biological reproduction or motherhood. They're examples of devalued and alienated unpaid labor. Let's organize for wages and better working conditions and get men involved in mothering. At the very least, male mothers will upgrade women's status as childcare workers."

Perhaps, but how can we deny that women have a profound and everlasting bond with the children they've birthed; that this bond begins in utero; that it is further strengthened by the experience of childbirth, breast-feeding and primary childcare, and by the socialization into motherhood that women (not men) receive?

How can we deny that children bond with their birth mothers in utero, and that children suffer terribly in all kinds of ways when this bond is prematurely or abruptly terminated?*

Acknowledging these truths does not doom women to the status of surrogate uteruses—or men to the status of sperm donors. Patriarchal "civilization" has already done so.

I n patriarchy, sexually promiscuous men are not taught to view themselves as sacredly connected to the children their sperm happens to conceive; and married men, for the most part, tend to relate to their genetic children as if they, the fathers, were no more than absentee landlords.

In patriarchy, men already view women as "body parts" (vaginas, uteruses, serving hands) to be traded or taken by force, for the moment or forever, in slavery or concubinage; to be rented by the hour in prostitution; to be indentured in polygamous or monogamous marriage; and to be cast off just as easily. (Some men treat inanimate property—such as their cars—more respectfully than they treat their wives and children.)

Why then are women, including feminists, so unaware of what it means to "prefer" Betsy Stern over Mary Beth Whitehead? According to Merle Hoffman, these two women

> are two sides of the same coin, the Janus head . . . Whitehead
> is passion where Stern is mind. Whitehead is blood, tissue,
> guts, need, sex. Stern is intellect, control and alienation.
> Whitehead is mother, Stern is career. Whitehead is bad girl,
> Stern is good girl. Whitehead is whore, Stern is virgin—
> indeed Stern is immaculate conception! The Janus head—
> both dark, both with bangs and similar long, gaunt, stark
> faces. Madonna/Whore, Elizabeth I and Mary, Queen of

*All the studies cited by experts such as Drs. Steven Nickman, Phyllis Silverman, Marshall Klaus, Reuben Pannor, and Betty Jean Lifton strongly suggest that being separated from one's birth mother constitutes a lasting trauma.

> *Scots. Locked in history and in life in the eternal struggle of*
> *mind and the body. The intellect and the sexual—Athena and*
> *Venus.*
>
> *Any wonder that public sentiment rides with Elizabeth*
> *Stern, the woman whose love is limited by the desire for genetic*
> *perfection, whose motherhood is not dependent upon sexual*
> *intercourse—whose body is somehow removed from the act*
> *that so traditionally defines woman?"[1]*

Do women view Betsy as trustworthy because she is more like a
man than like a woman *in that she can't or won't get pregnant*? Do
we unconsciously feel that women who remind us of men are more
trustworthy as mothers? Are we this male-identified, this mother-
hating, this fearful or ambivalent about being female?

How many women, including feminists, are so angry at our mothers and so mother-wounded that we don't easily trust or admire any
woman whose identity is first and foremost: mother?

Do women, including feminists, feel that a surrogacy arrangement
is the bloodless means by which to accomplish gender neutrality?
That surrogacy was the way in which Betsy and Bill neutralized or
destroyed their biologically based sex roles—for us all? Or that Betsy
is really Baby M's father and that Bill is her true mother? And that
this represents "progress" or women's liberation?

According to the New Jersey *Bergen Record,* on August 22, 1986,
Bill Stern became very angry when a reporter asked him whether he
couldn't just go out and hire another surrogate mother. Bill replied:
"That's like telling someone who's just had a miscarriage that they
can always go out and have another child. That's a cruel thing to say."

The day after Easter, Mary Beth came to retrieve her baby from
the Sterns. Both Mary Beth and Bill were upset.

How about Betsy Stern? According to Bill, his ever-efficient wife
was "upstairs calling Noel Keane on the telephone." According to
Mary Beth, Betsy was folding and packing layette items."[2]

According to Betsy—pale, gaunt, accomplished, incredibly narrow
at the wrist, waist, pelvis, and ankle, the most "masculine" (i.e., the
least emotionally expressive) of Baby M's four parents—she too was
crying. Betsy told her lawyer, Gary Skoloff, that she, Bill, and Mary
Beth's sister Joanne were all trying to convince Mary Beth *not* to take

the baby back, because "we feared . . . she [would] become more attached to her." Then Betsy said, "Bill was crying, Mary Beth was crying, [and] I was crying."

As well she might. The Virgin Queen is, like Mary Beth, under ironclad reproductive contract to Bill Stern. Did Betsy Stern, M.D., Ph.D., ever feel empowered *not* to use her body in Bill's reproductive service? Did she ever feel that she and Bill were *already* a family—without a child? Or that adopting a child might be fairer or more humane, especially to her?

Did Betsy herself really want a baby—as much as Bill did? Bill is quoted everywhere, ad nauseam, on his feelings about having a child. It is surprising how few public statements Betsy seems to have made on the subject. Betsy consulted a pastoral counselor about her "fear" of getting pregnant once she thought she had multiple sclerosis: "[The counselor] has a divinity degree, and . . . I was still—I still wanted to have my own child, like anybody else. Bill and I wanted to have a child of our own, you know, what any woman wants . . . as an act of love between the two of us. . . . So, I was still thinking of taking the risk . . . but nobody could give you any guarantees. . . ."[3]

Has Betsy thought motherhood through on her own?

On the stand, Bill said he was "stunned" and "so excited" when he heard that Baby M had been born. The next day Betsy testified that she too "was so stunned," and "we were so excited." Bill: "Our dream was coming true," and the next day Betsy: "My dream had come true." In fact, in her testimony Betsy kept referring to and supporting Bill's testimony. She said: "As my husband said yesterday . . ." and "Just as my husband testified . . ."[4]

What would happen to Bill's "right" to procreate if Betsy refused to get pregnant and refused to consider adoption or surrogacy? What would happen to Betsy's marriage if she questioned Bill's enormous sense of genetic entitlement, or opposed his desire to have a baby with another woman?

Despite her advanced degrees and despite her choice not to become pregnant, Betsy is hardly an emancipated woman. Betsy moves in the same patriarchal trance or fugue state that moves Mary Beth. According to Dr. Marshall D. Schechter, Betsy scored "high on submissiveness" (on the Cattell Personality Inventory). Dr. David Brodzinsky noted that Betsy was an "accommodating woman who was eager to please. In fact she impressed me as a little too eager and accepting."

Betsy did not allow herself to question whether wives are—or are not—their husband's surrogate uteruses. What Betsy said, in effect, was: I can't be a surrogate uterus because I'm medically sick; we'll hire another woman to do my compulsory reproductive service for me.

Betsy knows that a woman's first duty is to obey and please her husband and, in this case, to fight his battles for him: fiercely. Betsy is a much more obedient wife to Bill (and to all of patriarchy) than Mary Beth is—either to Bill or to her legal husband, Rick. The more obedient wife is always viewed as the "better" mother.

What kind of husband is Bill? He allowed Betsy, and she allowed herself, to endure a painful public ordeal, one that would bring stress to a woman far healthier than herself. What could such a trial do to someone who suffers from multiple sclerosis?

Mary Beth, the "uppity" wife, denied Bill her services and their genetic child. Unlike Betsy, she refused to sacrifice herself for Bill or to place her emotions second to his needs. Therefore, Mary Beth was diagnosed as having a personality disorder and viewed as if she were maternally unfit.

The experts made their pronouncements, the media reported what they said, and we assumed that Mary Beth was nuts. Didn't she have a "narcissistic" personality disorder? Wasn't she "immature," "histrionic," and "borderline"? If the experts, Drs. Schechter and Brodzinsky, and the media said so, it had to be true.

But the "news" is not the same as the "truth." Television images are often flashed at us out of context and explained superficially. People tend to believe what they hear first. Children believe what their parents tell them; juries believe the *first* witness they hear; and we, the people, believe the *first* expert whose words are reported in the media.

According to the mental-health experts, Mary Beth could do no right. They used everything she said and did against her. They disapproved of her *because* she was bonded to Baby M—as if this proved that she was no better than an animal.

It's as if these experts were nineteenth-century missionaries and Mary Beth a particularly stubborn native who refused to convert to Civilization, and what's more, refused to let them plunder her natural resources—not without a fight. The Sterns represent enlightened "progress." Mary Beth is all primitive "instinct."*

For example, Dr. Schechter described Mary Beth as "impulsive" (she decided to become a surrogate mother; she ran away to Florida); "immature" (she refused to regard her nursing infant as a separate individual); "exhibitionistic" (she seemed to enjoy media attention); "manipulative and destructive" (she fled and then threatened Bill on the phone); "paranoid" (she felt victimized by the custody trial); and "self-important" (she feels entitled to do whatever she wants to do).

Dr. Brodzinsky and Dr. Judith Brown Greif found something wrong with Mary Beth for thinking that she occupied a special or unique place as her daughter's mother. Dr. Brodzinsky described Mary Beth as "overreacting to minor events" and detected in her a "grandiose sense of giving." Dr. Greif described Mary Beth as suffering from "narcissistic thinking," because she "feels that Sara/Melissa belongs with her because she is the mother. Mrs. Whitehead is almost myopic in her view that her role as a biological mother enables her to understand her children better than anyone else."

However, the same (or similar) words: "impulsive," "immature," "inconsistent," "manipulative and destructive," "paranoid," "grandiose," "self-important," "myopic," can be used to describe the Sterns—based on information contained in the *pro-Stern* mental-health reports.[5]

Isn't Bill "impulsive"? (He decided to become a surrogate contract father; he chose Mary Beth instantly from a photograph and finalized the arrangements after a brief meeting with her in a restaurant.)[6]

*On October 16, 1986, the Bergen County Probation Department concluded that both couples would make "more than adequate parents" for Baby M. But Lorraine Abraham, the guardian ad litem, decided to hire three *outside* experts—who unanimously viewed the Sterns as "more fit" parents. The experts were: Marshall D. Schechter, M.D., of Wynnewood, Pennsylvania, a psychiatrist; David Brodzinsky, Ph.D., of South Orange, New Jersey, a psychologist; and Judith Brown Greif, D.S.W., of New York and New Jersey, an advocate of joint custody. The three experts met with Lorraine Abraham *in each others' presence* before they interviewed the involved parties. According to Schechter, their initial meeting with Abraham lasted approximately eight hours. According to Schechter, they all three met together again with Abraham at the conclusion of their "independent" evaluations.

Drs. Allwyne Levine and Lee Salk were hired separately by the Sterns. Dr. Salk never met Mary Beth; he read over and commented on the mental-health reports.

Isn't Bill "manipulative" and "destructive"? (He secretly taped Mary Beth on the phone when she was in Florida.) Isn't Bill "paranoid"? (He acts as if Baby M will be seriously harmed if she develops a loving relationship with her birth mother.) Doesn't he "overreact to minor events"? (He becomes enraptured because his daughter greets him upon his return from work each day.) Isn't he "grandiose," "self-important," and "myopic"? (He thinks that Baby M is his and not Mary Beth's because she has his genes and because he signed a surrogacy contract.)

Like Mary Beth, the Sterns are also "inconsistent": despite the fact that Betsy self-diagnosed her multiple sclerosis, and also functioned as Mary Beth's unofficial physician-dominatrix during pregnancy, she later claimed that there was no point in asking to review Mary Beth's psychological report—how could she or Bill have understood a complicated medical report?

The Sterns, too, are "impatient": For eleven years (from 1974 to 1985) they chose to delay having a child—but once they decided to have one, they didn't even try adoption because, as they said, that would mean a "multi-year wait."

Bill is not "exhibitionistic"—but he and Betsy are "reserved," "distant," perhaps secretive. Dr. Brodzinsky described Bill as "emotionally reserved" and "anxious"; he has "difficulty in handling emotions" and "does not have good access to his inner, emotional life"; he "protects himself . . . through such defenses as denial, distancing, intellectualization and rationalization." Dr. Greif found Bill "somewhat distant" and said he was a "private person" who felt survival was linked with anonymity and being cautious. Dr. Brodzinsky noted that he was a "loner."

Neighbors described the Sterns as "aloof" and "eccentric"; one clerk described them as "nasty" and "supercilious."* Unlike Mary Beth, the Sterns are "private" people, i.e., they are cold, very cold. The experts admire them for this.

In his appeal brief, Harold Cassidy portrayed the Sterns at the hospital, come to see the baby for the first time:

> *Mary brought them over to see the baby. Bill just looked at her [the baby] and smiled. The Sterns neither said anything*

*These people must remain anonymous.

else nor showed emotion in any other way. . . . Given that the scene was the maternity ward window, where usually everyone, including the friends and relatives of the parents, will act festive and celebratory, one would think that the Sterns could have found a way to react with somewhat more emotion while still not disclosing the full situation. It is an interesting and candid reflection of the Sterns [that they didn't]. *

T he expert witnesses never used any of Bill's or Betsy's beliefs or actions against them. In turn, the media rarely questioned anything the Sterns did. In fact, the media fell under their own spell. Photojournalists lovingly portrayed Bill as a "New Age" father who, always alone, lovingly carried Baby M to and from her one-hour visits with her "Old Age" mother, Mary Beth. Bill also felt that he (not Mary Beth) was the one who was "really" pregnant and who "really" gave birth. He was not alone in this perception.

Dr. Brodzinsky testified that "the loss of a birth mother is generally deeply felt. However, I believe this sense of loss will be mitigated

---

*The Whiteheads hired five mental-health experts. Burton Z. Sokoloff, M.D., an expert in the emotional problems of adopted children, recommended that "the baby be immediately restored to Mrs. Whitehead" in order that the "bonding" (which began in utero and continued for four months after birth and included breast-feeding) be "continued." Phyllis R. Silverman, Ph.D., an expert in bonding, separation, and mourning, testified that Mary Beth was not mentally ill, but was reacting to enormous stress and real loss. Steven L. Nickman, M.D., an adoption and custody expert, testified that Baby M could be exposed to grave emotional risk if separated from her birth mother.

Harold Kopliewicz, M.D., also testified for the Whiteheads, recommending joint custody. Donald Klein, M.D., the psychiatrist who *wrote the descriptions of suicide and depression* for the diagnostic manual used by the Sterns' experts, also testified. His testimony that Mary Beth was not suicidal was ignored by Judge Sorkow. Judge Sorkow completely barred testimony that was offered on behalf of Mary Beth, from two additional and significant experts: Dr. Reuben Pannor, an expert in adoption and its consequences and one of the authors of *The Adoption Triangle* (Garden City, N.Y.: Doubleday, 1978); and Marshall Klaus, M.D., described by Harold Cassidy as "perhaps the foremost expert in the world on parent-child bonding," who sought to give his opinion on the importance of Baby M's bond to her mother.

by the presence of the child's birth father." Dr. Schechter testified that "Mrs. Whitehead makes an assumption that because she is the mother that the child Baby M belongs to her. This gives no credence to or value to the genetic contribution of the birth father."

What is a "birth father"? Is he perhaps motivated by more than the usual amount of unacknowledged uterus envy—a phenomenon I described a decade ago in my book *About Men*, and as Karen Horney, Margaret Mead, Theodore Reik, Bruno Bettelheim, and others have done before me? In my section on "Womb-less Men," I wrote about the way men's uterus envy and death-terror led to the male control of mythic maternity (patriarchal religion) and to the male control of pregnancy and childbirth (patriarchal medicine and science).

In the Beginning, there was the word . . . Patriarchs appropriated female reproduction by telling a fabulous lie so often and with such force that everyone came to believe it, and no one noticed the deception any longer. They said that God the Father gave birth to Adam, and Adam the Man gave birth to Eve, and God the Father created Christ.

L isten children, said the men: even the pagan male gods gave birth, but in manly ways—without losing blood, without risking death. Zeus gave birth to Athena from his head, he used his head, he uttered the Word and she appeared, displaced upward from the dangerous, lower (female) regions to the lofty regions of the male eye and ear and brain.

Listen children, said the men: The Church is the Mother of us all. Naming is all. Unbaptized, you cannot get into Heaven. Only men in skirts (priests) can turn boys into men. Listen, children: Modern medicine is the midwife of us all. Science is all. Only men in aprons can carve up the female mysteries without risking death . . .

> *Now, [Motherhood, or] technological Paradise is within male/erotic grasp. Astronauts, both communist/and capitalist, lumber on the moon like/pregnant women, while scientists on earth/try to create life in baby-blue test tubes,/the color of death . . . In museums, in marble silence, women/are hanging, beautifully clothed and beautifully/naked, painted*

*by great artists who/loved the female body. Strange, how few
of/them are pregnant. ***

When Mary Beth insisted that she was Baby M's mother, we
experienced her as *mocking* or *negating* Bill's paternity—but why?
She was not claiming to be the father. Bill couldn't create a baby by
himself—no matter how much money he had.

So we all agreed that Bill conceived *of* Baby M (not that Mary Beth
conceived Baby M); that Bill *contracted* for the birth (not that Mary
Beth had *contractions* and gave birth); and that Bill *wanted* a baby
(not that Mary Beth *had* a baby). In order for the *idea* of fatherhood
to triumph over the *fact* of motherhood, we had to see Bill as the
"birth father" and Mary Beth as only the surrogate uterus.

Thus, everyone, including Judge Sorkow, believed that Bill Stern
was Baby M's "truest" parent—not only because his sperm was
involved in her creation, but because Bill had *thought* of and *wanted*
"a" baby long before Mary Beth actually became pregnant. (According to Dr. Marshall Schechter, Bill tried to transmit his values and
interests from afar to Baby M while she was growing in Mary Beth's
uterus.)

The male idea, word, and legal contract are viewed as more "civilized" than is a natural event such as pregnancy, or a natural relationship, such as that between a birth mother and her child. In my book
Mothers On Trial: The Battle for Children and Custody, one of my
interviewees, Rose, struggled with the tension between law and justice. She said: "Who are these men to tell me whether I can live with
my son or not? I'm his mother. They can't do away with that fact by
laws alone. They sin against nature when they use laws to do that."

No one, neither the judge nor the lawyers nor the mental-health
experts for the Sterns, thought that Mary Beth's experience of pregnancy, childbirth, and breast-feeding entitled her to anything but
ridicule and contempt.

Judge Sorkow refused to allow Mary Beth to testify about how this
pregnancy and childbirth led her to change her mind. Angrily, Sorkow stopped her from speaking about these experiences. According
to *The Bergen Record,* he said, "We don't have to go through the pain

*From my book *About Men,* Simon & Schuster, 1978.

of birth [here]. The child was born, the child was born.""[7] He did, however, allow both Bill and Betsy to describe in minute detail how they decorated the baby's room:

> BETSY: *Originally . . . we got these teddy bear stencils . . . that was one of the cutest patterns . . . we picked out some wallpaper . . . and it didn't match . . .*
> BILL: *Her room had this ugly old paper . . . I rented a steamer . . . I was ankle deep in pieces of paper . . . we found . . . a teddy bear print . . . and this little border to go with it . . .*

When Judge Sorkow ordered Baby M into the custody of the Sterns, they saw nothing wrong with weaning her abruptly and violently. Pediatrician Betsy Stern was widely quoted as saying that in her expert opinion, breast-feeding was not necessary at all—certainly not after the first six weeks. Judge Sorkow then forbade Mary Beth to ever breast-feed Sara again.

I have interviewed hundreds and heard from thousands of custodially embattled mothers. Those who breast-fed infants usually described how their breast-feeding was trivialized, ridiculed, closely supervised, or directly outlawed by their husbands and by psychiatrists, pediatricians, lawyers (both his and hers), by the departments of Corrections and Social Services, and by judges.

Why do so many experts act as if mothers' milk is of no value —or is actually dangerous? Is it because they, like so many of us, once yearned for their mothers' milk—but received too little or none at all? Or because we as adults yearn for the "milk of human kindness" and find it lacking, withheld from us still? Is the breast-feeding of infants, like pregnancy, dangerous because only women can do it? Or is it dangerous because it is meant for infants only, not adult men?

How else explain the revulsion both men and women feel toward the exposed, milky breast in public and the paradoxical male and female fetishizing of the "recreational" breast meant to please adult men, not infants?[8]

W

hat do you mean she was breast-feeding Baby M for four and a half months?" John asks. "Why was she allowed to do that?" I am having dinner with John and Marie, an infertile married couple with an adopted son and daughter.

"I can't believe that someone actually let her take the baby home," says Marie, drawn from her post at the stove by what I've said. "That was my worst nightmare: that our birth mother would change her mind."

"Did you hire a surrogate-contract mother?" I ask.

"Oh no," says Marie. "We couldn't do that. It was a traditional adoption, but our birth mother had six months to change her mind. She could have taken Johnnie back even though we were already bonded to him for life after a few hours together."

"Imagine you gave birth to Johnnie," I say, "and you decided you couldn't part from him, and you started to breast-feed him and continued to do so for four and a half months after he was born and *then* he was taken away from you forever. Because that's exactly what happened to Mary Beth Whitehead."

"But that's terrible," Marie exclaims. "Why didn't they print that in the papers?"

"They did," I answer, "but no one seems to remember it. It just doesn't seem to register."

If it really registered, people would have to give up all their hasty conclusions and start thinking for themselves; people might start to question the incredible sense of entitlement due men and the infertile that dominates every discussion of this case.

John stands up. "If that's what they did to her, it's terrible. But let me ask you this: Is Mary Beth a nut or what? Would you let her raise your son?"

"Mary Beth is a perfectly competent mother," I answer. "She's a more *traditional* mother than I am. And, no, I wouldn't let her raise my son. She's not his mother, and she hasn't been living with me and taking responsibility for my son. But should anyone have the right to prevent her from raising the daughter she *did* give birth to?"

"John, if Mary Beth bonded with the baby, how can they take the baby away from her?" asks Marie, almost to herself.

"What kind of people would do that?" I ask softly. "Send a lawyer, a judge, and the police in to separate a breast-feeding infant from her mother? That's exactly what happened when Sara/Baby M was two and one-half months old. That's why Mary Beth fled to Florida. She didn't want to lose her baby."

"But what about that phone call she made threatening to kill herself and the baby?" John is up again.

"The Sterns put a lien on her bank account. Mary Beth had absolutely no money. She was about to lose her New Jersey house. She was distraught and cornered. She made the kind of statements a normal mother might make if she were threatened with the loss of her baby."

"Okay, I believe you," John says. "But Mary Beth sounds like she has no control over her life or over her emotions. Maybe this doesn't prove that she's crazy. But she sure is limited. The Sterns sound like take-charge people. Don't you think they can provide his daughter— and it is his daughter, too—with a leg up in life? Don't tell me it's not Mary Beth's fault she's uneducated or poor. Maybe it's not. But why should this particular baby have to inherit her mother's hard luck when there's an alternative for her?"

"Yes, you have a point," I agree. "But John, your parents raised you in poverty. What if an educated couple with a leg up in the world had wanted to adopt you against your mother's will: should the state have helped them do it? By force?"

"But Bill Stern is the girl's father," he protests.

"And Mary Beth Whitehead is the girl's mother," I repeat.

M any women, including feminists, seem to dislike the way Mary Beth romanticizes her "instinctive" or natural bodily functions. They are disgusted by the way she relies on her fertility instead of seeking her identity in a career. Who does she think she is? Mother Nature? Is she actually proud to be so out-of-control, so fecund?

We admire Betsy Stern for refusing to be limited by any of her "natural" limitations, i.e., even if she refuses to risk pregnancy, we respect her for using low-level technology and the law to become the mother of Bill's genetic child.

On the other hand, we despise Mary Beth for refusing to be limited by any of the "unnatural" limitations (technology and the law) placed upon her. Despite her husband Rick's vasectomy and Judge Sorkow's ex parte order, Mary Beth was obviously determined to get pregnant and to mother any child she had birthed—as a fugitive in Florida or as the mother of other children.*

Any woman who gets pregnant out of wedlock, for her own "instinctive" pleasure *without being under reproductive contract to a man* is invariably seen as guilty of *all* the quintessential female crimes: fornication, adultery, having "illegitimate" babies, using birth control, having abortions, committing witchcraft, infanticide.

Any woman who is capable of breaking *male* law—sexually, reproductively, theologically, economically—is obviously also *capable* of destroying what men alone have created: children, people. Her *capacity* is unforgivable. The patriarchal fear of the disobedient woman is the fear of the unwed mother; is the fear of the spurned wife turned rebel; is the fear of the witch; is the fear of Medea. "And after all, didn't Mary Beth threaten to kill the baby?"

The fact that patriarchy has devalued and degraded biological mothers (and consequently all women) is one thing; the spectacle of women romanticizing their patriarchal condition is a shabby spectacle indeed. I think her pleasure in her biology is what may disgust so many feminists about Mary Beth.

Are we as women supposed to relax and enjoy being reproductively colonized? Are women incapable of availing ourselves of the various cures for the "disease" of being born female, e.g., celibacy, birth control, surrogacy?

What if we don't happen to share Mary Beth's reproductive frenzy? Does this mean that we're "unnatural" women? Are we the ones who deserve to be pitied or punished for refusing to bear children? Shouldn't we (the Betsy Sterns of the world) actually be *rewarded* for not giving in to our base animal instincts?

Aren't we the "good girls"? Isn't Mary Beth the "bad girl"? Look how maliciously Mary Beth traps men's sperm in her body and then

---

*On October 31, 1987, Mary Beth again created a sensation by revealing that she was approximately three months pregnant with an "out-of-wedlock" child. The "revelation" was treated as if she were the Miraculous Virgin or as if she were starring in "Dallas" or "Dynasty." Why is Mary Beth seen as mindless, heartless, pitiless—when like Nature, she responds to loss by creating life?

makes the men (and the babies) pay for it! Brainless Bitch. Shameless Hussy. Devouring Monster. Cow. Cunt. Mother. Mother?[9]

Mary Beth Whitehead is the lightning rod for all these unspoken questions. Women are very hard on her. We see ourselves—and our collective past—in her. What we see is too problematic and unacceptable.

Mary Beth symbolizes the struggle that *women* are having with Nature and with our own nature. Women (at least those with educational and economic options) are struggling to decide whether the woman of the future should ever be a pregnant woman.

Will the woman of the future only be allowed one pregnancy or one biological child? Will she have to share both her pregnancy and her only child—as well as "her" man—with other women? Who will attract a man and/or a high-status job in the future: the fertile, pregnant woman or the infertile woman or the one who uses birth control?

If biology is not what makes a woman a mother or a "good" mother, are we saying that adoptive and/or stepmothers, nannies, childcare centers—surrogate mothers—will do as well or even better? Does a study exist that proves that parents adopt only for the most altruistic of reasons; that because they want *a* child, they know how to take care of a *particular* child; and that adoptive parents are true miracle workers and can take the trauma out of being adopted?

"Don't think that all adoptive parents are perfect," Laura begins. "Far from it. We tend to keep quiet about the bad stuff. Making it public, really studying it, would make it even harder for us to adopt than it already is."

Laura and Nell are both adoptive mothers. Laura is married; Nell is single. We're spending the afternoon at Nell's to talk about adoption.

"We know a couple," Nell interrupts, "who had one biological child and then adopted a little girl from India. Since she arrived seven years ago, that girl's been the only one who wears any second-hand clothes in the entire family. Her older brother, the biological child, always attended a good private school. Her parents told everyone they didn't have enough money to send two children to private school. They probably feel that the girl is so much better off with them than in India, that anything they do is sufficient. I don't think they'd do this if their daughter was white. I really don't.''

"That's nothing," exclaims Laura. "How about you-know-who, I don't want to use any names, the people who actually sent their daughter back, after five years, to whatever organization was willing to take her, rather than pay for expensive surgery and live through a long period of convalescence? They had that child since she was two months old. And yes, she had been sickly, but how could they do this to—I was going to say their own flesh and blood? Maybe people can do this *only* to an adopted child. They ought to be arrested!''

Nell continues the story. "The other adoptive parents in their social circle stopped talking to them. How else could they convince their own adopted children that they would never be returned if and when they required surgery or convalescence?''

"How about that couple who arranged to adopt a child early in the birth mother's pregnancy?" asks Laura. "The woman gave birth prematurely and the child, a boy, arrived in Chicago two weeks early. This MBA couple arranged to have him boarded for ten days in an orphanage, like a dog in a kennel, just so they wouldn't have to give up their long-planned-for last vacation together alone. How's that for heart?''

Now Laura and Nell begin to outdo each other with horror stories. I hear about adoptees who have been tormented with threats of "being returned"; physically neglected and psychologically rejected once a biological child was "miraculously" born; assigned a disproportionate number of family chores; abused, battered, and killed.

Why am I shocked? Adoptive parents are human beings, not saints, and they can be as cruel to their children as can biological parents. Yet I've always given them the benefit of the doubt, considered their horror stories as exceptions, aberrations.

For example, I've always interpreted the consistently higher rates of psychiatric "problems" and help-seeking behavior among adoptees as due to their relatively higher socioeconomic class, that is, they can afford therapy and view it as an acceptable thing to do.

Perhaps the secrecy and shame that surrounds adoption is what accounts for these higher rates of help-seeking behavior. Perhaps the world's view of biological ties as "superior" is what constitutes the adoption trauma. I never let myself think that an adoptive parent might be even less suited for child-rearing than a biological parent might be—even though I knew about the high rates of abuse and incest among adopted and/or stepchildren.

How could I? This would be too cruel a sentence to pronounce against those whose lives are already unfairly warped by society's mandate to "procreate or else" when, through no fault of their own, they can't.

No. That's not it. If adoptive parents are our "fall-back" position when biological parents fail, then what is our "fall-back" position when adoptive parents fail? *We have none.* Such information puts us on notice that our species has chosen not to protect all of earth's children.

In a sense, Mary Beth is like any legal wife and mother who loses custody against her will—simply because she has less money than her husband and/or his new wife.

It's easier to blame Mary Beth than to face the possibility that this could happen to any one of us, that poverty could lead us (or our daughters) into losing our own children—who have been born as part of a marriage contract.

Mary Beth is also different from most women—who have *not* signed surrogacy contracts.

What kind of woman signs a surrogacy contract? Maybe our first question should be: What kind of man signs a surrogacy contract? Or profits from and promotes a surrogacy contract?*

In the nineteenth century, the American state routinely justified the incarceration of "sexually active," impoverished immigrant girls, including rape and incest victims—by diagnosing them as "mentally ill," "genetically imbecile," or "feeble-minded." By definition, how could someone diagnosed by the experts as an "imbecile" also be a fit mother? She's subhuman; she can't even speak English properly. If she's pregnant, wouldn't her child be better off without her, in a respectable household—even as an indentured servant?

*Some people blamed Mary Beth—but not Bill—for signing a surrogacy contract.

What a perfect model for the surrogacy industry! Today, even if a "surrogate uterus" changes its mind, who'd believe what a uterus had to say? How can any woman who is so psychologically and economically wounded (you'd have to be "crazy" to sign a surrogacy contract) ever win custody of her child?

Are we then in favor of impregnating a woman whom we believe is mentally incompetent—for the sole purpose of being able to remove her child from her? Are we in favor of using this mentally incompetent woman's signature against her? (She "consented." She "agreed." She "knew what she was doing.")

People said: anyone who'd agree to sell her own baby is worse than psychiatrically impaired. She's a moral degenerate. Well, then: *do we want a lot of children to have her genes?* Are we so convinced that genes don't matter and that environment (the right attitude and lots of money) will always overcome genetic and uterine history?

The judge, the mental-health experts, and the media all told us that the woman who gave birth to Baby M was not her "real" mother but only her "surrogate" mother. They said that her *real* mother was her father.

Actually, Baby M's true father may be—Phil Donahue! I say this because I have never interviewed a surrogacy-contract mother who didn't first hear about surrogacy on the Donahue program. Even Noel Keane, the founder of two surrogacy clinics and the man who arranged the birth of Baby M, credits Donahue with introducing surrogacy to the public. I imagine it went something like this:

One day, probably in 1978, a woman who was "nobody" instantly became "somebody" (at least for a full hour) when she appeared on the Donahue show to discuss her calling as a surrogate mother. Millions of female viewers saw her. Their hearts stood still, then soared.

"I could get on the Donahue show!" they thought. (Americans suffer anonymity as a fate worse than death.) Right then and there, hundreds of anonymous women decided to become well-known philanthropists.

Cinderella (a nobody) would become her own Fairy Godmother (a somebody) who, with one wave of her magic wand, would grant a baby to a childless couple and gold to her own children. All this attention would be hers for *doing nothing* (as if pregnancy and childbirth are "nothing," because men don't do it).

"Nobody would look down at me or be mean to me. Not if I were somebody," they must have thought. "I'll show them—my good side, that is. I'll sacrifice myself to give the 'gift of life' to a suffering world."

What does a surrogacy-contract mother really want? Here is what some of them have said:

"My real bond was with the baby's mother. We had lunch once a week. She took me shopping. She bought me special foods. She's the one I'm gonna miss."

"She was so nice to me while I was pregnant," said another surrogacy-contract mother. "My own mother never treated me as nicely."

"She is really sort of a mother to me, the mother I always needed and never had," a third surrogacy-contract mother wrote. "I thought of everything that she had done for me and I wished I could do something in return. The idea just hit me, it's very simple. Why, I can have a baby for her!"

According to an interview in *The Bergen Record* (June 23, 1987), surrogacy-contract mother Patty Adair said that she thought about her child's adoptive mother "more than I think about the baby, because my bond was with her. I think of her . . . like a sister." In the same article, contract mother Harilyn Quill "suffered from a loss seemingly unrelated to the baby—that of an especially close relationship with the adoptive mother." Contract mother Dara Powell needed contact with the couple and asked them to contact her, but she assured them she "wouldn't need such attention forever. . . . I told them I just needed to be let off gradually." Gradually weaned. Gently weaned.

What is going on here? Does the surrogacy-contract mother want to *be* a "surrogate" mother—or does she want to *have* a "surrogate" mother for herself? Does Mary Beth want to be adopted and adored by an older, higher-status mother figure?[10]

Do she and all the other contract mothers want those maternally solicitous phone calls, lunches, advice-giving sessions to go on forever? Do they want this so badly that they're willing to give their babies away in order to get it?

Does a contract mother think that *she* is the baby who is being adopted? Does she become unhappy, not only because she's suddenly missing her newborn but because she's also the one left behind, as maternally unadored as ever?

Does a contract mother get pregnant to competitively *replace* her (infertile surrogate) mother—or to please her? Is the contract mother really Electra, woman as Oedipus, in search of union with a surrogate father? Or is she trying to exorcise her dependence on men, and to make peace with other women? Is the baby her peace offering?

The contract mother would never have sex with her surrogate mother's husband. She hasn't used her youth, her sexuality, or her fertility to compete against her surrogate mother for the same man. She was impregnated techno-medically, not sexually. She is a "good girl."

The pregnant girl has a heart of gold and is as powerful as any goddess. Nothing can hurt her. How can we say she's being victim-ized? She volunteered herself for the job. How can you exploit a volunteer?

Everyone wants a (surrogate) mother. No one's real mother is ever good enough. It may seem farfetched, but who might Bill Stern's surrogate mother be? It's not Mary Beth and it's not Betsy—it's his daughter, Baby M!

He clings to that baby helplessly, desperately, as if his not knowing where he leaves off and she begins is actually an accomplishment, as if *he's* the infant who'll die without *her* . . .

The media portrayed Bill Stern very sympathetically, as a Holocaust victim. For example, on January 6, 1987, *The New York Times* reported Stern's testimony about why he felt "compelled" to have a genetic child: ". . . because he had no blood relatives 'anywhere in the world.' He said he was born in Berlin shortly after World War II, the only child of a banker and a clothier who had spent the war 'hiding' from the Nazis."

Six days later, on January 12, 1987, *The New York Times* reported Bill's past as if he himself were a Holocaust survivor (and not the child of survivors):

> *Baby M's father . . . felt "compelled" to continue his family's bloodlines. He was born 40 years ago in Berlin, the only son*

*of a banker and a clothier in prewar Germany. Both parents
had been hounded and economically destroyed by the Nazis.
They have since died. All other living relatives . . . were killed
in the Holocaust.*

The mental-health experts were as vague and sympathetic as the
media about these facts. Dr. Brodzinsky noted that when Bill's
mother died, he "became the sole surviving member of his family"
and that Bill consequently "developed a deep-seated need to re-
establish ties with biological kin—to see and feel and love someone
else to whom he is biologically connected."

Dr. Greif pointed out that Bill's extended family, "Mr. Stern's
cousins, uncles, and grandparents—were killed." She, too, saw surrogacy as the way to "enable him to have a biological link to another
person, something he has been lacking since the death of his
mother." Dr. Schechter explains it thus: "Mr. Stern's mother died in
December of 1983, leaving him bereft of any living relatives. Mr.
Stern, and increasingly Mrs. Stern [?] desired a genetic link to a child
and therefore began to consider surrogate parent programs."

Mary Beth's motives were questioned, criticized, and used to prove
that she was mentally unbalanced; Bill's motives were accepted,
romanticized, and used to absolve him of any wrongdoing in his
choice of surrogacy as a personal response to the Holocaust.

Bill grew up in the United States with his parents. According to
Dr. Greif's report, Bill loved and got along with his father, who died
when he was twelve, but (shades of Portnoy) had a "conflictual"
relationship with his mother: she was too pushy, she "wouldn't let
go." According to Dr. Allwyne J. Levine, when Bill's father died, Bill
said Kaddish (a prayer for the dead) every day for the required twelve
months. Once Bill moved away to attend the University of Michigan,
he visited his mother in New York only twice a year.

In 1973, Bill Stern married his Michigan girlfriend of five years,
Betsy—who is the daughter of a Methodist lay preacher and biochemist. In 1985, thirteen months after his mother's death, Bill began
trying to artificially inseminate Mary Beth—who is of German and
Irish Catholic descent.

Is Baby M Bill's surrogate *Christian* mother?

By Jewish law, a child is Jewish only if her mother is Jewish. Baby
M's two mothers are both Christian, and her father plans to raise her

as a Unitarian. According to Allwyn J. Levine, Bill and Betsy both regularly attended services at a Presbyterian church; Bill received counseling for nine months with a Presbyterian pastoral counselor named Tom Ward.

Can it be that Bill unconsciously thinks that Baby M will be everything Bill wishes his mother *was:* independent, self-controlled, educated, Christian, untainted by Jewish, guilt-provoking sorrow?

Like many children of Holocaust survivors, perhaps Bill felt he was born to serve his mother's purposes. Perhaps Bill wanted a child to serve *his* purposes; a child who would never try to control him or make him feel guilty, never place demands on him, never be too "pushy." An idealized Christian surrogate mother . . .

Just as Betsy may have been admired for being a "good" woman (she had a "male" career and, like a man, would never become pregnant), did people also unconsciously admire Bill for being a "good," forgiving, assimilated Jew? Despite Hitler's provocation, Bill is a Jew who attends church, marries or impregnates only Christian women, and who psychologically wants a Christian (surrogate) mother . . .

What if Bill's Miracle Baby turns out to be like her own mother, Mary Beth? Narcissistic, manipulative, dependent, academically lazy, and also out of control? What will the Sterns do to make sure this does not happen? What will they do if, despite their efforts, this happens anyway?

Why didn't the mental-health experts ever pause, just once, to wonder: What kind of man would use both contract and penal law to make sure that "his" daughter would never again see, smell, breast-feed from, play with—even come to know her birth mother?

What kind of father would, in addition, bequeath his daughter as if she were a piece of property, to his wife, Betsy—were he to die before her birth? What kind of husband would replace his wife's body piecemeal (uterus first) because of a medical disability, instead of sharing her life with her "for better or for worse, in sickness and in health"? What kind of husband would run off on a genetic shopping spree knowing his wife couldn't go along, instead of cementing their love by sharing the adoption of a baby with her?

What kind of father gives his daughter *no* mother—to guarantee himself the fast, inside track in any potential custody battle? If Bill and Betsy were to divorce, would Betsy have any claim to custody?

She is a career woman who refused to get pregnant, who took off as little time from her career as possible for primary childcare, and who is not biologically or genetically related to her adoptive daughter. Bill is Baby M's genetic and legal father. He is also bonded to her. He conceived of her. He needs her. He loves her.

N ow we can ask: What kind of woman signs a surrogacy contract? To find out, I conducted twenty-five interviews with unhappy surrogacy-contract mothers, surrogacy lawyers, psychiatrists, and others involved in the surrogacy issue. I read articles and books in which surrogacy-contract mothers were studied and interviewed.[11] I observed happy contract mothers and listened to public debates in which they participated. I found that each of the surrogacy-contract mothers shared some or all of the following characteristics.

She is a *fertile woman of childbearing years* who has already proven herself as a *biological mother;* a relatively *uneducated* and *impoverished* woman who is *married to a low-income husband* and whose own economic options are so limited that less than a dollar an hour (for doing "nothing"—that is, carrying a child) sounds good to her— given that she is also a *full-time but unpaid housewife and mother;* a *middle-born* child with anywhere from three to nineteen siblings who became *addicted to television* during the late 1950s and 1960s, and who is either *functionally illiterate,* dyslexic, or a very slow reader.

A *traditional* and *religious* woman who grew up in a rigorously *Christian household* where she was taught that a "good" woman is someone who sacrifices herself for others and who transcends suffering by minimizing or denying it.

A *rebellious and self-destructive* woman who is stubbornly and unconsciously interpreting church doctrine in a rather unique way; sometimes an *incestuously abused* woman who as a child learned how to disassociate herself from traumatic experiences that were simultaneously pleasurable and painful, undeniable and yet denied.

Such a woman has been primed by religious and/or sexual authoritarianism to minimize, deny, and justify all subsequent invasions of her mind/body. In an attempt to exorcise the incestuous invasion, she may reenact it. It is her way of telling us what happened to her.

She splits herself in two in order to experience herself as both guilty and innocent, profane and sacred. She punishes herself in order to redeem herself. She splits herself in two as a way of denying that there is anyone "out there" (in the real world) or "in here" (inside her).

Some victims of incestuous abuse do more than disassociate themselves from their minds/bodies. Some develop a "multiple-personality disorder." How else are we to understand the chillingly infanticidal, amnesiac, and disassociated behavior of Elizabeth Diane Downs, an exceptionally happy surrogacy-contract mother who is now imprisoned in Oregon for murdering one of her (own) children and for attempting to murder two others?[12]

In April of 1980, Elizabeth Diane Downs decided to become a contract mother after she watched the Donahue show. Downs applied for and was accepted into the Surrogate Parenting Associates Program in Louisville, Kentucky. Ann Rule recounts the stunning details of Downs's psychiatric and psychological exams, the first of which she "flunked." She was then sent to a psychiatrist in Phoenix who "passed" her.

At the time, Downs was a fertile, married (but secretly separated) mother of three young children, a one-semester Bible college dropout, and a U.S. mail carrier. She grew up in a strict, religious ("Christian Baptist") home where she had been sexually molested by her father. According to Ann Rule, she

> never cried or fought; it never occurred to her that she could. "He was the authority figure. I couldn't resist him. I couldn't tell. I would just blank out. It just didn't exist. I didn't exist. It's like a nightmare—not real . . ." How Diane hated him. But she hated herself more. Despite her revulsion, the incestuous fondling evoked an instinctual pleasure response. It felt good, even though it was wrong. She could not separate sex from terror and power . . . and pleasure, and she could not understand the sensations she felt.

Consequently, several psychiatrists observed that Downs could "shut her emotions down at will" and seemed "able to isolate her affect completely." Upon insemination she quickly became pregnant and gave birth to a girl in May of 1982.

Downs was "euphoric" during this pregnancy and delivery but felt no loss and no sadness when she surrendered her baby to the surrogate couple. She felt "special," "like a princess," and could "hardly wait to be inseminated again."

Downs says she does not remember trying to murder all three of her children—nor does she *feel* anything about her incestuous molestation or about her surrogate pregnancy. Downs's affect is reportedly as unemotional as that of all the "happy" contract mothers whom I've publicly debated. Like Downs, most contract mothers (whether they are happy or unhappy) exhibit a remarkable degree of disassociation from their feelings, from their bodies, and from reality.

The happy contract mother insists (proudly and self-righteously) that she "never felt connected to any baby during pregnancy. It was never my baby *to* feel," she says. "It was always the couple's baby." (No, it was never *my* body. My body always belonged to my father . . .)

In a sense, most mothers, whether they are marriage- or surrogacy-contract mothers, are economically impoverished apart from the sexual and reproductive contracts they have with men. Perhaps the widespread sexual and incestuous abuse of female children (coupled with women's internalized self-hatred) explains why so many women enter into surrogacy-like arrangements with men, including husbands—without noticing what they're doing.

I am not saying that every surrogacy-contract mother or every wife is an incest victim or suffers from "multiple personality syndrome" or is capable of committing infanticide.[13]

Everyone—you or I—incest victims, happy or unhappy contract mothers—all are able to disassociate ourselves from our feelings and/or from our bodies when they cause us too much pain. However, the kind of disassociation incest victims exhibit is strikingly similar to the behavior of most of the happy contract mothers whom I've interviewed, debated, or observed.

According to the June 23, 1987, *Bergen Record,* "Many surrogate mothers said they viewed themselves as a 'service' or a 'vehicle' for the couple. During the pregnancy, they carefully would avoid using phrases like 'my baby.' When the baby would kick for the first time, for example, many would tell the couple, 'Your baby kicked today.' "

Most of these women also seemed obsessed with "appearances." They described themselves as the kind of women who kept them-

selves, their homes, and their children in "very neat condition."
Mary Beth Whitehead made it a point to tell me (and everyone else)
about how in order to "feel good," she scrubbed her bathroom
tiles, washed her floors—and then did her nails. "Every day" if
need be.

The majority of the contract mothers I interviewed over the phone
unilaterally *chose* to describe their physical appearance to me or to
send me pictures of themselves. They asked me whether or not I
thought they looked "pretty." (Some, in person, asked me whether
or not I thought they resembled their photos.) It's as if these women
are afraid "they" don't really exist; that all they have is how they
appear to others and whether that appearance is pleasing.

The contract mothers were also "disassociated" from themselves
(or from reality) in this sense: they literally didn't know what they
or others were doing or what it meant. For example, in a May 18,
1986, letter to Judge Sorkow, Mary Beth (who had agreed to abandon
a child at birth) self-righteously criticized Betsy Stern for planning
to "abandon" that same child to the care of paid employees.

Even non–surrogacy contract mothers are disassociated from reality. For example, even though Betsy Stern wanted to be the psychological mother and the legal mother, she had little idea of how much
work was involved. After having the baby in the house for a time,
she said, "I didn't realize how much time is required to raise a child."

Both happy and unhappy contract mothers tried to convince me
that they were essentially "good" women, morally as well as physically. Most described themselves as "religious" Christians (Catholic,
Baptist, or Fundamentalist) who attended church regularly and/or
were still "true believers."

The fanatical, almost stubborn naïveté exhibited by these women
is impossible to convey. Happy or unhappy, they took great pride in
how they trusted and obeyed everyone blindly about everything.

These women believed whatever the surrogacy-clinic lawyers and
doctors told them. They rarely asked questions; they never disobeyed
an order. They did exactly what they were told to do—and therefore
couldn't "believe" that they'd been used for "one thing only"; that
they'd "never mattered," i.e., that their fantasies of being "above"
it all had little to do with the realities of trafficking in women for
profit.

> *DEBBIE: I thought my couple and I would always be the best of friends. I imagined we'd always spend our holidays together—just one big happy family. I can't believe that all along they planned to get rid of me once they had the baby.*
> *HELEN: Even now it's really hard for me to admit that the whole thing was a setup against me from the start. I can't even complain about being paid too little for all my suffering. I was ready to do it for nothing.*
> *MARY BETH WHITEHEAD: I didn't know I was allowed to pick out the couple. I thought I had to do what they told me to do. I really liked Bill and Betsy. I thought they liked me too.*

Contract mothers were emphatic about not being motivated solely by financial need. They wanted to be seen as lady-bountiful "helpers"—not as poorly paid employees. They needed to see themselves (and to convince others) that they could not be held down by anything as vulgar as money.

> *DEBBIE: I really wanted to bring joy to a childless couple. The money was secondary. I wanted to do a good deed.*
> *SALLY: I didn't take any money. I wanted to help our friends out. I never imagined that they'd turn on me.*
> *ALEJANDRA: The women in my family convinced me that this was a proper and helpful thing to do. No one said it would make me a bad person.*
> *MARY BETH WHITEHEAD: Knowing that I can give this most loving gift of happiness to an unfortunate couple, plus the benefit to my family would be a rewarding experience. (From her initial letter to ICNY.)*

In a sense, a "good girl" *is,* by definition, a happy contract mother, that is, she is under reproductive contract either to her husband or to God himself. She is giving the "gift of life" to the unborn, to her husband, to a childless couple or to the world.

There is enough of a similarity between what a surrogacy-contract mother is doing and what a "good" woman is supposed to do that we can't just dismiss her as "bad": incestuously dirty, economically greedy, mentally sick. She is doing exactly what Christianity has taught her to do—but in her own maddeningly unique way.

The contract mother is asexually pregnant with a strange man's sperm. She and her task are sacred. But she isn't bearing her husband's sperm, nor is she bearing God's. Unlike the Virgin Mary and other married ladies, she isn't planning to rear the divine child herself: she has in fact executed a business or employment contract for her services and/or for her "product."

For a long time, I couldn't understand why more women, feminist and antifeminist alike, didn't view Mary Beth as a heroine. After all, look at what she was saying: "Money be damned! I made a mistake. I can't abandon my own flesh and blood. It's my body and it's my baby." Diverse groups of women should have found something here to admire. Most didn't—because Mary Beth's choice of surrogacy and then her change of heart about that choice put them (and her) into conflict with two opposing female role models: the Christian/religious one and the feminist/secular one. This conflict—really a head-on collision—is what fueled women's extraordinary passion over Mary Beth.

Surrogacy, or postindustrialized polygamy, has emerged at this moment for any number of reasons, among them an increase in sterility and a shortage of adoptable white infants. At this precise moment in history, surrogacy and how we feel about it is also a reflection of the war currently raging between secular feminism and religious patriarchy. In a sense, the surrogacy-contract mother is an example of feminism half-baked or religious fervor in crackpot form.

How can a *feminist* view Mary Beth as a heroic role model? Is a feminist role model someone who drops out of high school in order to get married or who glorifies being a pregnant and economically dependent housewife? Or someone who glorifies being a poorly paid womb-for-hire? But here's where the headaches begin. Even if Mary Beth hasn't quit domestic servitude for a higher-status career, she's at least charging men for her reproductive services. She may also represent "the" solution for the career woman who is infertile, or who for some reason doesn't want to get pregnant and/or to marry—but who definitely wants a child of her own. Some feminists might devalue Mary Beth's identity as a womb-for-hire but still wish to reserve the right to hire her for themselves.

But how can a *Christian* or a genuinely *religious* person view Mary Beth as a heroic role model? Is a Christian someone who allows herself to be impregnated by a strange man's sperm—outside of marriage and for money? From the Christian point of view, the whole thing is immoral, against God and Nature. And then the next headache begins.

Isn't childbearing one of woman's most important obligations and accomplishments? Isn't it an act of pure Christian love to have a baby for someone less fortunate than oneself? Don't people need to marry in order to create a stable society? Don't married people need children in order to be a "real" family?

What's being done to Mary Beth is done to hundreds or thousands of custodially challenged American mothers every day. What's different is not only that she signed a surrogacy rather than a marriage contract, but that we were actually invited to witness Mary Beth's trial through the media. (Usually these legal crucifixions take place without witnesses.)

Many people were entertained watching Mary Beth be condemned and tormented, day after day, as if she were "really" a character in a soap opera or one of the President's Men, suddenly and deservedly upended.

It could be any woman up there on that witness stand in Hackensack, New Jersey. At this moment in history, I am willing to stand up and be counted. Will so bloodthirsty (and so pro-male, pro-adoption, pro-science, and pro—middle class) an audience listen to anyone who threatens to interfere with their entertainment?

CHAPTER 3

INDUSTRIALIZED PREGNANCY: A DECADE OF SURROGACY

The use of women as "surrogate mothers" is as old as patriarchy. In the Old Testament, Abraham and Sarah's handmaid, Hagar, was a surrogate mother. What's new is our ability to industrialize pregnancy and to mass-produce custom-ordered children as if they were "products." Otherwise what's new is simply what's old—with a vengeance.[1]

Liberals tell us that women deserve equality because they are the same as or identical to men. Thus, men and women can both "parent."

The state tells us that a father is a better "parent" than a mother; that a sperm donor can be a "father" but that a birth mother is not necessarily a "mother"; and that sperm is more custodially entitling than is nine months of pregnancy and childbirth.

This is what the state is saying when it awards custody of a newborn infant to a sperm donor, a contract father, a boyfriend, a husband, or an adoption agency—over the objection of a perfectly fit birth mother; and when it treats a birth mother as if she's a criminal—or more harshly than a criminal for demanding to be recognized as her child's mother or custodian.

For example, men accused of murder are often treated more carefully (advised of their rights, allowed to hire a lawyer) than Mary Beth Whitehead was when Judge Sorkow issued his ex parte order against her.*

Mary Beth had not yet "kidnapped" her breast-feeding infant when, with no prior notice, no chance to hire a lawyer, Judge Sorkow sent the police in to seize her baby.

Judges increasingly allow a sperm donor or unwed boyfriend to change his mind about surrendering a child for adoption—but as often and increasingly have denied this same right to a birth mother.

For example, in 1977, in New Jersey, a "friendly" sperm donor sought paternal rights to a child conceived with his sperm. He had donated his sperm to a woman he knew who wanted a child—but who didn't want to marry or have sexual intercourse with him. He was under the impression that she would marry him after the birth of the child. However, the relationship ended when she was three months pregnant. Once the child was born, he sued for paternal rights. Over the birth mother's objection, a judge ruled that the sperm donor *was* the legal father, and was therefore entitled to parental rights, including visitation.

The mother can now be jailed if she in any way interferes with (or fails to "facilitate") paternal visitation; she can also be custodially challenged at any time. Her constitutional right to travel may be restricted until her child is eighteen so that paternal visitation can occur; her parental rights may even be terminated by a judge who values sperm plus a male income more highly than pregnancy and maternal-infant bonding—the scenario involved in the Baby M case.

In the New Jersey case (known as *CC* v. *CM*) described above, the sperm donor or father surrogate was permitted to assert his rights and to change his mind. The mother surrogate in the Baby M case was not. There are many cases in adoption law that illustrate this rather horrifying double standard. Let me contrast only two.

In 1985, in Tennessee, an unwed, pregnant eighteen-year-old, alone, penniless, afraid, approached a private adoption agency a week before she gave birth. They agreed to shelter her and pay her medical

---

*Race and class are also crucial factors. A white man or woman is usually treated more carefully than is a man or woman of color.

expenses if she would agree to surrender the baby for adoption. She signed adoption papers right after she gave birth, but changed her mind almost immediately. Within days, she and her newly helpful family began calling the agency. They hired a lawyer, who apparently didn't file court papers until eleven months after her *thirty-day* time limit had elapsed. The court denied her any parental rights and found that she hadn't acted quickly enough or been subjected to any "duress."[2]

In Arkansas in 1985, an unwed man successfully filed a petition to set aside an adoption *two and one-half years* after the birth of his genetic child. The child had been born in the fall of 1982; the man learned about the birth in March of 1984. He waited for nearly a full year until February of 1985 before he decided to act. That same year, the court decided that to impose the *one-year* statute of limitations would violate his due-process rights as an unwed father.[3]

A sperm donor and a "surrogate mother" are neither identical nor equal. Sperm donation is more like blood donation than it is like pregnancy-and-childbirth. However, sperm donation takes less time, involves less risk, and is perhaps more pleasurable than is being intravenously pierced and drained of a pint of blood.

A "surrogate father" or sperm donor can masturbate to orgasm in less than five minutes. A "surrogate mother" must be artificially inseminated (a time-consuming, stressful, and sometimes uncomfortable procedure) over and over again until she conceives; then, she must endure all the pain and risk associated with nine months of pregnancy and with childbirth.

Sperm cells are different from living children; the labor of pregnancy and childbirth is different from the "labor" required to produce the sperm. Without demeaning or diminishing men's role in biological reproduction, the fact is that the man contributes his sperm; the woman contributes herself.

An anonymous sperm donor (especially if he never has a genetic child of his own) may eventually want to find his (only) genetic child. However, such men are probably fewer in number than are birth mothers who were forced to give up their children. Also, whatever such an anonymous sperm donor may feel, *it is not the same as or equal to* the feelings that a birth mother feels about her "disappeared" child.

Sperm donors, inseminating physicians, and businessmen comprise an industry that caters to infertile men and their wives. If a wife conceives via artificial insemination, her husband automatically becomes the child's legal father. The infertile husband is protected from any challenge to his legal paternity that a sperm donor might make.*

In general, most anonymous sperm donors do not sue for paternity. Those who do are most often successful when the inseminated woman is unmarried, divorced, or a lesbian—when she is not under reproductive contract to any one man. As such, she is easily seen as "unfit" because she is often both poor and manless.

I n 1976, a Michigan lawyer named Noel Keane read about a man from San Francisco who had paid a woman seven thousand dollars to bear his genetic child. (They'd met through a newspaper ad.) Keane thought it was a great idea. However, under Michigan law, cash payments were illegal; initially he recruited unpaid volunteers. Keane was able to arrange only five surrogate births. He took a three-thousand-dollar "finder's fee" for each one.[4]

Keane knew that in order for surrogacy or contract motherhood to become an industry, women would have to be paid and contractually bound. He and other lawyers began to examine the loopholes and to publicize the "cause." Positive media coverage would ensure that even if contracts could not be enforced, surrogacy profiteers would not be criminally prosecuted as baby sellers. Noel Keane became a frequent guest on the Donahue show.

In 1979, lawyer Katie Brophy and infertility specialist Dr. Richard Levin founded Surrogate Parenting Associates, Inc. (SPA), in Louisville, Kentucky. They advertised for surrogates in newspapers; they

---

*This is not Betsy Stern's position. Betsy had to *adopt* Baby M; the baby was not automatically legally hers, even though she was married to the child's genetic father.

were paying ten thousand dollars per head.* Their first recruit was an Illinois woman, who now uses the name Elizabeth Kane. She conceived in February 1980 and gave birth in November. The case received a great deal of publicity; Kane said the publicity led to her husband's being fired even before the baby was born.[5]

In April of 1980, Elizabeth Diane Downs (whom I wrote about in chapter 2) wrote to Dr. Levin and expressed her desire to "help" others by "giving" them a baby. She flew to Louisville to be inseminated. According to Ann Rule:

> *Louisville charmed Diane. She was waited on, served hot soup, tucked in at night, totally pampered. It was as marvelous as she had hoped. . . . The whole experience was exhilarating and fun. Dr. Levin even drove a Corvette with personalized license plates: BABY 4 U. Diane speculated to herself that the surrogate project must have made him very wealthy.*
>
> *[On May 7, 1982, Diane flew back to Louisville to have labor induced.] It was like a magical carnival; the princess had come here to give birth to a perfect child. Louisville welcomed her with flowers and lights.*
>
> *Just before midnight, Diane was rolled into the delivery room. There, holding on to the "other mother's" hand, she gave birth to a baby girl. With tears running down her face, Diane held the baby for a moment, and then she placed it in the arms of the real mother who was to raise this child.*[6]

Lawyers, physicians, and other business people have organized the surrogacy or contract-motherhood industry into "clinics" or "programs." They are essentially business companies. The company lawyer and administrative staff represent the contract father. Their job is to ensure that the contract father gets his genetic child and that the contract mother does *not*. If the contract father is married, the company lawyer can also arrange for his wife to adopt the child.

The company recruits and screens the contract mothers. The inseminating physician may be a partner in the company or part of the company's lucrative business network. The physician may monitor the contract pregnancy and/or deliver the baby.

*This fee did not increase from 1979 to 1988.

A standard surrogacy contract requires the contract father to pay ten thousand dollars *plus* medical expenses to the birth mother; and from seven thousand five hundred up to ten thousand dollars to the agency for its matchmaking services. If the contract mother miscarries late in the pregnancy or delivers a stillborn, her payment is one thousand dollars.

Once a contract mother becomes pregnant, her life is no longer her own. She is specifically prohibited from engaging in any activities perceived as potentially harmful to the fetus (smoking, taking aspirin or prescription drugs, drinking, overeating, undereating, etc.); she may be required to inform the company of her whereabouts at all times; she may be required to undergo amniocentesis—and an abortion if "defects" are detected.

However, even Judge Sorkow decided that the legal right to abortion couldn't be lost (or waived) by a contract mother, no matter how many contracts she signed promising to give up that right. For this reason, surrogacy companies are interested in making sure that their contract mothers are "happy" or at least "under their control" during pregnancy.

Surrogacy companies generally employ psychiatrists or psychologists to screen out those applicants likely to change their minds. Whether they can do this (and how hard they try) varies. Dr. Philip Parker, Keane's Detroit psychologist, admits to rejecting only one out of more than five hundred applicants; he believes that prospective "surrogates" are "self-selecting."[7]

Los Angeles lawyer Bill Handel claims that his company, Center for Surrogate Parenting, Inc. (CSP), rejects nineteen out of twenty applicants in the course of a four-month screening process. From chapter 2 you may remember that Elizabeth Diane Downs "flunked" one set of psychological tests but "passed" another.

Some surrogacy companies introduce the contract mother to the contract couple as a way of making them feel loved and important. Some companies absolutely forbid any contact between contracting parties. Philadelphia's Surrogate Mothering, Limited, keeps both parties anonymous; Louisville's SPA allows the contract mother to write a one-page letter to "her couple"—but only later in the pregnancy.

Los Angeles's CSP believes that "mother-couple bonding" cuts down on problems; they match contract mothers and couples on the basis of their personal characteristics and insist that the three first spend a full day together to build up trust. According to Hilary Hanafin, CSP's psychologist: "It works for us because [the surrogate] cannot imagine hurting this couple whom she knows and likes so much."[8]

D ebbie was a surrogacy mother from Texas. She learned about a surrogacy broker after she read about a professor and his wife who were registered with the broker. Debbie was lonely; she "needed something" to make her feel "fulfilled." The couple in the article seemed "warm and loving"; Debbie "just knew" that if she became "their surrogate" that the three of them would have a "wonderful" and "lifelong relationship." I interviewed Debbie in the summer of 1987.

PHYLLIS: You really chose the couple from an article? You know their real names?

DEBBIE: Know their names? God, I was in their house on a weekly basis for a year and a half. They became so involved in my life, they were the closest people in my life, full time. Their names are Ben and Harriet. They're each twelve years older than I am.

PHYLLIS: How did you pick them?

DEBBIE: The broker sent me their picture. He's a professor and she's a housewife. They got married so they could have a baby through the program. They might not be married otherwise.

PHYLLIS: Did you look like Harriet?

DEBBIE: Oh, no. He wanted a baby that looked like him. He set out to find a blue-eyed, blond-haired surrogate. They definitely wanted a blond, blue-eyed baby. This is his first child.

PHYLLIS: So you chose each other? What happened then?

DEBBIE: The broker put together the paperwork. But we sort of agreed among ourselves, even before we signed anything. I was a student and he was a professor. It made me think I could meet people and that would be good for me.

PHYLLIS: *You mean maybe you could find a husband or a better job?*

DEBBIE: *Yes. If I had a baby for somebody, they would help me with the rest of my life. I know that sounds awful, but I just thought I'd have a relationship with these people all my life. Harriet said I'd always be with them on holidays. I told my son that I was going to have a baby for Ben and Harriet and that the baby would be like a cousin to him. He would always be able to see it, play with it, grow up knowing the baby. These people showered my son with gifts and gave me a lot of things for him. They took him out, bought him clothes, gave him a big birthday party. I tried to back out of giving them the baby. But they were holding—they had my son.*

PHYLLIS: *Wait a minute, what do you mean they had your son?*

DEBBIE: *I was in the last weeks of my pregnancy. It was summer. He was bored. "Oh, Mommy, you can't do anything with me," he'd been saying. So Harriet and Ben said they would keep him for me. So they had my son and I was due any day. I'd been trying to get out of the whole thing.*

PHYLLIS: *When did you tell them you wanted to back out? What happened?*

DEBBIE: *I mentioned it in my fourth month. That's when our relationship was a real constant thing. Harriet started taking me to lunch once a week. She took me swimming. She introduced me to all her friends. I didn't want to complain, but I had no money for maternity clothes. I was embarrassed to tell her I needed the money.*

In the meanwhile, Ben's mother wanted to meet me so I spent the weekend with her. She was going on and on about me having blue eyes. She kept feeding me. She showed me pictures of Ben when he was a baby. It was a very strange situation. Once she really yelled at me because I fell down. I had only skinned my knee. She and Harriet and Ben acted like they owned my body. I couldn't do anything without getting permission.

When I was eight months pregnant, I was going to take off and hide. But I had no money. I had health problems. I was on welfare. My son was in school. My mother hated that I was a surrogate. She also hated the fact that I had my son out of wedlock.

PHYLLIS: *What kind of woman is Harriet?*

DEBBIE: *Homey. She bakes and cooks and sews. She's very submissive to her husband. He's the boss.*

PHYLLIS: *What's he like?*

DEBBIE: *He thinks he's God's gift to women. He's extremely handsome and he's the type of man women look at twice and he knows it. He's in charge. He's not a "homebody." He's a workaholic. He works at the university and does private consulting and teaches. I don't think he's ever home.*

Debbie found it hard to be assertive. It took her two months to tell Ben and Harriet that she'd "rather not have them with her in the delivery room." It took her two months after she gave birth to tell Ben and Harriet that she'd "rather keep her baby." As time passed, Debbie began to realize that she hadn't been adopted along with the baby. I agree that Debbie sounds naïve. Why is such a woman being allowed to sign a surrogacy contract?

PHYLLIS: *What was your relationship like after you gave up the baby?*

DEBBIE: *Friendly at first. I called Harriet and asked what the baby looked like, other things. Everything was okay until I hit the real reason I was calling. Then she—God, she was very angry with me. I just couldn't believe she was acting that way to me. So I said, "I gave you my baby, and look how you're treating me." She said to me, "If you ever say that word to me again I'm going to hang up on you." I said, "What word?" She said, "Your baby. He's not your baby. He's my baby." So I never said that word again.*

But I couldn't stop crying or thinking about the baby. So Ben and Harriet agreed to pay for some therapy for me. Then Ben and Harriet took me out to lunch but they refused to bring

> *the baby. Harriet said I couldn't see him yet, I wasn't ready,*
> *I was still too attached; the therapy obviously wasn't working.*
> *She called my therapist and said they're not paying the bills*
> *anymore.*

Most contract couples are very grateful to the contract mother. They also want nothing more to do with her after the baby is safely "theirs."

Journalist Anne Taylor Fleming described a California "surrogate" who "had meant to make the couple like her so much that 'afterwards' she would be part of their extended family and could watch her son growing up." But she writes, "the couple did not want her around. And she was not unattached from her son, and clearly never would be." One adoptive mother refused to give her last name or address because she was afraid the birth mother would "try to send the child birthday presents in the future."[9]

Some surrogacy companies set up "support" groups for their contract mothers. An older woman or "mother" figure (analogous to a convent mother superior or to a brothel madam) is often in charge of keeping the "girls" in line.

Debbie had a support group—but it dropped her when her couple started fighting with the broker about money; and because Debbie had started saying she wanted to keep her baby. Debbie says the support group "kept telling her to keep her feelings quiet." Debbie was not emotionally supported by her "support" group; nevertheless two group members were "there" for her during labor.

> *Two of them from the group were in the hospital with me when*
> *I had the baby. They were like spies. The hospital people all*
> *cooperated in this thing—it was impossible for me to oppose*
> *it, and there were these two surrogate spies there, too. I was*
> *actually friendly with those women until recently. Now they*
> *refuse to talk to me because I talk against surrogate parenting.*
> *It's like I said something bad about their religion.*

Debbie also described being medically abused by the physician selected by the broker.

They first had me examined by a physician's assistant. He told me I wouldn't be able to get pregnant unless I took fertility drugs. So I took them but the drugs were having horrible side effects. My face broke out and my vision blurred and I was dizzy and my ovaries were swollen. Then a pharmacist told me I was getting a triple dose of Clomid, and it was a male hormone, and really dangerous. I complained to my support group but they didn't do anything.

Before I was inseminated they tested me for everything. Turns out they didn't test Ben very carefully, only for AIDS and syphilis. His sperm gave me a sexually transmitted virus. I had an infection for two months. Maybe nobody thought a man would have a disease. He was a professor; they just thought he was perfect.

Whom does the broker's physician represent: the contract mother, the contract couple, or the company? Are American physicians actually harming patients in the interest of "scientific" research? In the interest of profit margins?

A number of women have sued surrogacy brokers, for example. Gannett News Service reported that at least ten former clients of Noel Keane's cited problems with his programs. Malcolm Gladwell and Rochelle Sharpe, writing in the *New Republic,* described some of them: "One surrogate underwent artificial insemination before any contract had been signed; another was approved despite a history of heart disease; in two other cases, the surrogate mother bore her husband's child—not the client's."

Another example described by Gladwell and Sharpe concerns "Jane Doe," a twenty-five-year-old woman from Michigan whose medical history had not been taken into consideration—including the fact that she had recently had an operation for cervical cancer, and that out of nine previous pregnancies, she had had five miscarriages. Doe, who was not certain in the first place that she wanted to be a surrogate mother, claims Keane coerced her, a charge he denies. He has filed a libel suit against her and her lawyer. The case was summarily dismissed by the federal court on the grounds that she had failed to state a federal cause of action. The court noted that the issues raised by the case were new and unsettled and the problem was better left to state courts and legislatures.

What if a contract mother refuses to surrender her baby? That's easy. A company can always threaten her. Chances are she'll believe their threats. She knows they can sue, jail, bankrupt, or custodially challenge her. I asked Debbie if anyone had ever threatened her when she first talked about changing her mind.

> DEBBIE: *The broker threatened me. He said they'd make things really hard for me to keep my baby. He didn't get explicit. But I knew he'd threatened other surrogate mothers. One surrogate said he had threatened to get her husband fired. Another surrogate said this guy could make your life absolute hell. He'd have a battery of lawyers against you. He'd make sure you had to pay every penny back or get you into jail if you couldn't pay it back fast enough. The broker told me that he had a hunch I was on welfare and that he was going to check the county welfare records and report me for trying to earn money as a surrogate if I backed out of the deal.*
> PHYLLIS: *How did that make you feel?*
> DEBBIE: *Angry. Very angry. Mostly scared, very intimidated. He has an overpowering voice!*
> PHYLLIS: *You believed him, you were afraid of him?*
> DEBBIE: *I'm still afraid of him!*

The director of Debbie's surrogacy broker did report her to welfare when it was clear that a lawsuit was in the offing.

Not all initially "happy" contract mothers remain "happy." Within a year of her baby's birth, Elizabeth Kane, the nation's first paid surrogate contract mother, began to publicly express her change of heart. She now opposes surrogacy and has written a book against it. In a follow-up study of thirty contract mothers, Dr. Philip Parker found that "several" had "severe grief reactions and had received treatment."[10]

A birth mother who wants to keep her baby has no support—and must battle some powerful opponents. Society at large will not help her; her own family may refuse to support her; private adoption agencies and the surrogacy companies will fight her for her child.

Despite this, at least nine contract mothers have received media attention in their fight to keep their babies.[11]

In 1981, for instance, one contract mother got into a custody battle over her newborn after she surmised that the would-be "legal" mother had had a sex-change operation. (In fact, according to Keane, the woman had not been a transsexual; she had instead been a "sexual anomaly" at birth, indistinguishable as either man or woman, and had had an operation to correct the problem.)

Not every case involved a surrogacy company or contract. For example, in Milwaukee, a contract father pursued custody in court although no contract had been signed and no payment made. The birth mother was single and a friend of the sperm donor's wife. She had wanted to give them a "gift of love," and then found she couldn't give up her child. The judge treated the matter as a straightforward custody case. He decided that although both parents were fit, the father was more fit because he had more money and could also provide the child with a two-parent home. The birth mother's parental rights were preserved and she received visitation.[12]

In October 1987, a Michigan court awarded temporary custody of month-old twins to Laurie Yates, the mother who had signed a surrogacy contract. Halfway through her pregnancy, Yates realized that she'd made a mistake and couldn't give up her children. Yates said she felt surrogacy was sinful and wrong. Mike Wallace presented her story on "60 Minutes"; State Senator Connie Binsfield called a press conference on her behalf.

According to the legal briefs and to Dr. Judianne Denson-Gerber's psychiatric testimony, Laurie Yates's husband had been rendered sterile at work; the couple were simply too poor to afford artificial insemination. Laurie Yates therefore decided to become a "surrogate mother" in order to earn money for artificial insemination. Laurie's goal in life was to be the mother of as many children as possible. Her own mother had nineteen children. Yates is also a Keane surrogate mother.*

---

*Yates was subsequently discovered to have abused, neglected and abandoned a child. Her lawyers withdrew from the case. She is entitled to visitation.

On November 12, 1987, the first contract mother died as a result of being pregnant. It was not a surrogate death; it was a *real* death. The headlines read: NO LEGAL ACTION POSSIBLE IN CASE OF SURROGATE MOM WHO DIED.[13]

One case that has erupted in litigation, with charges and countercharges on all sides, is the surrogacy arrangement between Judy Stiver and Alexander Malahoff. Stiver bore a severely defective child whom the contract father (Malahoff) refused to accept. He claimed he was not the child's father. Phil Donahue aired the results of the paternity test live: Malahoff was not the genetic father. Stiver claimed that she had not been advised to refrain from marital intercourse during the insemination period, and the child's deformity was the result of an infection transmitted to her during the insemination process.

A disproportionate number of the highly publicized surrogacy "disasters" have been on contract to Keane's companies. But even "bad" publicity seems to be good for business. Keane boasts that the Baby M case has quadrupled client inquiries. "Jane Doe" admits that she first approached his company to be a "surrogate" after reading the news about the Judy Stiver case.[14]

Women don't have to sign surrogacy contracts in order to be reproductively or custodially exploited or abused. This happens every day to married mothers who are custodially challenged by their husbands. However, what if the surrogacy arrangement involves no middlemen, no contract, no coercion, no sexual intercourse, and takes place privately between two consenting adults? What if a fertile woman desires to help an infertile woman, simply out of compassion? What, if anything, is wrong with this scenario?

Sally is a birth mother. She lives in a small midwestern town, has been married for ten years, and is the mother of three children: nine-year-old Abraham, seven-year-old Rebekkah, and four-year-old Matthew. Sally became pregnant for "friends": Frank and his infertile wife, Dawn. Like Debbie, Sally was "surprised" and "hurt" when, afterward, her couple refused to have anything more to do with her. She was also "surprised" by her children's reactions: they were "devastated" by what happened.

Sally had "no idea" that surrogacy could be "bad." She read Keane's book, watched "Donahue," read "glowing" articles on the subject. She didn't want money or middlemen: her husband Christopher artificially inseminated her. Christopher and Frank had known each other since childhood. Sally hoped that her "act of love" would turn the two couples from "just being friends" into "being a kind of family."

Indeed, once Sally became pregnant the two couples saw each other more often. Weekends, they all went to the movies together. Dawn followed Sally around the house "all starry-eyed" and "inspired" by Sally's "growing belly and the life inside." Both couples attended Sally's childbirth classes.

However, Sally wasn't "all starry-eyed." In fact, she was increasingly becoming afraid of Frank—who wanted to "control everything." He wanted to assist with the birth, take pictures. Sally felt that Frank was becoming "more important" than her and, with some support from the home-birth midwife, barred Frank from her childbed (but not from her home).

> SALLY: *Frank felt like a threat to me. I had a nightmare that I was in that science-fiction film,* Invasion of the Body Snatchers. *Have you seen that movie? Creatures come from outer space—come to earth as pods, and they grow into persons, and they take over your body. I felt like that in the nightmare. Frank was my pod. And he was taking over my body. That was the worst fear—it stuck with me the whole pregnancy.* I decided that I'd only be rid of Frank if I had him cut the umbilical cord.
> PHYLLIS: *How did you feel when Frank cut the cord?*
> SALLY: *A big rush. Like—Frank was out of my life now. Like the whole darn time I was pregnant, I felt like he was in there!*

Frank and Dawn stayed with Sally for three days after Jason's birth. Then, they left with the baby. Sally expected to see Jason "as soon as they felt like a family." But Frank kept putting her off. He needed "more time." Sally persisted; Frank became angry. He finally told Sally "flat out" that she could "never have anything to do with his son."

SALLY: *He admitted that they'd lied to me about the visitation and holidays. They were afraid I wouldn't give them the baby otherwise. After two months went by I dropped in unannounced. Dawn was alone. She threw a fit. But first, I held Jason for a few minutes. Dawn grabbed him out of my arms and made me leave. Frank was furious. He threatened me.*

PHYLLIS: What happened once it was clear that Frank and Dawn weren't going to let you have a relationship with them or with Jason?

SALLY: *I got very blue. I started seeing a psychiatrist. She got me to thinking about how my body had been used by men over many years, and I never had anything to say about it. Because I was a victim of incest. My father had incest with me for six years, since I was eight years old.*

PHYLLIS: (Long pause) Would you say that deciding to be a "surrogate" is related to being an incest victim?

SALLY: *Definitely. I hadn't reckoned how to cleanse my soul. How do I get my father's semen out of my body? I could accomplish this in the surrogate process. I could offer my body. This time, I was the one offering. Freely. This would somehow cleanse my soul.*

PHYLLIS: You thought being a surrogate would give you more control or retroactive control over your own body?

SALLY: *Right. But it turned out to be totally wrong. The first insemination was the most horrible thing I ever went through in my whole life. It was like being an incest victim again! But I felt like I had to go through with it. Once I was pregnant, I couldn't have an abortion. I felt like I had to work this pregnancy through to heal myself. But what I did was to punish myself, not heal myself.*

PHYLLIS: By the way, what's Frank's last name?

SALLY: *Oh, I could never tell you that.* (Pause) *Oh, I know I'm being forced to protect those who victimized me. Again. I hate it. I'm protecting Dawn and Frank because of my love for Jason. I hate it. It makes me sick.*

PHYLLIS: Do your children ask about Jason?

SALLY: *Yes. Quite often. My daughter Rebekkah says that if she has a baby she'll never give it away. She's been asking me, "Did you really have to give Jason away?" It's on her*

*mind a lot. It's on my son Matthew's mind, too, but he tries
not to talk about it. I've begun to encourage them to talk about
it.*

*You know, I have one picture of Jason. He's got my eyes.
So does Rebekkah. I can see Jason just by looking in a mirror,
just by looking at my daughter Rebekkah.*

Both Debbie and Sally voluntarily signed contracts. Alejandra
Munoz, a Mexican peasant, claims she did not become a surrogate
voluntarily. She says that her Mexican-American relatives lied to her
and tricked her into it, a charge that they deny.

What happened to Alejandra is not about surrogacy companies or
contracts. It is about the routine exploitation of women *by their own
families,* and about how wives and mothers exploit and abuse other
women—domestics, concubines, surrogates, their own daughters—in
order to please and protect husbands and sons.

In 1985, at the request of her relatives, Alejandra, then nineteen, illegally crossed the border into Southern California with her
two-year-old daughter. She had agreed to be a surrogate mother for
her second cousin, thirty-eight-year-old Natividad (Nattie), who was
no longer fertile. In an interview, Alejandra told me that her great
aunt, grandmother, and second cousin had promised her fifteen
hundred dollars if she would be a "good girl" and allow herself to
be inseminated with the sperm of Mario Haro, Nattie's husband.
Nattie was a bank auditor, Mario a high school science teacher. The
procedure would be "small and painless" and would take only "two
or three weeks." Once Alejandra became pregnant, a physician
would remove the fertilized ovum and re-implant it in Nattie. Alejandra said that both her great aunt and her grandmother believed
this story.

The Haros deny everything about the intention to transplant the
embryo. They claim that Alejandra agreed to have the baby in return
for help in obtaining a visa. They say that once pregnant, Alejandra
demanded five thousand dollars to carry the baby. The Haros couldn't
afford that much. They drew up a contract promising her fifteen
hundred dollars. After the baby was born, Alejandra demanded more
money in exchange for the baby. (Alejandra denies ever having
signed a contract voluntarily.)

I first read about Alejandra in *The New York Times* in September 1986. I interviewed her in June 1987. Her cousin Angela Garcia, who is Nattie's half sister, translated for her.

> PHYLLIS: *When did Alejandra first realize that she'd been tricked?*
>
> ANGELA: *When she was already three weeks pregnant. The Haros, mainly Nattie, did the insemination themselves, at home. They didn't want to pay a penny for anything, not even medical expenses. They told Alejandra to use the name "Nattie Haro" when she went to the doctor, "otherwise they will find out you are an illegal alien." The Haros wanted all the medical expenses covered. They didn't want to pay anything to adopt the baby. After about three weeks, my aunt and I went to ask them: when would they flush the ovum out? Then, Nattie burst out with the real story: Alejandra would have to carry the baby to full term! Alejandra was so mad, she said she'd have an abortion. But Alejandra is Catholic and doesn't believe in abortion. Alejandra couldn't think what to do, because she couldn't return to Mexico pregnant. People would never believe what happened. They would believe she got herself pregnant, and life would be unbearable for her.*
>
> PHYLLIS: *No escape?*
>
> ANGELA: *None. Now she was pregnant without money, alone in a strange country, with relatives she didn't know. Nattie made Alejandra sign a paper promising to give up the rights to the baby. If not, they threatened to have her deported, shamed. Alejandra was too scared to tell anybody. We didn't find out until afterwards, the terrible treatment they were giving her. . . . Mario's family was told that Nattie was having the baby; Nattie wore a pillow under her clothes.*

Unlike Debbie or Sally (or even Mary Beth Whitehead), Alejandra lived with her sperm donor and his wife. From the way she described it, Alejandra had *less* freedom than any other contract mother I interviewed. Perhaps her pregnancy was more like that of a woman whose husband or boyfriend mistreats her.

On June 25, 1986, Alejandra gave birth to a girl—by caesarean. She did not want to give up her baby. While she was recovering in the hospital, the Haros took the baby home and Alejandra enlisted Angela's support. They went to the police; the police said that Alejandra had to prove that she was the mother. Nattie's name was on the birth certificate.

Alejandra finally found a lawyer to take her case pro bono and sued the Haros for custody. Judge William Pate did not award Alejandra custody; he did award her varying amounts of visitation. Immigration Commissioner Harold Ezell allowed Alejandra to remain in California for another year to fight for her child. Ezell agreed that Alejandra had been "conned." In our interview, Angela spoke for Alejandra.

> ANGELA: *The judge appointed a lawyer for the baby. The Haros have a nice house, careers, money. They are professionals. They speak English. Alejandra is a "nobody." The baby's lawyer ordered Alejandra to have a psychological evaluation. Not the Haros! They're supposed to be perfect. Nobody cares about what they did. The social services people got involved. They sent an American man to interview Alejandra. He spoke Spanish. He said, "You can have more babies, but they can't."*
> PHYLLIS: *What did Alejandra say?*
> ANGELA: *That she loved her daughter.*

The Haros maintain that Alejandra asked for money and never asked for the baby. They initially argued, as did the Sterns, that they had a binding contractual right to custody; they later argued that custody awarded to them would be in the child's best interests. The court's latest ruling: the Haros have the girl every night and every weekend; Alejandra has her during the day, Monday through Thursday, until she is three years old. We have not heard the last of this case.

Would the state have protected Alejandra more manfully if she'd been Mario Haro's legal wife? How often and to what extent does the state protect a mother from her husband's physical, economic, or custodial violence? Would Alejandra have been better off if she'd voluntarily signed a surrogacy contract?

In what sense does a woman's right to sign a surrogacy contract empower her? It certainly doesn't empower her economically. Ten thousand dollars per baby represents a wage of less than a dollar an hour for nine months of pregnancy and childbirth, plus the time it takes to be administratively processed, genetically, gynecologically, and psychiatrically screened, and then successfully inseminated.

Does a woman's right to sign a surrogacy contract empower her reproductively or custodially? Did Debbie or Mary Beth have any power? Obviously, women are as much—or as little—empowered by contract motherhood as they are by marriage. In other words, both contract and married mothers remain at a disadvantage *precisely where they are most different from men,* namely in the areas of biological reproduction and custody.

Most people believe that a "deal is a deal"—and it is a deal when it empowers a man at a woman's expense; not when it empowers a woman at a man's expense. Also, most people don't expect a man to live up to all his promises; only women are expected to do this.

CHAPTER 4

JOURNAL OF A BRIEF CAMPAIGN, 1987

Surrogacy has caught the imagination of the nation—but why? Probably no more than one thousand surrogate contract mothers exist in the whole country; probably more than one thousand children are taken from their birth mothers in custody battles every single day. Why should I put my energies into one New Jersey baby who was conceived on contract?

The media and the public do not remember that hundreds of Mary Beth Whiteheads are on trial every day in America; this case is unusual only because we're paying attention to it. Maybe, just maybe, a birth mother may be seen as having a right to her child—even if she's signed a surrogacy contract or adoption papers or a marriage contract. This case is about the reproductive and custodial rights of all women.

I need to remind people that millions of mothers have been forced into the position of "surrogate uteruses." We have ignored these women. We have claimed that they're unfit. They fade out of court, out of sight, out of their children's lives.

This journal, kept in 1987, is a partial record of what it means to try and change history by an inch.

FEBRUARY 4

"Where do you stand on the Baby M case?" At least ten of my students want to know.

"Where do *you* all stand?" I respond, and I propose a debate on the Baby M case. "Who wants to represent Mary Beth?" I ask.

Not a single hand is raised.

"Who wants to represent the Sterns?" Twenty hands go up.

FEBRUARY 5

Mary Beth may have signed a contract but she's still the birth mother. The Sterns and Mary Beth are not having a "fair" fight among "equals." Mary Beth is outnumbered and outclassed. Where's our sympathy for the underdog?

Call Mary Beth's current lawyer, Harold J. Cassidy, to offer my support. Make an appointment to meet him. Start calling people to sound them out. Will they join me at a press conference at the trial in Hackensack?

Call Andrea Dworkin, who, in 1983, first wrote about reproductive technologies and surrogacy in *Right Wing Women.* I ask whether she or other feminists have been in touch with Mary Beth. Yes. Early on, Gena Corea (who in 1985 wrote about surrogacy in *The Mother Machine*) had worked on a brief with Mary Beth's first lawyer. According to Andrea, she and Gena had a meeting with Mary Beth in the fall of 1986.

FEBRUARY 8

Call the brash and brilliant Kathleen Lahey and the calm and cautious Sarah Salter in Massachusetts, two radical lawyers whom I've previously consulted on custody matters and who organized a custody conference in July of 1986 in Canada. I suggest we draft a position paper on the reproductive and custodial implications of the Baby M case and present it to the nation at a press conference in

Hackensack on the eighteenth day of this month. Agree to fly to Boston next weekend.

FEBRUARY 9

Have my assistant, Carrie, call La Leche League for support. She calls at least ten different branch offices. Every woman contacted says that she can't get involved in anything "political" or that she doesn't "like" Mary Beth Whitehead. How can someone not "like" a woman she doesn't know? How can someone be so "fanatically" in favor of breast-feeding that she's involved with La Leche, and not care that Baby M was breast-feeding when she was "legally" snatched? Don't the La Leche women see this as child abuse? If *they* don't—who does?

FEBRUARY 10

Just talked to Alison Ward, a birth mother, a former vice-president of Concerned United Birthparents (CUB) and Mary Beth's liaison to the world. Alison spent three hours with me on the phone. Talked on the phone with Mary Beth for two hours. She sounds young and scared, but extremely well spoken. It's as if she's waited all her life to say these lines. She doesn't sound "crazy." She has guts and humor. She'll need both. She's involved in a trial by fire. The ordeal is bound to disfigure and enlarge her. Can I make her understand this? I probably can't. We agree to meet.

I'm afraid to meet her. What if I meet her and don't like her? Will I refuse to stand by the issues if she's not a good enough public heroine for me?

FEBRUARY 11

Today was a teaching day. My class held our debate on the Baby M case. Constance, a single, twenty-nine-year-old "yuppie," argued the case for the Sterns. She is eloquent, hard-as-nails, and fanatical about the sacredness of contracts—as if no contract is ever broken or renegotiated.

Agnes, a married forty-two-year-old birth mother of four, argues the case for Mary Beth Whitehead. Agnes is not eloquent. She keeps apologizing for "speaking as a mother," and wonders whether "a mother's feelings for her children can be used in a debate."

"That's the question, isn't it?" I say.

"The baby is half Mr. Stern's," Constance begins. "And since the Sterns wanted the child, and Mary Beth didn't, it's really more than half theirs, isn't it? Mary Beth turned out to be an unfit mother, so the judge gave the baby to the Sterns. What's done is done. Baby M is already bonded to them." Constance looks triumphant.

"How do you know that Mary Beth is an unfit mother?" Agnes asks. "The Sterns kidnapped her . . ."

"How can you call the Sterns kidnappers?" Constance's temper flares. "The Sterns have so much more to offer Baby M. Why not let the baby have what's good for her?"

"Do you think that the person with more money is automatically the better parent?" Agnes stands up. "I think if someone tried to take my nursing infant away from me, I'd try to kill them. I'd definitely threaten them. You know, your hormones *do change* after you give birth. You're emotional about everything."

"So, you're admitting that *mothers* are chemically different from men," says Constance. "Maybe women shouldn't become mothers then. Obviously it drives them crazy and then men use the truth about *mothers* to keep women out of the job market."

"But motherhood is a very beautiful experience . . ." Agnes begins.

"You're making me very angry!" Constance yells. "Are you saying that women shouldn't do anything but have children, because nothing else is as 'beautiful'? I don't want to have any children. My mother had lots of kids and it got her nowhere fast. I don't want to be treated like half a woman because I'm choosing not to ruin my life."

"I'm not saying that all women have to become mothers, am I?" Agnes turns to me, then back to Constance. "Dear, one day you may change your mind about this."

Nina, a married woman in her fifties, raises her hand. She speaks slowly. "I never thought I'd be telling you this, but I am infertile. My husband and I have no children. But I can't help feeling that surrogate arrangements are unfair to both mother and child.

"We know that mothers who give their children away for adoption feel guilty and tormented about it. Why do we think that surrogate mothers won't suffer as much? Don't we care? We know that adopted children have many problems and want to know all about their biological mothers. Do we think that children conceived in surrogacy will not suffer similarly? Or don't we care?"

Nina takes a deep breath and stands up. "I think Mary Beth Whitehead is Baby M's true mother. She is entitled to the child of her body."

So, one woman stood up for Mary Beth.

Stacey is already standing and talking. "I agree. Mary Beth should have some rights. But so should the baby. How do we know that babies are better off with fathers than with mothers? Men and women aren't socialized into motherhood in the same way."

Agnes raises her hand and waits patiently to be recognized. "I've always felt closer to my children than their father has. I never thought that maybe it was because I gave birth to them or spent more time with them. I thought: Well that's how my husband was raised and that's okay because he's a good provider."

Mothers themselves do not value their own labor nor are they allowed to understand that what they feel about motherhood is a form of truth that should be admissible as evidence in the courts of law and public opinion.

"I want to get back to surrogacy," Constance says. "If a woman decides to sell her services as a surrogate, we have no right to interfere with her decision. It's her body to do with as she chooses. If we let women go around making and breaking contracts, no one will make contracts with women."

"What if legalized surrogacy makes it possible for men not to marry women?" This is Agnes. "What if a man can hire a different woman every week for sex and a woman to bear his children for him? He could live with his mother until the cows come home . . ."

The "marrying" women are silent. Then, all at once four women proclaim that they're "for Mary Beth too."

They may not trust Mary Beth but they mistrust men as husbands even more. They don't want to lose their boyfriends or husbands to sex prostitutes or to mothers-for-hire.

Before the debate, 95 percent of the class raised their hands in a show of support for the Sterns. Afterward, only 50 percent were definitely pro-Stern.

FEBRUARY 12

I wave to Lois Gould at a book party. I hope Lois and I end up agreeing about surrogacy. I hear she's planning a meeting of feminists to discuss surrogacy, reproductive technology, the Baby M case, etc.

It's hard to know how feminists will go. I'm afraid that many feminists will be pro-Stern and prosurrogacy. (It's a woman's right to sell her uterus, it's a woman's right to *hire* another woman to be pregnant for her, etc.)

FEBRUARY 14–15

Rockport, Massachusetts, with Kathleen and Sarah. Kathleen is in bed drafting our position paper on yellow legal pads. Sarah brings each page to me for corrections and approval. I ask whomever I'm talking to on the phone (I've called at least fifty people this weekend) to please hold on; then Sarah goes upstairs and types everything into the computer. Everyone I call is glad that "someone" is doing "something." No one wants to do the grunt work. A few feminist academics don't want to blow their image as neutral experts by appearing to take sides. Others just don't want to be associated with any (more) "losers."

I've invited Michelle Harrison, a physician, to come for lunch. Michelle is excited by what Kathleen, Sarah, and I are doing. I ask her to join us.

FEBRUARY 16

Drive out to Red Bank, New Jersey, to met Harold Cassidy. He looks very tired. He is grateful for any support for Mary Beth.

FEBRUARY 17

My phone rings. Absentmindedly I pick it up. A woman is crying. "Dr. Chesler," she says, "I've just lost custody of my boys to a man who only ignored or bullied them—a man who spent the last seven years battering me senseless in front of them! How could a *judge* do this? What will happen to my boys without me? They're four and seven: too little to be without their mother.

"Oh," she weeps, "I'm feeling desperate. I have no income, none. I weigh one hundred and seven pounds and I'm five feet eight inches tall. I'm physically and emotionally exhausted. I need help. Someone who cares. Is there really a God?"

On the phone with Mary Beth again. "What do you want me to say on your behalf?" I ask her.

"Tell everyone that I made a mistake and that I'm trying to make up for it best as I can," she replies.

I'll do that, Mary Beth. Sleep well, Mary Beth.

FEBRUARY 18

Noon. Hackensack, New Jersey. Sixty journalists and cameramen are in the room. It looks like a joint House-Senate hearing on crimes in the White House. What has Mary Beth Whitehead done to merit such attention? We push through the crush of media people to the same bank of microphones used by the lawyers and their daily witnesses.

There are eight of us: myself and Kathleen Lahey, who specializes in custody, adoption, and reproductive issues; Michelle Harrison; Karen Malpede, a playwright and peace activist; Ynestra King, a peace and environmental activist; Sybil Shainwald, a lawyer and past president of the National Women's Health Network; Sarah Salter, who is a tax specialist; and Bettye Lane, a photographer.

Together, the eight of us are biological and adoptive mothers, fertile and infertile women, and nonmothers by choice. Bettye Lane backs away, crouches down, and aims her camera at us. And now we are "on" the stage of history. I introduce us and begin.

"We are here today to denounce this trial as a form of child abuse and sex discrimination. It represents a brutal use of state power on behalf of one man against one woman and her child. Without mercy, policemen, armed and dangerous, removed Baby Sara, a nursing infant, from her mother's breast; Judge Sorkow, armed and dangerous, made sure Mary Beth Whitehead would never see her daughter Sara alone again. He made sure that Sara would be safely 'bonded' to the Sterns long before this trial began.

"This is child abuse. Sara Elizabeth Whitehead is the victim of a legal kidnapping. We call for her immediate return to her birth mother, Mary Beth Whitehead."

I have their attention. They'll listen for a little while.

"The entire Catholic working class of America is on trial here. And together with them, we are all unfit. How many mothers of any class or religion would be pronounced 'fit'?

"Mary Beth made a terrible mistake. She knows this and is trying to set it right. It is barbaric to punish her so savagely. Who amongst us dares cast the first stone?"

"What do you women want?" a reporter calls out.

"We want the judge to remove himself from the case . . ."

"What are you going to *do*?" another reporter asks.

"We're not going to chain ourselves to the courthouse steps, if that's what you mean," I respond. "At least not yet. We're going to keep talking to you if you'll keep listening." I motion to Kathleen Lahey, our next speaker. Stepping smartly up to the microphone, Kathleen proceeds to cover every imaginable legal, contractual and constitutional issue involved. She ends on a note of passion:

"For years, the 'fathers' rights movement' has been working to devalue biological motherhood and to glorify genetic fatherhood. Central to this shift in values is the glorification of male sperm as the basis for defining fathering at the expense of looking at the *quality* of fathering.

"What kind of father would use such legal tactics to grab an infant from her mother's arms, without regard for the effect it would have on the child? It is quite probable that Baby Sara will suffer emotional damage from having been snatched from her mother's breast at the age of four months, interrupting her attachment to her mother and interfering with her emotional development in ways that will affect her permanently. And this is unforgivable."

One by one, our women speak. Michelle Harrison also speaks with passion and great assurance:

"The pain of infertility cannot be used to rationalize the pain of a woman forced to relinquish her child. People say that Mary Beth initially said she'd give up the baby and I think: If every man who said to his pregnant wife or girlfriend, 'I don't want that child,' was held to his words, far fewer children would have fathers. Over and over, we have recognized for men that one cannot know in advance the effect of becoming a parent, that how a man feels in advance of the birth cannot be held against him in determining the nature of his future involvement with a child."

And now Karen Malpede is speaking. She asks: "Would anyone be making such a fuss if the child in question were not a healthy, blond-haired, blue-eyed infant? And would the case even be in court if the sperm donor were not a privileged professional, or if the mother was not married to a mere sanitation worker?

"Again we must ask: What kind of people would bring legal proceedings against a child's natural mother which are intended to slander and malign her character and which will cause enormous suffering to her and her children, Baby Sara's half-sister and brother? Do the Sterns truly believe they can raise Baby Sara without her ever finding out about her natural mother, the tremendous love her mother bears for her, or the ugly record of this case?"

Ynestra King is asking hard questions in a magnificently gentle tone.

"Why don't people confront the true causes of sterility: birth control and a nuclear-poisoned environment, before they so violently plunder the fertility of poor women? Those behind surrogate motherhood assume that everything can be quantified, bought and sold. Human life is not a commodity to be sold or owned. There are some things that can't be bought and sold."

Sybil Shainwald closes our presentation with a speech about contracts and the Constitution.

"Women cannot be held to a pre-conception contract. The contract is not valid and can't be enforced. It violates our laws against baby selling and both the Thirteenth and Fourteenth Amendments to the Constitution, which prohibit involuntary servitude and slavery, i.e., the selling of human life."

The press conference is over. We've done it: carried out a "commando raid" on the media; we stood up and were seen and heard on the five o'clock, six o'clock, and ten o'clock news all over the country.

Mary Beth has come to gaze in wonder at us: *women* on her side. She hides her tears, comes over to meet us. We are awkward, embarrassed, paranoid. Will shaking hands or embracing us be used against her? If we repeat what she tells us will she be accused of "manipulating" us, will we be accused of stupidity—as if nothing Mary Beth says can be trusted or used in her defense? As if she must prove her innocence by miraculous means only?

Here come two of my favorite columnists: Murray Kempton and Jimmy Breslin. Murray is surprised that feminists would be "gentleman enough" to come out in support of Mary Beth. He shakes my hand. In his column tomorrow he will write that:

> The Sterns had bought themselves a cow, and the cow had kicked over the milk can. That view of the case is in no way meant to reflect upon the Sterns. Every aspect of Elizabeth Stern suggests a woman as good in her different way as Mary Beth Whitehead. The distinction is that Mary Beth Whitehead knows the perils and risks life extorts and the Sterns don't seem to.
>
> If they were not somehow so disablingly innocent, they could not have thought to purchase life's warmth with a bargain so chill.
>
> [Mary Beth] is likely to lose Baby M; she was intermittently harried all through yesterday by a court that has inescapably made up its mind. So, too, have I, and have thus lost the right to report upon her any further, a pity because, for all her vagaries, she is of stuff heroic and that is too seldom available for viewing.

Toward the end of our conference an armed sheriff singles me out and motions me to the side. "You have to tell your people to move it on out," he says. "Now."

"But we're not doing anything illegal," I say as authoritatively as possible.

"Look. Mr. Skoloff spoke to the judge and the judge doesn't want you in this courtroom."

So we're bothering Harvey and Gary. They want to gag us just as they've gagged Mary Beth.

"But this isn't his courtroom," I reply schoolmarmishly. "This is an area open to the public in the courthouse, specially set aside for press conferences."

For a minute the sheriff looks uncertain. Then he says: "Mr. Skoloff knows what he wants. I gotta do what he says."

Is Gary Skoloff Judge Sorkow's boss, too?

"We can't leave the press in midsentence," I counter, walking the sheriff out into the hallway, "but we're nearly done."

"You'd better not try this again," he tells me.

"Oh, we'll be back," I say rather sweetly. "You can count on it."

Mary Beth gets no credit for having the guts to stand up and tell her story to the whole mother-blaming world. Bridgette was a severely battered wife and the mother of an incestuously abused child. Unlike Mary Beth, Bridgette had never disobeyed a court order, run away, been artificially inseminated, or signed a surrogacy contract. She did lose custody temporarily—but for trying to protect her daughter Nicole, who'd been sexually abused by her ex-husband Anthony.

The testimony was conflicting. The judge, a woman, said she had "no reason . . . to believe that there has ever been any abuse" by the child's father. Just seven months later, the judge had to reverse herself, saying, "Something is happening to this child. I do not know what that is." Despite testimony that the father had sexually abused the child, the judge allowed him visitation.

Bridgette described her plight at our Speak-Out on Mothers and Custody of Children on March 1, 1986, in New York City. She spoke "out"—in a muffled voice from behind a thick black veil. She wore it to protect herself from any more of Anthony's retaliation.

FEBRUARY 19

At least thirty calls from the media and ten calls from women, mostly mothers—who want to help. "Come to our next demonstration on the twenty-fifth," I tell everyone.

Joan Wile, singer and songwriter, offers to help for the next few weeks. She says she's not a feminist but that she's a mother and a veteran of antiwar and peace campaigns. I'm grateful for her offer— no ideological questions asked. She knows how to write a press release and where to send it.

FEBRUARY 20

Very few feminists or feminist organizations have called to say
. . . anything. I think feminist organizations should be a presence in
the courthouse. Several of them have noted that their most vocal
members seem to be adoptive mothers, or infertile, or married to
infertile men, or the second wives of men who have custody of their
children (or who pay what they think is too much child support), or
are women who have no children and/or who are completely disinter-
ested in mother-and-child issues.

One woman was verbally supportive but advised me not to "take
sides" and to "proceed with the utmost caution." I ask her if her
organization, which has some wealth, could cover some expenses; she
says she'll ask her board. (I'm not surprised that I don't hear from
her again.)

A number of prominent feminists, including Betty Friedan, Gloria
Steinem, Kate Stimpson, Paula Caplan, Blanche Cook, Ann Snitow,
Kate Millett, Barbara Ehrenreich, Andrea Dworkin, Letty Pogrebin,
and Pauline Bart *have* returned my phone calls.* Laurie Woods and
Myra Sun, of the National Center for Women and Family Law, are
extremely excited by what we're doing. But they're federally funded
and have zero access to discretionary funds. Their meager funding
would be jeopardized if they ever participated in anything "political"
or tried to help any one woman directly. Their mandate allows them
to help lawyers, not people.[1]

Margery Ratner and Ann Simon of the Center for Constitutional
Rights and Nadine Taub of the Rutgers Women's Rights Law Clinic
already are, or plan to become, involved. (Nadine has submitted an
amicus brief.)

FEBRUARY 21

The Baby M case is the best way I have of showing people what
an average custody battle is like—and how much it resembles a witch

---

*At my request, Doctors Paula Caplan and Pauline Bart assisted in the preparation
of the mental health data for Harold Cassidy's appeal brief.

trial. But since Mary Beth is so unsympathetic a figure, am I help-ing—or hurting—other custodially embattled mothers by associating them with her?

Why didn't the millions of custody mothers rise up, en masse, and march on Hackensack and then on Washington? Why haven't they yet? Some cannot accept Mary Beth's persecution as similar to their own: *she* signed a surrogacy agreement; they never did. Others have found their individual struggles so demoralizing and destructive that they no longer have the capacity to join in political action.

In contrast to themselves, Mary Beth has held the attention of the media constantly, has received pro bono work and other help. Moth-ers resent having been *treated as monstrously as Mary Beth*—even though they never signed surrogacy contracts. They also resent the fact that neither feminist organizations nor the ACLU ever tried to help them and that their own lawyers routinely blamed them for their own victimization.

Did two consultations today with custodially embattled mothers. Caroline's three teenagers opted to live with their father. "My own children look down at me because I have no money. They laugh at me when I cry. They say: 'Grow up, Mom.' The only people I can share this with are the men in this Fathers' Rights Group [!] I'm too ashamed to tell anyone I work with (I'm a nurse, but their father's a doctor) that my own children don't want to live with me, don't even want to see me."

Rhoda, the other mother, is a Wall Street investment banker who's just completed three years of an internship program. Rhoda is afraid she can't win custody of Isobel and Nathalie, her two-year-old twins. "My husband did all the childcare," she says.

"I bet you did a lot of childcare for an investment banker," I venture. And then I hear a story I've already heard a hundred times before.

It seems that Rhoda is the one who rushed home early every day after work to shop and cook dinner. Evenings and weekends, unas-sisted by her husband or by any paid employee, Rhoda did all the housecleaning and laundry. She chose all of her daughters' clothes ("my husband didn't understand girls' dresses"), took them to doc-tors and dentists and nursed them through any illness, interviewed and hired babysitters . . .

"Stop," I say, "I can't stand any more. What exactly did their father do?"

"Oh, he did a lot," Rhoda says. "He dropped the girls off in the morning at the special daycare program that I'd researched, and he picked them up at five P.M. every day. In the beginning, when I was still breast-feeding, he'd bring them over to me at work. And, oh, yes. He'd take them out to eat when I had to work late at night on a deal. Most nights, he stayed home and watched TV with the children and the babysitter I'd hired.

"I should have known better. Of course he began an affair with the babysitter. My husband is a newspaper reporter. He says he knows his rights and he wants the house we paid for with money from my parents, plus alimony and child support."

FEBRUARY 22

Mary Beth's not the only one who wants her name in lights. We all do, God help us: you, me, the other surrogate-contract mothers, the surrogacy profiteers, the feminists, the lawyers, the infertility doctors, the ethicists, the mental-illness experts, the judges—the media itself. (Who'll play the lawyer, who'll play the judge in the movie?)

FEBRUARY 24

Am deluged with calls from the media. Are we having another press conference? Will we "choreograph" a demonstration that looks good on television? Will anyone famous be there? History is competing with Hollywood for audience ratings.

My hope is that the demonstrations will give feminists and others the time and the incentive to join us or to do something else. It's important to maintain a visible opposition to surrogacy and to mother-blaming. I'm frightened by how *respectable* surrogacy can be made to appear. Watching people defend surrogacy suggests how respectable slavery must once have seemed—as discussed or explained by well-dressed and cultured ladies and gentlemen in the nineteenth century.

FEBRUARY 25

D Day. At Michelle's suggestion, we've assembled an empty crib outside the courthouse and filled it with a giant panda bear. Local New Jersey mothers are here. They've brought their own amazing signs: WOMEN ARE NOT DOGS FOR BREEDING PURPOSES, MOTHERS WITH FEELINGS, MARY BETH IS A FIT AND LOVING MOTHER, SARA WHITEHEAD IS HER NAME, BERGEN COUNTY 1987—THE SPANISH INQUISITION 1692.

We circle the crib: twenty-five women ranging in age from our mid-thirties to our mid-seventies on a picket line together, braving the bitterly cold weather.

"Every woman will have an empty crib in her life if Mary Beth doesn't get her baby back," I say. "We call on people of conscience to challenge the cruelty that has characterized this trial. We ask you to write directly to the judge, to your local newspaper, to your state and federal representatives and to us, the Committee for Mary Beth Whitehead." (After much agonizing we've decided it would be cowardly to call ourselves something safe like "The Task Force on Surrogacy.")

A black grandmother in her seventies, Viola Hanon, is here. She is retired and very quiet. She is to come to every one of our demonstrations. "I couldn't sleep thinking about this," she tells me.

"Mrs. Whitehead's ordeal is like feeding the Christians to the lions," says Francesca McPhee, who helped organize a small New Jersey group, Mothers With Feelings. Francesca and Rosemary Bailey *look* like solid citizens, U.S.A.: I imagine them Republicans, churchgoers, wives of American Legion members. I'm glad they're here to cover my radical feminist ass.

"How come Stern hired Mary Beth as the ideal mother and now he says she's unfit?" asks demonstrator Elsie Peterson.

"Everything is being turned against her," says Michelle Harrison. "The experts are worried that Mary Beth doesn't play patty-cake correctly. Do they care that Bill Stern doesn't play it at all?"

"Why are the experts destroying this woman's character?" asks Karen Malpede. "So that a new industry may be formed that profits from human misery, sterility, and poverty?" Karen has brought Sybil Claiborne and several other women from the Women's Pentagon Action Project and the Seneca Falls encampment.

I read a letter written on baby-blue child's stationery. It has been written by eleven-year-old Tuesday Whitehead to her sister Sara Whitehead. In it, Tuesday affirms their sisterhood; she describes their separation as a tragedy, and she tells her, "I love you. . . . WE ARE SISTERS!"

At least ten journalists try to grab the letter out of my hand; at least five patiently stand in line to copy it down. Only *one* local New Jersey newspaper ever mentions it.

Funny. Mary Beth can do the smallest thing and if it can be used against her, it's blown up to gigantic proportions. Here, Tuesday is trying to remind people that the judge has barred her (and her testimony) from the court and the media censors her, too.

"We'll be back next week," we tell everyone.

Today is the day Dr. Phyllis Silverman, a psychiatric social worker from Boston, testifies for Mary Beth. She testified that:

> *Mrs. Whitehead's reaction is like that of other "birth mothers" who suffer pain, grief, and rage for as long as thirty years after giving up a child. The bond of a nursing mother with a child is very powerful.*
>
> *Mary Beth Whitehead['s] . . . behavior in my view was appropriate. She's grieving, . . . and her coping mechanisms are very taxed. One can sometimes get crazy behavior in a crazy situation.*

Mary Beth is "crazy" for trying to escape from a "crazy" situation—one she has brought on herself by signing a surrogacy contract. We often think a battered wife is "crazy," too. ("She chose the wrong guy and she chose to stay with him.") We have little sympathy for her—but if her husband abuses, rapes, or kills their children, we blame her, not her husband.

Studies suggest that judges rarely protect her—but if she tries to escape, they do order the children into paternal custody. The escaping mothers are then swiftly hunted down, arrested, jailed, fined, and deprived of custody and all but minimal and supervised visitation, like Mary Beth Whitehead.

For example, Dorothy was an executive secretary in the Midwest who married Steve, a policeman, who, she says, used his badge, his gun, and his fists to harass, manipulate, terrorize, and physically and sexually assault her. After years of domestic hell, Dorothy took their children, aged five and six, with her when she moved out and took an apartment in a nearby town. According to Dorothy, Steve's fury escalated and expanded to include physical and life-threatening assaults on his children and on Dorothy's female relatives.

The courts didn't protect Dorothy, and in 1984, she finally fled the state. According to Bob, her second husband (who knew her during this period), Steve proceeded to post false police circulars, use police computers, and alert the "missing children" network. Dorothy turned herself in after her children's pictures were broadcast on television. In 1985, she was briefly jailed and then forbidden to contact her children.

Althea is a Southern mother who wrote, called and participated in the New York National Speakout on Custody. Althea claims she had valiantly tried to protect herself and her son from her husband's physical and verbal attacks. After years of legal and physical harassment, Althea's ex-husband beat her bloody while their four-year-old son watched, sobbing. Although Althea no longer had custody, she fled, taking her son with her.

Althea became a counselor in a shelter for battered women. She made a "new life" for herself and for her son. Four years later, Althea's ex-boyfriend informed Althea's ex-husband of her whereabouts. Althea was arrested, jailed, fined, placed on five years' probation, and given highly restricted, supervised visitation.

Dorothy and Althea—and not their emotionally and physically violent husbands—were treated as dangerous. Mary Beth was treated like any other of these "runaway wives" who try to protect their children or to maintain a nonbattered connection to these children.

FEBRUARY 26

A miracle! Merle Hoffman, president of CHOICES [a New York women's medical facility], was so moved by the demonstration yesterday (which she participated in and photographed) that she gave me a check to help defray expenses. Bless her!

I'm overworked and on a limb financially. I ask each woman who joined me on February 18 to please do some of the "grunt work" or cover some of my expenses. Michelle Harrison and Sybil Shainwald (to their everlasting credit) promise to send—and do send—money.

When I tell everyone that my health is bad (which it is), that I'm tired all the time (which I am), that I can't do it all, that I need help, that I'll have to drop out, my comrades all say: "C'mon Phyllis, you can do it"; "You're so strong"; "It's really *your* issue"; "We wish we could help but we can't so you'd better keep it up."

Where is Harold getting the energy, the time—the money to subsidize himself? He's not a Fortune 500 lawyer with a large staff and an inheritance of his own. Mary Beth certainly has no money. Alison and Harold have each asked me separately to raise money for Mary Beth's appeal.

Harold is uncomfortable about having to ask anyone for help. He doesn't like the media and thinks Mary Beth should steer clear of it. He isn't happy about having to court (or avoid) the media. Rather proudly, somewhat naïvely, he's refused to resort to Gary Skoloff's courtroom tactics. He wants to win on the issues. He knows he can't win in Sorkow's courtroom; he's conducting the trial with the appeal in mind.

The phone is ringing off the hook—with questions and offers of support from mothers all over the country from as far away as California, Hawaii, Florida. Some say they want to send Mary Beth a one-, five-, or ten-dollar bill. I refer them to a fund that's been set up by Kathy Rutler, a New Jersey mother, for just this purpose.

Too tired to attend the meeting at Lois Gould's last night. I'll be at the next one. Lois tells me it drew a large number of feminist academics, journalists, lawyers, and other professionals. Ann Snitow, who chaired the meeting, sent me a note wishing me "luck" in Hackensack.

FEBRUARY 27

I'm on the phone with at least thirty to fifty people every day. I've been trying to get various organizations involved on Rick Whitehead's behalf. Rick is a decorated Vietnam veteran and a sanitation worker. Are children to be routinely removed from all such fathers?

My contact at the civil-service union agrees with me that class bias is involved in the case. He wants to help but is in the midst of a bitter election battle.

A formerly embattled "custody mother" who began a mothers'- and childrens'-rights newsletter, called me from her hospital bed. "What can I do?" she asks. "Rest and get out of the hospital," I tell her. "We're getting it done."

What about the Catholic church? Mary Beth is Catholic and says she has been going to church for strength and solace. Sister Margaret Traxler is "our" woman at the Vatican: she's one of the nuns who publicly opposed the pope on abortion and refused to recant or desist.

"Anything I can do to help that poor girl," says Sister Margaret. She sounds as tired as I am, but agrees to write a personal letter of support for Mary Beth.

FEBRUARY 28

Call Jan Peterson at the Congress for Neighborhood Women in Brooklyn. Would she, her staff, or the people they serve want to join our next demonstration? Turns out that Jan has some staff women who are interested in the surrogacy issue and who want to come to our March 4 demonstration—if I can drive them to Hackensack and back.

MARCH 1

I have my assistant Carrie systematically calling every New Jersey woman who attended the first National Speakout on Mothers and

Custody of Children that took place exactly one year ago today at John Jay College.

Carrie tells me that some women literally hang up on her when they hear that I'm "for" Mary Beth, i.e., against her mistreatment and against surrogacy as an industry. Other women are delighted or promise to come to Hackensack.

MARCH 2

Nora Ephron, Lois Gould, Marilyn French, and I are involved in writing the Great "We Are All Unfit Mothers" Letter. (Something like the "We Have All Had Abortions" letter signed and published in France in the early seventies.) We feel that Hollywood stars will only sign a very low-key letter; and that feminists may not sign any letter that's perceived as a pro–Mary Beth letter.

"Look, Phyllis, Mary Beth is perceived as a loser," Lois says. "As I call around for signers, I've never run into such dislike of one woman before. If we're going to win the fight against surrogacy we've almost got to divorce ourselves from Mary Beth!"

What if she's right? But most women are losers. That's one of the reasons I'm there: so that Mary Beth doesn't have to go down alone.

"Lois," I say, "we can't order our heroines from Bloomingdale's. They always come to us raw, out of the bowels of history . . . but no matter what anyone thinks of Mary Beth personally, she *is* fighting against the surrogacy industry actually and symbolically."

Lois is right. I'm right too. I'm glad there are two of us. Lois seems to me to have literary and media connections. And I'm hoping that this is true.

I'm willing to "take to the streets" so that our views and activities can be reported as hard news in the press and on TV, nightly. Between the two of us I know we'll affect public opinion.

It's time for it to change anyway.

MARCH 4

More very cold weather. There are about twenty-five women and children quietly lining the first-floor corridor outside the press room.

We are nowhere near Judge Sorkow's courtroom. People—plaintiffs, defendants, witnesses, children, police officers, lawyers, stenographers, judges—are constantly entering and leaving the courthouse. People congregate on every floor waiting to be called. We—mainly mothers with infants and toddlers—are also waiting. We have three women in their sixties and seventies with us today.

"Ahh, you," the sheriff says, "the judge wants you to move your people outside."

"We're pretty quiet," I say. "We're just waiting inside until the press breaks for lunch. Then we'll brave the ten-degree weather for our demonstration."

"Naw. You'll go now." And that man, and two others, start herding us out just as if we're cattle.

A few reporters watch this. They ask me what I think of what's happening.

"Well," I say, "it's the same system that herded Mary Beth out of her baby's life. Such a system doesn't hesitate to treat other women and children the same way . . ."

Mary Beth comes over to say hello. I give her Sister Margaret Traxler's letter of support and tell her that Barbara Katz Rothman has gotten the Sociologists for Women in Society to condemn Mary Beth's mistreatment by the experts and the media.

And now something interesting occurs. A mother has brought her nine-week-old daughter with her. The baby wears a sign: NOT FOR SALE. The woman hands Mary Beth the baby and, as if on cue, photographers and TV cameras go crazy, pushing and shoving to film Mary Beth cradling the baby, weeping. (Mary Beth gets accused of "rigging" this scene for the sake of publicity—as if the national press is there against its will and at her command, as if the publicity is an unfair advantage that Mary Beth has.)

Betsy Stern is walking back to court after lunch. Two or three of our demonstrators break away and run after her, one yelling, "How does it feel to take another woman's child?"

I'm appalled and surprised. I shouldn't be. These women are not exactly "political." They're here rather spontaneously to express themselves as mothers. This is their strength—and their weakness. It's what keeps them coming back. It's what makes them unpredictable. And potentially embarrassing.

I wonder what Betsy Stern is really like? Betsy is completely armored, hidden. She's something of a mystery figure.

March 5

I've been going through the mental-health reports for nearly two weeks. They're quite unbelievable. Mary Beth's lawyers should have distributed them to every American—and used them to conduct a national teach-in on mother-blaming and class and gender bias among the experts.

It's really hard to pick out the *worst* examples of bias. There are so many. I've finally decided on four quotes (from Doctors Brodzinsky, Greif, and Schechter) for the "We Are All Unfit Mothers" letter.

I work on this at least twelve to fifteen hours a day, seven days a week, as if it were a political campaign. No: I work as if I'm in hard labor, driven and assisted by forces beyond my control. Whether I want to or not, even when I feel I can't do it, I still deliver one demonstration a week.

Carrie and I do virtually nothing else. I've begged, demanded, and bartered for volunteer hours from friends, relatives, strangers. I have them handling the phones, doing the layout for flyers, writing press releases, driving demonstrators to and from Hackensack in cars and buses that I've commandeered or rented; typing, filing, Xeroxing, rushing off to post and Federal Express offices, picking up legal briefs; buying stamps, typewriter ribbon, typing paper, pens, pencils, markers, oaktag for signs, Advil, Excedrin, aspirin.

Expenses mount. Savings dwindle. I must be crazy to subsidize so huge a campaign. I *am* crazy.

March 9

Today, *The New York Times* published an editorial: "There Is Nothing Surrogate About the Pain" that condemned the trial as biased against both women and the working class and that called for joint custody! (The usually vocal advocates of joint custody have remained absolutely silent. These folks tend to be interested in joint custody when it benefits a father; less so when it only benefits a child; never when it might benefit a mother.)

Harold, Alison, Michelle, Karen, Kathleen, Sybil, Joan—even Mary Beth are all thrilled by the editorial. So am I. It's a magnificent victory.

Otherwise, too little sleep—and my ear is falling off. I'm on the phone constantly. "Can you drive a bus out to Hackensack?" "Can you just pick it up from the rental place and drive it over to the Congress of Neighborhood Women?" "Can you donate some money toward the bus rental?" "Can you do an interview with this radio or television program?"

I'm thrilled that ninety women have signed the "We Are All Unfit Mothers" letter in less than a week. Ultimately 129 women will sign the letter, including nonpoliticals, nonfeminists, and feminists at war with each other on other issues.*

MARCH 10

It's a cold and windy day on Wall Street. Just finished testifying for a career mother in a custody battle. My pretrial deposition took five full hours. (Mary Beth is custodially "unworthy" because she has no economic resources; my career mother is "unworthy" because she has a career—she's a businesswoman.)

SIX P.M. and Lois Gould's loft is a madhouse. Lois is on the phone trying to reach Dolly Parton, Lily Tomlin, Elizabeth Taylor. Letty Cottin Pogrebin is giving an interview about The Great Letter to a reporter from *The Washington Post.* The MacNeil-Lehrer people are here with lots of lights, cameras, wires, and hysteria. We've all invited guests to watch surrogacy-clinic owner Betsy Aigen, one of her "happy" surrogate mothers, physician Wendy Chavkin, lawyer Janet Gallagher, novelist Lois Gould, journalist Letty Pogrebin, and myself spend five hours verbally competing for twelve or fifteen minutes of prime airtime. I feel sure that most of what I say about Mary Beth will be edited out; that the program will show feminists "fighting" and will use "happy" surrogates to defend or justify surrogacy profiteering. That's like having underpaid and overworked

---

*See Appendix D for the letter itself and the list of signatories.

factory workers defend their boss's right to own the only factory in town. Where else can factory workers get a job? What other kind of work can they do?

Betsy Aigen runs a surrogacy business and is herself an adoptive mother through a surrogacy arrangement. On camera, Betsy becomes rhapsodic about pregnancy and childbirth as the quintessential female orgasm.

"Oh the joy of giving birth . . ." Betsy exclaims. Lois and I look at each other and start talking about varicose veins, loosened teeth and hair, leg cramps, backaches, nausea, heart attacks, phlebitis, sterility, loss of bladder control, death—all known to accompany or result from pregnancy and childbirth.

MARCH 11

Seven A.M. A friend wakes me up. "Well, Phyllis, you got the pope to come out against surrogacy just in time for your next demonstration. Congratulations!"

"Sure," I respond, "some of my best friends are really powerful."

I'm afraid the pope's position makes my work harder, not easier. By this afternoon, I'll probably be accused of jumping into bed with all the men in the Vatican. ("If Chesler agrees with the pope that means she's fronting for the Church . . .")

If the Church really wanted to stop surrogacy, why haven't they helped Mary Beth? I thought the Church believed in condemning the sin but not the sinner.

I still admire the spiritual context in which the Vatican discusses surrogacy. All life is sacred; ends never justify the means. Reproductive and genetic experiments do not exist in a moral vacuum. When they do, they exploit the many for the sake of the few.

All day today, feminists flinch when I say I respect the "seamless garment" of logic worn by the Vatican. But why should my recognition of the Vatican's consistency imperil my feminist credentials? Do I have to agree with my comrades on everything and with our "enemies" on nothing?

MARCH 12

Today is our largest and most energizing demonstration yet. We're about sixty people. Two busloads from the Congress of Neighborhood Women in Brooklyn have delivered forty people to Hackensack: men and women, young and middle-aged, Hispanic, black, brown, yellow, white.

The Brooklyn-born signs are wonderful: FATHERHOOD IS MORE THAN A ONE-NIGHT STAND IN A PETRI DISH carried by a young black man; NO BREEDER CLASS OF THIRD WORLD WOMEN carried by a young Hispanic woman; RICH MEN BUY POOR WOMEN carried by a young black woman. Their energy is infectious. We sing civil-rights songs and chant, "Bring that baby home," in rock and Caribbean rhythm, over and over again.

Mary Beth comes out to greet us. At the sight of her, everyone stops and begins singing, "You've Got a Friend." Despite the heavy, wet snow, Mary Beth begins to shake the hand of every demonstrator to personally thank us for coming. It is a dignified gesture.

My friend the sheriff asks us to please stop singing or better yet, to end our demonstration altogether. "Some of the judges are complaining that your noise is interfering with their cases this afternoon."

"What!" I cry. "Interfering with the miscarriages of justice that go on in this courthouse"—and we sing with renewed vigor for as long as our strength holds out.

Not a single brown, black, or male face appears on any television screen. We are free to demonstrate; the networks are free not to cover us. Today is the last day of the trial. Sorkow will hand down his decision by the end of the month.

News of The Great Letter is everywhere. Phil Donahue mentioned it today on his program on reproductive technologies and surrogacy.

MARCH 13

The Washington Post, The Bergen Record, and *Newsday* all have morning stories on the letter. Betty Friedan, Nora Ephron, Marilyn French, and Erica Jong are quoted.

NORA: The catalyzing factor for the letter had been women's feelings that anyone could come into our homes and twist our lives into allegations that we were unfit. We owe a great debt to Marshall Schechter. The day he made his comment about hair dye, it converted half my friends. I don't pretend to have a solution in the Baby M case, but I do think that it's a kind of grotesque parody of all custody cases.

MARILYN: It's like the whole male middle-class world is standing arms linked against this poor woman who dared to open her mouth and say, "I want my baby." The woman who spends nine months in intense emotional interaction with a fetus has a right to say whether she wants that child or not and whether she changes her mind. She has the first choice.

BETTY: Mrs. Whitehead is being treated as if she is some sort of a thing, that she can be forced to sign away the rights of her child, that this is like a contract to sell an automobile. It's an invasion of her privacy.

ERICA: Maternal instincts should override a legal contract. This must seem like an odd alliance, but I really think the pope is right on this one. This is the first time in my life that I've ever agreed with the Vatican on anything.

Mary Beth is quoted as saying that "It's a nice feeling to know I'm not standing alone." But Mary Beth *is* standing alone—even if world-famous women are signing letters on the issues. (Few have pulled out their checkbooks or opened their hearts to her as an individual.)

Mary Beth *is* alone: except she's so surrounded by media that she's never physically alone. If fifty reporters ask Mary Beth what she's eaten for breakfast and then actually publish stories about what she ate, then is she or isn't she as much news as the queen of England? Will Judge Sorkow actually hurt her the way judges routinely hurt other custodially embattled mothers? How can he—with so many journalists watching him?

By now, does Mary Beth herself think she's starring in "Dallas" or "Dynasty," that she's not really a grieving mother, but an actress who'll soon move on to other roles? That she's not really a condemned woman, but an about-to-be-published world-famous author and millionaire?

Mary Beth may see herself as powerful and important; she is not the only one with this view. She is surrounded by do-gooders, opportunists, activists, and ideologues who see her as their way to educate people about women's reproductive and custodial rights (that's me); or to outlaw surrogacy, run for political office, make legal history, testify at congressional hearings, relive the seventies, challenge the apathy of the Reagan years, forge a new career, etc.

The competition to control Mary Beth at the Gateway to Media Heaven is particularly fierce. The air around her is thick with intrigue. So many careers clashing in midair, so many egos vying for her favors. Whoever wants to win this dead-heat competition must be prepared to lend Mary Beth money (she has none); give her free medical attention (she and her children need doctors, as well as lawyers); accompany her on shopping sprees (she is now a public figure and must dress the part) and on vacations (she must also "get away from it all"). Everyone who wants "in" must spend a great deal of time functioning as a "surrogate family" for her as she grows increasingly isolated by and addicted to public attention.

As anyone would. Me, too. Five weeks ago, yes, I wanted to show "the world" that Mary Beth's ordeal was precisely what I'd been describing in *Mothers On Trial*; yes, I wanted to rescue Mary Beth in order to redeem the reproductive and custodial rights of all women. But this is becoming a circus and a nightmare.

MARCH 15

Dr. Elizabeth Morgan's brother Jim has been trying to reach me. Elizabeth is the Washington, D.C., plastic surgeon who had been jailed for "interfering" with her ex-husband's unsupervised visitation, although some experts believed that her four-year-old daughter, Hilary, was being sexually molested during visitation. There was disagreement among the experts, and in separate cases, both a judge and a jury ruled for the father. However, Elizabeth Morgan believed so strongly that her daughter was in danger that she was willing to spend months in jail rather than leave the daughter with her father.

Elizabeth and her brother want me to do for Elizabeth what I've done for Mary Beth—"put her case on the map." Oh, dear man! I didn't do that. The media went after Mary Beth on their own. I neither enchanted nor shamed them into it. I agree to read Elizabeth's papers and to speak to her lawyer and to her daughter's therapist.*

So, Mary Beth's visitation is supervised by an armed sheriff and a nurse-matron. If she were a sexually or physically violent father, she might have liberal, unsupervised visitation—even custody. In one case a Chicago mother, Andrea, sent me color photos of her children's puffed, purple and bruised faces. The story she told me was horrifying but not unusual.

According to Andrea, in 1982, she was divorced. A child psychiatrist described her ex-husband Larry as "explosive" and "dangerous." The judge did not order her son and daughter, then ages two and four, to visit their father; he was convinced that they were afraid of him. In 1984, their father sued for a change of custody because the children had refused visitation with him. In 1985, another judge sent both children into sole paternal custody. Larry beat them severely. On Andrea's next visit, she brought them to a pediatric trauma expert. The abuse was carefully documented; the children were interviewed; it was clear that Larry had done it.

Andrea did not "kidnap" her children. She appealed to the authorities. As a result, her son and her daughter were taken from her, put into foster care, and then returned to their father—who moved away to another state without informing Andrea. Felony child abuse charges were issued against him and then dropped.

Andrea's own lawyer pressured her not to pursue any more litigation on behalf of her children. Finally, Andrea signed an agreement not to litigate any further, in return for minimal visitation at her own expense. The children are afraid to talk to anyone about their lives with their father. In a telephone interview, Andrea said:

> *My son is afraid to talk any more. He was so brave. But nobody listened. What he's most afraid of now is that I'll try to help him and it won't work, and I'll be blamed again, and*

*In March 1987 I spoke with Hilary's therapist, who reiterated that she continued to believe the child had been sexually abused. On August 28, 1987, Dr. Elizabeth Morgan was jailed again. She was still in jail as of March 1988.

*they'll be separated from me forever. So we're all paralyzed
in fear for each other. I live in constant dread for the safety
of my children. They live in fear for me. They're afraid for
each other. We're all afraid for all of us.*

MARCH 29

Angela Hanlon, Francesca McPhee, Rosemary Bailey, and Richard
Kruse, of the New Jersey Citizens Against Surrogacy, have organized
a private birthday luncheon for Mary Beth.

Earlier today, for the first time since the Sterns seized custody, the
Whiteheads (Mary Beth, Richard, Tuesday, and Ryan) were allowed
to see the baby for three hours—at the home of Lorraine Abraham,
the guardian ad litem.

"Do you think this means I'll get good visitation?" Mary Beth asks
me. "Why else would they let us see her all together? They can't just
cut us off, can they?"

"Let's hope for the best and expect the worst," I say. What *does*
such unusual visitation two days before the decision mean? Is it a
hopeful sign—or the equivalent of the condemned prisoner's favorite
last meal?

Alison Ward and Michelle Harrison are both here with their pre-
school-age children. Bob Hanley of *The New York Times* and Michael
Kelly of *The Bergen Record* want to talk to us about what today's
visitation may mean.

There are at least twenty-five other people here, many of whom
have been out demonstrating with us. I ask each person to stand up
and "speak" to Mary Beth publicly—"give her a birthday wish or
tell her what her struggle means to you."

"Mary Beth, we're proud of you for standing up to those people,"
says Professor Richard Kruse.

"Mary Beth, don't let this get you down. You're the mother and
you're doing everything you can to get your child back," says Angela
Hanlon.

"Chin up, Mary Beth," say demonstrators Catherine and Mary
Margaret McLeod.

I give Mary Beth a telegram I've just received from actress Susan
Anspach and Betty Friedan, which reads:

Dear Mary Beth,

   Your capacity to love and your courage to fight are amazing and admirable. Keep up the fight for all of us, not just mothers, not just women, but for the best, most important qualities in all human beings.

                                   Sincerely,
                                   Susan Anspach and Betty Friedan

Mary Beth rises and tells everyone that her extended family (except for her parents in Florida, and Rick and the children) has deserted her and that she is all alone; that we, all of us in this room, are her family now.

"Thank you, thank you for being here for me." And now she is crying and Tuesday is comforting her.

MARCH 30

The phone keeps ringing. "Are you planning a demonstration for tomorrow?" "Will you come and talk to us about the case?" "What kind of help does Mary Beth need?" This question from "Nightline": "Will you come to the studio if Harold Cassidy won't?"

MARCH 31

Decision Day. Harvey Sorkow is reading his 121-page opinion out loud to the assembled press. There are at least 150 press people here. A new and larger room has been set aside for them—and for Los Angeles lawyer Bill Handel's "stable" of surrogate mothers (The National Association of [Happy] Surrogate Mothers). Bill, along with a Los Angeles psychologist and a local publicist, are here to hold a press conference in favor of surrogacy no matter what the decision is.

Alison keeps Mary Beth company away from the courthouse. We're edgy, desultory, and don't know whether to hold a rally or a press conference, give interviews one-on-one, charge into the packed courtroom—or weep. When in doubt, do a little of everything—which we proceed to do.

What's taking so long? It's already 4:30 P.M. Harvey's been at it for four hours.

We decide to hold a small press conference—but the Happy Surrogates have "beat us at our own game," their publicist tells me. And so they have. They are physically guarding the bank of microphones. "We'll only move over for Mr. Skoloff," one says. "If you get in our way you'll be real sorry."

News begins to circulate: the surrogacy contract has been upheld, the Sterns have gotten custody, Mary Beth has no visitation—the judge has severed her parental rights. The judge has held an impromptu adoption proceeding; Betsy Stern is now the baby's legal mother.

As the extent of the victory becomes known the press falls strangely silent. But when the Sterns and Gary Skoloff enter the press room, they break into roars and cheers. The world press gives the Sterns a standing ovation that lasts for at least two minutes.

"Shame," I say standing up. "Shame." The New Jersey mothers and grandmothers cover their ears, look terrified, flee the stage of history. Richard Kruse stands with me, large and mournful.

And now I'm being interviewed by a correspondent who's come from Moscow to cover the decision.

"Imagine," he says, "a mother and child actually separated from each other because of money."

"Yes, it's barbaric," I say. "But in Soviet Russia many children have been separated from their politically 'incorrect' mothers and fathers by the state. In your country, children are viewed as state property. Here, they're viewed as men's private property."

I tell reporter after reporter that Mary Beth has been extraordinarily courageous: she has fought cruel and powerful opponents and been publicly crucified every day since August of last year. How many women or men could survive such a trial?

I'm having trouble today—and I'm not even the mother on trial whose parental rights have just been severed. I'm exhausted and feel deserted, abandoned.

The New Jersey mothers say, over and over again, that they're "afraid, afraid," and "what else can they do?" I'm too busy, too tired, to comfort them, but feel I should be able to. I haven't seen or talked to or heard about Mary Beth. How is she? How can she be?

I have thirty phone calls from the media waiting for me at home—and no time to respond. I call Gena, Sybil, Kathleen, and Karen, persuade them to start calling the media back. I'm too tired to eat. I just manage to pack an overnight bag and drive into Manhattan for the "CBS Morning Show." Tomorrow, I debate Noel Keane.

APRIL 1

Eight A.M. in the CBS Green Room. Noel Keane (all smiles and deference) approaches me to shake my hand.

"I'm really a nice guy," he says earnestly. "I want you to know that Noel Keane doesn't think he's doing anything wrong. I'm sure if we sat down and talked we'd agree on a lot of things."

He talks about himself in the third person (like Mary Beth sometimes does). He sees himself as a saint and martyr (like Mary Beth sometimes does). Why is it so important to "Noel Keane" that I *personally* like him? I don't dislike him on personal grounds.

"Joining us today on 'The CBS Morning Show' are Noel Keane, Phyllis Chesler, and two very happy surrogate mothers"—and we're on the air with Mariette Hartley.

The surrogate mothers are very ladylike in their silks and pearls and demure expressions.

I discuss the issues with Noel. I want to know why his clinic never informed Mary Beth that she hadn't "passed" her psychological test.

"Noel," I ask, "why didn't you have her screened a second time, as your own psychologist, Dr. Joan Einwohner, recommended? Why didn't you give Mary Beth's test results to the Sterns?"

Noel gets red in the face and waves a sheet of paper in the air. "Why don't you read the report?" he demands.*

As I describe the increase in custody battles and the paternal kidnapping of children, the audience (mainly women in their sixties

---

*I've practically memorized that particular report. As I've noted in the Introduction, it says that "it would be important to explore with [Mary Beth] in somewhat more depth whether she will be able to relinquish the child at the end. . . . She may have more needs to have another child than she is admitting."

and seventies) gasps, then begins to boo. Loudly. And for a long time. I go on without pausing.

I wonder how many are churchwomen who believe in and defend the father-dominated family? They might attack any woman who stepped out of the Chain of Command: God, Country, Father, Father-Controlled wife, and Father-Owned Children.

APRIL 2

Afternoon in Red Bank, New Jersey. We are gathered together— eighty members of the national press and I—to hear Mary Beth's response to Sorkow's decision. One woman (whose name I do not want to use—let's call her the first woman) has been handing out a press release entitled: SARA ELIZABETH WHITEHEAD AWARDED TO THE HIGHEST BIDDER; MOTHER NOT TO SEE CHILD AGAIN; CASH-AND-CARRY DECISION SEEN AS THREAT TO CORE OF FAMILY.

This woman is outraged that Harold hasn't invited the lawyer of her choice to join him at the podium.

"Why should he do that?" I ask. "He must know you're leaning on Mary Beth to fire him and hire this other lawyer."

"Harold would step down if he really cared about winning the case," she says matter-of-factly.

From September of 1986, another woman (whose name I do not want to use) has been "like a mother" to Mary Beth. She spent all her hours at work on the phone *for* Mary Beth, and all her hours after work *with* Mary Beth. This woman functioned as Mary Beth's press agent, social secretary, cleaning woman, errand-runner, chauffeur, and all-round companion.

Since mid-February, the first woman has spent hours every week on the phone with Mary Beth. Last week she left her business and moved to New Jersey for three weeks, in order to be near Mary Beth at this "historic moment." Since then she has been functioning as Mary Beth's family pediatrician, personal psychiatrist, media consultant, legal advisor, chauffeur, dinner companion, and mother figure.

These women are a "team" competing for exclusive control of Mary Beth, just as if she were an economic, media or ideological commodity. It may not be illegal but it is unscrupulous to treat a political victim as if she's a psychiatric patient (or a surrogate daughter) in order to use her as a symbolic weapon in one's own battle against the world. It's unscrupulous to allow someone like Mary Beth to think that you're her "friend" in order to get her to confide in or depend on you.

How can Mary Beth know whom to trust, whom to choose? She's utterly vulnerable. She thinks she can exploit her exploiters—and to some extent, she exacts her price. Mary Beth is the only custodially embattled mother I've ever met whose lawyers are worrying about how to raise money for her! It's usually the other way around.

I know custodially embattled mothers who can't get a return call from their lawyers' *secretaries* after they've left twenty phone messages, sent certified letters, lost their child support, their visitation, their children, and their minds.

Poor Mary Beth! She thinks she's supposed to profit from her victimization, *too.* She doesn't understand that her role is that of the sacrificial victim.

APRIL 5

People—including feminists—don't "take to the streets" spontaneously. We chose an April date in February, after our first demonstration in Hackensack. We knew it would take at least two months of demonstrating, letter writing, and media interviews to attract "steady" demonstrators and to establish our credibility. I still wasn't sure we'd have enough demonstrators for an April protest unless we timed it to coincide with some large feminist conference. Luckily, one was organized by Women Against Pornography and planned for April 4 at the NYU Law School.

The conference planners were very helpful. They posted notices; they allowed me to address the plenary session. I urged, begged, demanded that women turn out today at 14 East 60th Street—Noel Keane's Infertility Center of New York.

And here they are: 125 placard-carrying demonstrators, from California, Canada, Illinois, Massachusetts, Minnesota, New Jersey, New Hampshire, New York, Pennsylvania, Washington State, and Wisconsin. At least twenty-five men are demonstrating with us. Bullhorns, police barricades, and TV crews are with us, too.

Janice Raymond, of FINRRAGE (Feminist International Network to Resist Reproductive and Genetic Engineering), introduces the speakers. Milagros Hernandez, of the National Congress of Neighborhood Women, performs street theater. Joan Wile, of the Committee for Mary Beth Whitehead, leads us in a song she's written entitled "We're Unfit." Richard Kruse, of the New Jersey Citizens Against Surrogacy, condemns Sorkow's decision as "unconstitutional and ludicrous."

Norma Ramos, general counsel for Women Against Pornography, says that "New York's hospitals are being turned into involuntary orphanages for black, Latin, and Asian babies whom wealthy white couples do not wish to adopt. The middlemen like Noel Keane do surrogacy for profit, not out of compassion for infertile women."

Gena Corea demands that "surrogacy be criminalized" as it has been in some other countries. Kathleen Lahey, founding editor of *Canadian Journal of Women and the Law,* suggests that it's dangerous to make surrogacy illegal "because we don't want the state monitoring pregnancies or seizing a woman's child by force on the basis of a purchase."

Karen Malpede, of the Women's Pentagon Action Project, reminds us that "the rich are colonizing women's bodies as violently and as profitably as they've colonized the earth. Must we organize massive sit-ins at surrogacy clinics *and* nuclear silos?"

Our demonstration is momentarily wonderful. The questions remain: Will the media publicize all the lawsuits being brought by other unhappy surrogate mothers? Will lawyers—including the ACLU and NOW's Legal Defense and Education Fund, begin to take these cases pro bono? Will people start lobbying their legislatures against surrogacy and for women's reproductive rights—including the right to *have* and to *keep* a child? Will activists emerge who'll demonstrate outside the surrogacy clinics in Philadelphia, New York, Dearborn, Chevy Chase, Louisville, San Francisco, and Los Angeles?

April 10

We're holding a vigil on Mary Beth's lawn as a way of sharing the waiting with her. Today the New Jersey supreme court will decide whether she can see the baby while the appeal is pending. This morning, a feminist amicus brief supporting Mary Beth's visitation rights was hand delivered to the supreme court. Noreen Connell, president of NOW–NY State issued the first NOW statement on surrogacy: birth mothers should be allowed to change their minds; money should not be allowed to change hands.

Today is also the day the New Jersey Highway Department is paving its Brick Township roads. DETOUR! CLOSED FOR CONSTRUCTION roadblocks are everywhere. Will people be able to find Mary Beth's house? This must be a coincidence—or does Gary Skoloff run Brick Township too? I finally decide to drive through all the DETOUR signs. (Not an easy decision to make. How would it look for Mary Beth if we were arrested in Brick Township?)

The day is a blaze of unexpected summer sunlight. Mary Beth is serving lemonade (!) to about thirty mothers, fathers, toddlers, and infants—who have come from Long Island, Manhattan, Brooklyn, Staten Island, and from all over New Jersey.

It's a heartbreakingly peaceful scene. People sunbathing on the lawn. Signs leaning against trees: NO DISPOSABLE WOMEN, PUT THE BABY BROKERS ON TRIAL, BABY SELLING IS SLAVERY, BABY BROKERS PROFIT FROM WOMEN'S PAIN. It is very quiet, very hot.

Fifteen journalists in slow motion move from mother to mother, perspiring, smiling. "Why are you here?" "I just couldn't sleep because of this case." "What do you want?" "Justice for mothers and children."

High noon—and no news from the New Jersey supreme court. By twelve-thirty we decide to hold a press conference. With Mary Beth at my side I refer to Baby Sara as a legally kidnapped hostage who is being held—not in Beirut or Teheran but right here in Tenafly, New Jersey. I introduce Richard Kruse (looking professorial in a suit) and Angela Hanlon (nervously fingering her crucifix) as the founders of the New Jersey Citizens Against Surrogacy.

Richard: "We believe that Judge Harvey R. Sorkow's decision epitomizes all that is rotten about an otherwise beautiful system. It's an illegal, immoral, illogical, and stupid decision."

Angela: "We've sent letters to our legislators asking them to outlaw surrogate parenting. Please start lobbying, too. Artificial insemination has been used to create a stronger breed of animal. To apply the principle to humans is an immoral act of tremendous proportions."

Mary Beth (in gray shorts and loafers) thanks everyone for "being there—but my neighbors really hate the commotion." We go back to waiting. And waiting. Mary Beth sits on the front steps playing with other people's children. Two o'clock and Rick comes home. Three o'clock and Ryan and Tuesday come home.

Mary Beth starts calling Harold's office every fifteen minutes. (If she didn't, I would.) I go outside and disappear behind the house. I'm actually *praying:* Goddess dear, please have those seven judges reinstate her visitation. Five o'clock and still no news. People start to leave. The press starts to leave. I leave, too.

I call Mary Beth the minute I get home. "They told me I can see her," she says. "For two hours. Once a week. They're giving me a chance. It's a beginning."

Mary Beth is right. It's the "beginning" of our contemporary fight against commercialized surrogacy and for women's reproductive and custodial rights.

I wonder: how similar is Mary Beth to other working-class mothers who've signed surrogacy contracts?

How different is Mary Beth's situation from that of any birth mother who's promised to sign adoption papers—and who then changes her mind? Does the fact that a pregnancy began with a surrogacy contract make the adoption experience different or safer for the child who is being adopted away from his birth mother?

CHAPTER 5

A POUND OF FLESH: SURROGACY, ADOPTION, AND CONTRACTS

A woman may promise to marry a man. What if she changes her mind? Should we force her to marry him anyway? Should we punish her for not keeping her promise?

What if she changes her mind after she marries him—or after they have children? Should we forbid a divorce once a child has been born? Should we imprison a runaway wife—or punish her by severing her parental rights?

What if a woman agrees to be a man's slave? Should a judge force her into slavery against her will because "a deal is a deal"—even when that "deal" violates conventional morality or state and constitutional law?

Are contracts sacred? Are they more sacred than the bond between a mother and child? What makes a contract more important than a contraction? A legal conception more honorable than a biological one? Is legalism's "pound of flesh" more worthy of a human being than "the quality of mercy"?

People condemn a surrogacy-contract mother, first for signing an unnatural agreement, then for trying to back out of it. People actually say: "If she's allowed to change her mind, then no man can trust a woman." Consider what our reactions might have been to a slightly different scenario.

A house husband needs money for his children's education. (His wife is a poor earner and unstable besides.) He himself is something of a dreamer. He'd like to earn easy money in an altruistic way—perhaps by helping science find a cure for cancer.

He writes to his local cancer research center, which has advertised for male volunteers. The center interviews and quickly accepts him into their program. He contractually agrees to have a scientist implant a foreign body into one of his testicles; after nine months she will remove the implant in order to study the formation of antibodies.

The man agrees to carry the implant for nine months and to bear the risks and pain involved. He will receive ten thousand dollars for this—but only if his body produces the scientifically desired antibodies. If not, he will receive only one thousand dollars. His fee will be determined after the implant has been surgically removed and studied.

The man undergoes treatments for six months before the implant "takes hold." Then something unexpected happens. His body completely encysts or incorporates the foreign implant. (The scientist knew that this *could* happen; the man did not.) The man refuses the money; the idea of surgery is now too traumatic. "The implant is part of me," he says. "Surgery would be like an amputation."

The scientist is now more eager than ever to retrieve the implant. She strongly believes its value (both to science and to her career) is much greater than the man's temporary discomfort. However, the law requires the man's written consent prior to surgery—no matter that he agreed to it before.

The scientist goes to court; a judge decides that a living part of the man's living flesh indeed belongs to the scientist. The surgery won't kill him; he knew what was expected of him when he signed the contract; he can't just change his mind. A judge orders the surgical removal to take place against the man's will.

Would we sympathize with the scientist or with the house husband? Would we respect the scientist because she was smart enough to get the man's signature on the dotted line and strong-minded enough to take him to court when he refused to honor his commitment?

Or would we sympathize with the man who was desperate enough to sell himself or parts of himself as an experimental subject? Would we blame the scientist because she did not inform him of the complete risk he was to take? Would we forgive the man because he was "idealistic" and initially meant well? Would we ultimately want to protect this man from his mistake—not for his sake but for ours?

Let's think of his implant as analogous to an organ, like a kidney. It's illegal to sell our organs, no matter how much we may need the money. We can, however, *donate* our organs out of love or altruism. Would legalizing the sale of human organs make it an acceptable practice?

What if a poor man agreed to sell one of his kidneys but then changed his mind? Would we want a judge to enforce the contract against the man's will? Perhaps we could hold a trial to determine who most deserved the kidney, who was a more "worthy" human being? How would we feel if a judge decided to seize the less "worthy" man's kidney?

What if we didn't trust the judge, the lawyers, or the expert witnesses? What if we felt they were biased, both against poor men and perhaps against all people who had two healthy kidneys? What if the lawyers and the experts had been trying to purchase kidneys for themselves or for their relatives? What if we thought a legal decision could be bought—just as easily as a kidney? What if everything and everybody was for sale?

"Look," you might say, "no one forced this man to agree to sell his kidney in the first place. Anyway, it's *his* kidney. He can do whatever he wants with it"—except, apparently, keep it, now that he's changed his mind, now that a man richer and worthier than himself wants it for his very own.

"Look," you might say, "this sale-of-a-kidney isn't the worst deal a poor person can make. Anyone lucky enough to be paid for his labor is by definition always selling or losing a piece of himself in order to survive. Why draw the line at kidneys? Is there something sacred about them?"

Yes, there is, I say. In my opinion, it is immoral to buy and sell the flesh of a living human being for profit; to trade human organs (or whole humans) as if they were sugar, coffee, bananas; to act as if living human flesh, once cornered, slaughtered, or contractually acquired, can, with impunity, be turned into soap or lampshades or used for industrial, scientific, or consumer purposes.

The removal of a child from his birth mother—against her will and for profit—is even more heinous than the forced removal of a woman's kidney. A birth mother (her body and her mind) is connected to and remembers her missing baby more vividly than she remembers her missing kidney. Both she and her child are likely to remain bonded to each other for as long as they both shall live.

Why are so many people more concerned with the sanctity of a contract than with the sanctity of human life and human bonds? Can a full-blooded human being really comply with the terms of the surrogate-parenting contract? Can a judge really enforce it?

> THE SURROGATE understands and agrees that . . . she will not form or attempt to form a parent-child relationship with any child she may conceive . . . and shall freely surrender custody to the Natural Father, immediately upon birth of the child; and terminate all parental rights to said child pursuant to this Agreement.

This contract was written by people who believe that *words* can prevent a woman from forming a "parent-child relationship" with a baby growing inside her. There is no way that a judge can enforce such an agreement; any attempt to do so is ultimately a sham.

For example, Judge Sorkow could and did physically remove Baby Sara from her mother; he could and did remove Mary Beth's name from the birth certificate. But a birth mother and her child have a connection with each other that is neither subject to contractual annulment nor subject to court order. Sara's bond to her birth mother is not a bond Judge Sorkow can revoke.

In fact, neither can the birth mother. Even if Mary Beth Whitehead had signed the adoption papers and surrendered the baby, it still wouldn't mean that she complied with the terms of the contract— which called for her to form *no* parent-child relationship. A mother cannot contract a bond out of existence. She can, under pressure, contract it into a distorted form.*

---

*Adoptive parents often point out that the "birth bond" is one thing but that "parenting" is another. They are right. However, birth mothers also point out that

The surrogate-parenting contract betrays as little understanding of normal human psychology as it does of man-made laws. According to lawyer Harold Cassidy's appeal brief and according to fourteen additional amicus curiae ("friend of the court") briefs filed in the Baby M case, the contract breaks many important laws and violates public policy.*

For example, the surrogate-parenting contract discriminates illegally both against women and against labor. There is no such thing as a contract for services without a "consideration" (a payment of some sort).

If a "surrogate" is *not* being paid for the baby, but only for her gestational "services," then, according to state law, she is being grossly and illegally underpaid, i.e., she is not earning the minimum wage per hour, nor is she being paid in cash or on a weekly basis.

If, on the other hand, a "surrogate" *is* being paid to surrender the baby (a "product"), then the contract violates both state and federal laws against baby-selling and against peonage or indentured servitude, i.e., a citizen and human being cannot be *forced* to perform against her will; nor can she be jailed for refusing to "specifically perform." For example, no one can force a football player to "play ball" or an opera singer to "sing" against his will once he's quit— even if he's contractually promised to do so.

The surrogate-parenting agreement also violates the Thirteenth and Fourteenth Amendments to the Constitution, which prohibit slavery and ensure to us all equal protection (due process) under the law. A human being cannot be bought or sold—whether one is a baby fathered by a slave owner and therefore "half his"; or a whole woman who is "rented" for a period of nine months.

In Whitehead's case, her right to due process and equal protection under the law (guaranteed by the Fourteenth Amendment) was violated by the ex parte order that transferred custody to Bill Stern without giving her notice or the opportunity to be heard. Nor did the state have a "compelling interest" to suspend her Fourteenth Amendment rights.

"anyone can parent" but "only one woman can give birth to a child," and that it is preferable for the woman who has the "birth bond" to continue the bond begun in utero or at birth by parenting the child.

*These briefs are summarized in Appendix E.

In addition, no citizen can ever sell or promise to sell any of her inalienable constitutional rights. For example, Mary Beth Whitehead may choose not to exercise her right to vote—but she cannot sell that right to Bill Stern.

Similarly, no woman, including one who signs a surrogacy contract, can sell her parental rights; they are also inalienable and constitutionally protected. The sperm donor and the natural mother (that is, the pregnant woman who gives birth) are, at birth, the child's *parents;* they are the only *(two)* people whose parental rights are constitutionally protected. Only the state can sever their parental rights. It must do so in a lawful and orderly way—and then, only if the parents have agreed, or have abandoned that child or been shown to be unfit as parents.

If this weren't enough, the surrogate-parenting contract also breaks the adoption laws. At birth, the "surrogate" is the child's only mother—which is why she must sign adoption papers. However, it is illegal to force a birth mother to surrender her child to adoption before she gives birth to that child. It is also illegal to buy or sell a child for the express purpose of adoption.

How can we expect a judge to uphold and enforce a contract that is essentially unenforceable; that breaks criminal laws; and that also violates civil contract law in that it constitutes an unfair agreement between unequals, each of whom assume very different risks and liabilities.*

For example, the surrogate risks pain, disease, surgery, and death; the natural father is not even contractually obligated to accept custody of his baby. If, during the pregnancy, the natural father and his wife should disappear or die or simply change their minds; if the natural father refuses to accept a less than perfect infant—then what?

The state (but not the surrogate-parenting contract) *may* oblige the natural father to pay a minimum level of child support. However, neither the state nor the contract can force him to accept custody of an unacceptable baby. In fact, the state can oblige the father to pay minimum child support for only eighteen years. If the child is a paraplegic, retarded, emotionally disturbed, delinquent or, at eigh-

---

*If a contract is shown to be unfair or is obtained by fraud or duress, a judge may refuse to uphold or enforce it.

teen, criminally insane, future liability rests solely with the state, i.e., the taxpayers.

Who is responsible if the surrogate mother also refuses to accept custody of the infant? Is the state (or taxpayer) supposed to subsidize the surrogacy industry entirely? To date, the surrogacy industry has been subsidized by the taxpayer and by health-care consumers.

For example, the costs of pregnancy and childbirth are paid by the surrogate's own medical insurance; the natural father (not the entrepreneur) pays for whatever her insurance doesn't cover. The state also makes it possible for many housewife-mothers of young children to work round the clock for anywhere from one to two years without having to be paid—by subsidizing her surrogacy with state (or taxpayer) Aid to Dependent Children.

In a sense, the state has unknowingly assumed all of the financial liabilities; the surrogacy entrepreneur, all of the financial advantages; the surrogate *and the baby* have assumed all of the medical and psychological liabilities; and the natural father, all of the psychological advantages.

The baby. What are our responsibilities toward newborn infants and to children? In general, it is against public policy to create an industry that is hazardous to our social health. This is true even if a particular individual is willing to take certain risks for himself.

"But," people may ask, "doesn't he have the right to do so? Then, if something goes wrong, isn't it his own fault?"

Once, not long ago, if a railroad worker was dismembered on the job, people said, "He has only himself to blame! He chose a risky job." Over the years, we have come to believe that the public, including railroad workers, should be protected from certain hazards—even if they choose not to protect themselves.

Witness the seat-belt laws. Some people would—if they could—buy cheaper cars, without seat belts. However, auto manufacturers no longer have the right to sell such cars. We are not free to make or buy cars that society considers hazardous and therefore against public policy. Perhaps too many car accidents would create too many grieving mothers (as well as fathers) and too many grieving and orphaned children . . .

We must also question any practice or industry that systematically exposes both women and children to serious physical risk and profound psychological trauma—even if the women volunteer to work in such an industry; even if the children are never told that they've been volunteered long before they were even conceived.

As yet, we have no studies that document either the short- or the long-term effects of surrogacy on women and children. However, according to Alison Ward, a birth mother and the former vice-president of Concerned United Birthparents (CUB), surrogacy is similar to closed and/or coerced adoption in many important ways. She says that:

> *In both cases they hold a contract over the birth mother's head. They tell both the "surrogate" and the "adoption" birth mother that once she signs the contract, she can never change her mind. They tell both of us as birth mothers that since we're not married to the child's genetic father, that we aren't good for—and can only hurt, our own child; that we should not try to keep or to find our child.*

Ward describes the plight of a surrogacy-contract birth mother as analogous to that of an adoption-contract birth mother. She says:

> *Look at Elizabeth Kane [the first woman to be hired as a surrogate and to do publicity about it]. Seven years ago [in 1981] she was saying that surrogacy was the greatest thing since sliced bread. Now she realizes that, like any birth mother, she lost her child to adoption. She is going through the grieving process. She hopes one day to reunite.*

The purpose of the surrogacy industry is to create a situation that leads to adoption. It encourages mothers to bear children for whom they will have no responsibility and to promise to relinquish their infants even before they have been conceived; it brings children into being for the express purpose of separating them from their birth mothers. The surrogacy industry also allows an unscreened couple to legally adopt the child.

Why should we knowingly encourage a practice or create an industry—surrogacy—that is potentially so hazardous to the health of the human race?*

---

*This is a question that Mary Beth Whitehead's lawyer, Harold Cassidy, asked again and again in his appeal to the New Jersey supreme court.

We already know something about how losing a child to adoption affects a birth mother. Numerous studies and first-person accounts have been published.[1] Hundreds of thousands of women in the United States in the twentieth century have lost a child to adoption.

Birth mothers tell us that the pain they feel often gets worse with time. Like the mothers of kidnapped children, birth mothers describe their suffering as similar to mourning for the dead—except their mourning never ends. Birth mothers report: "I have a gnawing feeling in my abdomen"; "a haunting shadow of sadness"; "I feel like the pieces of a person." Many birth mothers have bouts of "irrational" anger and self-blame. "Enduring anguish" is common as much as twenty years later.*[2]

In 1982, Dr. Edward Rynearson described the experience of twenty of his adult patients who, as teenagers, surrendered their first child to adoption:

> *Nineteen of them established an intense private monologue with the fetus [during pregnancy], including a rescue fantasy in which they and the newborn infant could somehow be "saved" from the relinquishment. . . . All of the women had dreaded delivery. They remembered labor as a time of loneliness and painful panic. All received general anesthesia at the time of delivery. Eighteen of the women were not allowed to see their babies after delivery.* [3]

A 1984 study of more than two thousand Australian birth mothers found that virtually all of them felt a great sense of loss—which was not alleviated by the passage of time[4]; a 1984 study of more than three hundred American birth mothers found that within three years, 60 percent had experienced significant gynecological, medical, and psychiatric problems[5]; a 1985 study confirmed that 82 percent of the birth mothers surveyed said they wished to see their children again, and that the pain of giving up their babies was "like nothing they could have imagined."[6]

---

*It is possible (but not likely) that some birth mothers have adjusted more positively. It is also possible that some birth mothers are essentially angry at *themselves* for having failed their children. They may direct this anger toward others who have stolen their children or who have refused to support their right-to-mother.

In interviews with fifty birth mothers in 1986, Dr. Phyllis Silverman found that many were

> *not aware until years afterwards that they were grieving. They all reported a sense of malaise . . . they thought something was wrong with them since they had been told [by professionals] that they would be able to carry on as if nothing happened. . . . It took many of these women from 5 to 20 years before they could talk about what they had done.* [7]

Birth mothers often have recurring dreams of their lost children, and they may even follow children on the street whom they fantasize may be their own.[8] Statements from more than two hundred birth mothers include: "I was always aware, always looking for him in people I saw"; "I wondered how a loving God could do such a thing"; "Separation from my child has been a constant source of pain, worse than torture."[9]

Birth mothers often imagine that their children are either already dead or still alive but suffering. According to one birth mother:

> *I used to read the paper and torture myself about every boy his age mentioned in the news. There was a boy two years old struck and killed by a train in 1966, the year he was two. I phoned the agency and they told me it wasn't him, but I never forgot it, and to tell the truth, I didn't believe them. I couldn't trust them after what I had been through with them before.* [10]

Year after year, newspapers, studies, and first-person accounts inform us of children (both biological and adoptive) who have been neglected, abused, raped, tortured, and murdered in the United States at the hands of their foster, adoptive, and biological parents and at the hands of live-in boyfriends, stepmothers, strangers—and the state.

Unfortunately, we rarely read about these many little deaths. They are not unborn fetuses; they are too "routine" for the media to dramatize; these children are too small to organize on their own behalf; and we cannot bear to absorb such unending sorrow.

The cruelty with which white unwed teenage birth mothers have been treated by their own families and with which all birth mothers have been treated by social workers, pregnancy counselors, adoption agencies, organized patriarchal churches, and judges and lawyers is truly astounding. This is especially true since such adults already know that surrendering birth mothers suffer intensely and forever; and that adoption does not necessarily guarantee that a child will have a good life. Enormous pressure is generally exerted on the birth mother to give up her child.

Some parents, mainly in white families, have literally locked their teenage daughters up at home, spirited them out of state, and threatened them with mental hospitalization or worse for getting pregnant—and for staying pregnant; for wanting an abortion—and for refusing to have an abortion. According to one fifteen-year-old birth mother: "My parents threatened to sign me away if I refused to release [my baby] for adoption. I was really terrified of the social worker, that cold, old bitch who really looked down on me. She had only one goal, and that was to get me to sign. There were no alternatives offered."[11]

Pregnancy "counselors" have warned pregnant teenagers and adults that they, the birth mothers, will probably abuse their own children[12]; assured them that their initial sadness will quickly subside[13]; and convinced them that wanting to keep their babies is "unrealistic"[14] and exceedingly "selfish."[15] According to one young and vulnerable birth mother:

> I had a social worker who was a nun. From the time a Catholic girl is very small, she is taught there is something special about "Sister." She demands unquestioned obedience. . . . Such a one you didn't cross. You were afraid. She had the idea I wasn't good enough for my own child, someone else could do better. So I surrendered her, but not in my heart. I just kept on loving her.[16]

A birth mother who refused to relinquish her baby immediately nevertheless was persuaded to allow him to be placed in foster care. She says:

> I was only allowed to visit him once a month at the agency. I was too scared and passive to ask for anything. I felt they

*were doing me a favor in letting me see my own child.
. . . And all the while the social worker was counseling me
to forget "my own selfish needs" and do what was best for the
child. I was presented with a totally unrealistic picture of
adoptive parents as incarnate gods, perfect parents hand-
picked by the agency to give my child everything I could not
provide. . . . As it was, I felt utterly beaten, defeated, worth-
less. I surrendered. I never heard from the agency again.* [17]

Overall, the often ineffective helping profession is remarkably
effective in persuading birth mothers to give up their children. A
1982 study of nineteen thousand pregnant teenagers revealed that
pregnancy counselors who promoted adoption managed to persuade
36 percent to surrender their babies; of the women counseled by
counselors who did not promote adoption, only 2 percent decided to
give up their babies.[18]

The counselors are all being honest: it *is* a hard world for the
unwed mother. (Indeed, it is also hard for the wed mother.) It is an
indictment of our society that motherhood is such a heavy cross to
bear. But a recitation of the difficulties does not give the frightened
pregnant woman the full story.*

There are some services and alternatives available and counselors
can explain them and help the pregnant woman to keep her baby.
Counselors could also encourage a pregnant woman to withdraw from
or creatively outwit an environment that is systematically and routinely hostile to mothers, women, children, and the nurturance of life.

In 1985, in Portland, Oregon, an unusually inspired arrangement
(known as the "Soham Project," named for the mother) was developed in order to help an unwed mother and her infant. The mother
had no family, religious, or other effective support; she turned to a
large group of friends and acquaintances, both married and single,
male and female, who organized themselves into a "preindustrial" or
"tribal" extended-family network. No state agency, and few nuclear
families, could ever have provided her with such humane and human
support.

Few pregnancy counselors or adoption "facilitators" have ever
tried to develop such civilized arrangements for their clients—who

---

*It is important to remember that when a birth mother does give her baby up for
altruistic reasons, she is still reviled, feared, hated, and unendingly punished.

could, with some help, even form such a network with each other. Instead, everyone—the girl's family, the specialists, and the state— concentrate on separating birth mothers from their children, even when that is decidedly *not* what the birth mother wants.

For example, in 1980, Christina Landaverde fled her native El Salvador. Like so many immigrants before her, she arrived in the United States destitute, pregnant, and with a poor knowledge of English. Soon after he was born, social workers persuaded Christina to part "temporarily" from her son, Mauricio. The document Christina signed contains the following clause: "I understand that this declaration is not a consent to adoption and that in signing this document I retain rights to the custody, control, earnings, and support of said child." She said that the lawyers and social workers assured her that she was not giving away her baby and was reserving her option to change her mind.

Within three weeks, Christina wanted her son back. She was too late. The social workers had already found Mauricio a "real" family: a white, married American couple, both of whom spoke English perfectly, and neither of whom worked as a domestic.

From 1980 to 1983, Christina Landaverde waged a heroic and lonely war for custody of her son. The court confirmed that Christina had not surrendered, abandoned, persistently neglected, or been an unfit mother to Mauricio. On the contrary:

> *This mother has ever been very devoted, dedicated to the struggle to regain her child—overcoming her lack of language and her paucity of funds, by her trek across America, by her persistent visits to the child, as well as by her legal efforts . . . [It is] difficult to avoid measuring the relationship of parent and child by our own North American standards of culture, language and nature of family constellations.*

In August of 1983, a New York court returned custody of her son to Christina.[19]

A birth mother may actually think that she's entitled to change her mind about giving up her baby; that she has thirty or sixty days to do so, because a law says that she may "revoke" her consent to adoption.

It doesn't mean that at all.

It may mean (depending on the state, the year, the judge, and exactly who wants the child) that the birth mother may "revoke" her consent and be custodially reunited with her baby; or that she may "revoke" her consent and be entitled to a custody trial—one she's not likely to win. (She's unwed; she's already parted from her baby; she has no money, etc.)

What else is it but "duress" to obtain a birth mother's signature by offering her hospital care or money when she's about to go into labor or has literally just given birth; when she's experiencing the most stressful moment of her life; when she has no legal advice, no job or housing or prospects, and no help from her family or from the ubiquitous "birth father"?

Most adoption papers are signed under "duress," and most should therefore be considered illegal. We choose not to view it this way. Extracting consent from women who are in a state of distress and who don't know the law is the *daily work* of the adoption business. It is much easier to coerce and control the individual woman than to change our whole approach to adoption and motherhood.

It is relatively easy to destroy birth mothers one by one; it is much harder to rethink what we mean by "family" and what uncoerced adoption might be like.

Married as well as unwed birth mothers do die in childbirth or when their child is still underage; there may be no father and no family willing or able to mother the maternally orphaned child. Also, married and birth mothers—like fathers, and like foster or adoptive parents—do abandon, neglect, or seriously abuse their children. Sometimes, very rarely, usually during a war, a birth mother may "freely" and forever give up her child to a stranger in order to save that child's life.* For such reasons, adoption must exist—child-oriented, open, altruistic adoption, not parent-oriented, closed, and coerced adoption.

Altruistic adoption, like genuinely altruistic parenting, does exist. It is unfortunately rare in both cases. Most people have biological children in order to satisfy or "complete" themselves; people also adopt for the same reasons.

Birth mothers and adoptive mothers, genetic fathers and adoptive fathers, do treat healthy and able children differently from "difficult"

---

*This is still coercion.

children. Over the years, I have interviewed and counseled at least
ten mothers who have sacrificed both their marriages and their careers, as well as any semblance of a sexual, social, or cultural life,
in order to mother and nurse chronically sick or exceptionally demanding children.*

Similarly, there are saintly adoptive parents who adopt children
who have already been rejected by their biological families, including
children who are physically and emotionally disabled. The truly
uncoerced relinquishment together with the truly altruistic adoption
of these children provides the least harmful alternative available in
a bad situation.

I in no way oppose such adoptions; I applaud them. The pain these
children feel at having been given up by, or taken away from, their
mothers is a pain their adoptive parents cannot remove and may or
may not be able to ease; most important, it is a pain the adoptive
parents had absolutely no part in creating.

Saints and altruists are usually in short supply; they are unfortunately not overrepresented among adoptive parents—who, like white
middle-class biological parents, have also put the needs of already
living and "damaged" children—in urgent need of loving families—
second to their own needs to have a biological or newborn and
near-perfect child of their "own."

Today, adoption is not primarily about the welfare of children; it
is about the welfare of those adults who want to "have" children.
Many dedicated social workers try to turn that desire to good purpose,
by persuading child-starved people to be parents to children who
would have been "unadoptable" fifteen years ago. But it is undeniable that there is a market in babies, similar in many ways to markets
in other crops.

There is a "black market" and a "gray market." There are grada-
tions of children, as of coffee, with the prime, white, North American
baby commanding the best price. There are profits for the brokers,
traders, and middlemen.[20]

---

*There are of course many mothers who refuse to do this or who do a very imperfect
job. It is important to note that eight of these ten saintly mothers were deserted
by their husbands. These fathers were unable to cope with having to put their
permanently disabled children *first* and their own need to be mothered by their
wives *second*.

Judge Richard Posner, appointed by President Reagan in 1981 to the U.S. Court of Appeals for the Seventh Circuit, is an outspoken advocate of deregulated free-market adoption. Impoverished birth mothers would get money; by paying more, adoptive parents could get the genetic characteristics they wanted; even the baby would benefit. He writes: "Willingness to pay money for a baby would seem on the whole a reassuring factor from the standpoint of child welfare. Few people buy a car or a television set in order to smash it. In general, the more costly a purchase, the more care the purchaser will lavish on it."[21]

Critics of private adoption call it a "gray market." Fees change hands; babies cross state lines; birth mothers are, as ever, shabbily treated.[22] A network of private adoption "facilitators" (lawyers, doctors, businessmen) has rapidly grown. Two 1978 studies show that parents who go to private "facilitators" have three chances in four of getting the baby they want within a year.[23] Furthermore, they usually get them very young; according to one study, 89 percent before they are two weeks old.[24]

This currently costs anywhere from ten to fifty thousand dollars.

Infertility is not a late-twentieth-century phenomenon. Infertility (and its pain) has always existed. However, in the past, the infertile were probably more resigned to their fate; possibly they were also able to adopt children informally, within their own extended families or communities.

Today, resignation and the belief in an afterlife have been replaced with a demand for Paradise Now, on the installment plan. There is no reason not to want the best of everything; there is nothing that can't be bought or overcome. Accordingly, noses, teeth, breasts, hearts, spouses, families—can all be fixed, discarded, replaced.

A society obsessed with acquiring and consuming material commodities has increased the pain of the infertile. Now, "having" a child is neither a blessing nor a burden sent by God. A child is a "life-style" commodity to be acquired; a symbol of potency, fertility, normalcy, perhaps the only lifelong relationship we can count on in an age of divorce and massive family disruption. A child is also seen as the one "little" thing that we as individuals can still control—in a world no longer in our individual control.

Consequently, many otherwise decent people have lost their moral bearings in their pursuit of a child. In 1979, Betty Jean Lifton described such (closed) adoptive parents in this way: "[First they] spend years trying to conceive a baby of their own, . . . [then] they pretend that adoption is the superior way of parenting. [Then they tell their adopted child that] other people had to take what they got, but we were able to choose you."[25]

The kind of sealed-record adoptive parents in America whom Lifton is describing are increasingly white, middle-class, professional men and women,[26] who have demanded that the adoption records be sealed. As an English judge said: a "veil" was drawn between the baby and its unwed mother "as opaque and impenetrable as possible, like the veil which God has placed between the living and the dead."[27]

Traditionally, most birth mothers who surrendered their children to adoption were white and middle class.[28] Poor and nonwhite women were, then as now, more often assisted by informal or formal adoptions by relatives.

The adoption of white "illegitimate" children was relatively simple until fifteen or twenty years ago. Then the supply dried up. The middle-class white women who had produced the "product" either went on the pill, had abortions, or kept their babies. The crushing stigma of unwed motherhood lost some of its power; women were sometimes complimented for keeping their babies, for having chosen *not* to abort them.[29]

Once, 80 percent of out-of-wedlock babies were surrendered for adoption; now only 4 percent are. The result is that the pool of healthy white babies available for adoption has diminished to near zero; just as the number of white couples who want or need to adopt has skyrocketed.[30]

These adoptive parents wanted babies who looked like themselves; and/or who were newborn, nearly perfect, and if not white, then light-skinned with Caucasian features.

In 1978, an estimated one hundred thousand to one hundred fifty thousand children were available for adoption in the United States. Most were not "acceptable." When 131 parents who adopted privately were asked what "categories" of children they would *not* take under any circumstances, here were the results:

WOULDN'T TAKE:	PERCENTAGE
Older black child	85%
Normal black infant	74%
Older child of another ethnic group	66%
White child with noncorrectible handicap	61%
Normal white child over six years old	48%
White child with mental illness in background	29%
Infant of another ethnic group (Oriental, Chicano, Indian)	27%
Normal white child over two years old	22%
White child with correctible handicap	17%*[31]

In 1983, the Spence-Chapin. Agency in New York placed one hundred and ninety Asian, fifty-five black, and thirty-two white children—but there were several thousand requests for these thirty-two white children.[32] Spence-Chapin tries to encourage the adoption of older black children in foster care, "special needs" children, then Korean babies, then the handful of healthy white infants. It holds group seminars and is unusually gentle with the seekers of white babies. Most agencies now bluntly inform callers that their waiting lists are closed or that there are no healthy white newborns to be had.

Parents who decide to adopt "special needs" children have to deal with the foster-care system. For years, older, disabled, and black children were treated as virtually unadoptable. This is not because black people refuse to adopt children. When income and age are taken into account, blacks adopt children four and a half times as often as whites and Hispanics.[33]

---

*Incidentally, the wealthier the parent, the less accepting. Nearly half the parents with incomes under twenty thousand dollars a year, but only one out of six of those with annual incomes over thirty thousand dollars, scored as "highly accepting of non-typical children."

The number of black children in foster care is so large, though, that even the strong commitment of the black community to adopt "needier" children doesn't help. And traditional agencies have often rejected black couples as adoptive parents because they didn't own their own homes, were economically "unimpressive," or couldn't afford to have one parent stay at home.[34]

The fact is that there is a shortage of both babies (newborn, perfect, white) *and* of adoptive parents (for older, handicapped, and nonwhite children). To survive, voluntary adoption agencies have had to establish new "product lines."

In 1966, 1,206 foreign children were brought into this country to be adopted; by 1975, the figure was steadily climbing, at 5,672. It is no longer considered unusual for a middle-class white couple to have a family of Asian or Latin American children, and airfare to Colombia may be part of the cost of adopting a healthy infant.[35]

The Spence-Chapin Agency has actually established ties with the Korean government in order to offer Korean babies. Our ability to obtain Korean babies is in one sense not much different from our ability to buy cheap Korean cars and electronics. According to Lifton:

> *We see infants being imported like precious saplings from Korea, Thailand, Latin America—harvested by the ingenious rich in the fields of the demoralized poor. We see these children's roots being severed just like ours before them . . . and we wonder in what manner, what code, they will someday seek what is lost to them.*[36]

American adoptive parents apparently prefer to adopt foreign babies. The birth mothers are very far away. Their ability to locate their children is quite limited. Such birth mothers (and their pain) are practically invisible. That is their chief advantage. According to one social worker:

> *A Korean child who is born out of wedlock is a prime candidate for an orphanage. The mother absolutely cannot keep you. It just is not sanctioned over there. They just automatically give them up, or if they try to keep them they find they can't get a job. There's no welfare, there's no aid to dependent children, their families have kicked them out; there's just nothing.*[37]

In 1986, seven years after Lifton's *Lost and Found: The Adoption Experience* first appeared, an adoptive mother published a book about her and her husband's struggle to adopt children. The couple hadn't wanted a black or disabled child; they wanted a healthy white infant. They tried private agencies; they tried public agencies; they tried private adoption facilitators. Finally, the wife (and author) received a call from her own fertility specialist. A sixteen-year-old girl from a white middle-class home was pregnant and due to deliver in a few weeks. She and her parents had decided it would be best for her to give the infant up for adoption immediately.

The couple selected names while they waited. They purchased baby clothes and furniture; they arranged to pay the girl's medical bills. (In other words, they did the same sorts of things the Sterns did during Mary Beth Whitehead's pregnancy.) Then—the phone rings. It's a boy! But they've lost him! The maternal grandmother has persuaded her daughter to keep the baby.

The couple were devastated. The wife says, "We had lost our son"—whom they had already named Jonathan. The husband expresses his reaction this way: "Rage swept over me. What could I do to punish them, make them suffer?"[38] After discussing their grief, the couple continued their search for children to adopt. They had no luck with their domestic contacts, and they considered foreign adoption, which the author describes as having one significant advantage: "There would be no possibility of birthparents tracking down children."[39] Eventually, this couple adopted a Chinese baby whom they named Nicholas. In the epilogue, the adoptive mother sums up her philosophy about adoption and her experiences: "The loss of Jonathan was a 'stillbirth.' Nicholas and Ruth [a second adopted child] are 'of our blood.' . . . I am their real mother. There is nothing about my identity that I know in a more primal way."[40]

The author's husband is an editor at an academic press. One day a writer approached him with a book about open adoption, which he said could be publishable if the author made an intelligent objective case for her point of view. This is how his wife describes the incident:

> *It became clear her stance was not objective: she had 'given up her baby,' had never recovered from it, had never forgiven herself for 'cutting him off from his roots.' It was clear that to her the birthmother was the real mother, the adoptive par-*

ents simply caretakers. It was hard for [my husband] to remain
calm, but he managed to survive the encounter, telling her
finally that the book didn't sound quite right for an academic
press. . . . He never mentioned he was an adoptive father.[41]

These adoptive parents are not objective on the subject of adoption; few people are on either side. However, sealed-record adoptive parents do belong to a large and rather diverse group of people who favor adoption in general—or the rights of sperm donors and adoptive parents over the rights of birth mothers and their children. This group includes:

The infertile; those who *fear* they may be infertile; most adoptive parents; those who profit from or are employed by adoption agencies;

Idealists and ideologues of all persuasions, including: advocates of zero-population growth, sterilization, birth control, and celibacy;

Those who believe in progress and in human perfectibility, including Brave New World scientists, genetic engineers, and "master race" theorists;

Materialists—those who worship *things* and want every child to have as many as possible;

Those who fear, hate, and wish to punish women (especially when they are too independent or disobedient) and who seize the opportunity to do so whenever an unwed woman gets pregnant;

Those who fear, hate, and do not want to subsidize the children of dark-skinned, ethnic, or native women (even those who are obediently married) and who favor the employment of such women as "surrogate uteruses" or "incubators" for their sperm- and egg-donating social superiors;

Child-haters who don't want more children to be born; and definitely not if it means their tax dollars will have to support them (bombs and highways—yes, babies—no);

Those women who have chosen *not* to become biological (or adoptive) mothers but who may unconsciously be bitter about having had to make this sacrifice. Such women often deny (to themselves) that birthing and mothering a child may, despite patriarchy, still be an intrinsically valuable activity;

Men whose identity (both sexual and otherwise) is so insecure that they wish to appropriate motherhood as one of their "God-given" functions;

Women and men who have been so maternally deprived and/or mother-wounded that they are angry at all biological mothers including (or instead of) their own;

Those who identify with and value male, middle-class professions—and pregnancy and biological motherhood are not middle-class, male professions;

Men and women who are terrified by biological events and who don't want such bloody, "repulsive" processes to contaminate them or their children;

All those who, for whatever reasons, now view the adoption bond as more sacred and more civilized than the birth bond.

This is a long and rather formidable list of middle-class and educated people—who are used to getting their way and their "money's worth." They take this for granted; it is their due. They are not guilty about this. These are the kind of people who are perfectly willing to steal from others if they themselves feel unjustly robbed—as long as the theft is legal or unpunishable.

Playwright Edward Albee, in *The American Dream,* and novelist Margaret Atwood, in *The Handmaid's Tale,* have portrayed a certain kind of adoptive parent. In Albee's play, the "Bye Bye Adoption Service" has sold a "bumble" to an unsuspecting couple. The "bumble" didn't "look like" either one of its parents; it cried too much, misbehaved—it even masturbated! The "bumble's" adoptive parents were forced to "gouge its eyes out," cut off its hands and its "you-know-what" in order to socialize it. No matter how hard they tried, nothing worked.

> *For a last straw, it finally up and died; and you can imagine how* that *made them feel, their having paid for it and all. So, they called up the lady who sold them the bumble in the first*

place and told her to come right over to their apartment. They wanted satisfaction; they wanted their money back. That's what they wanted. [42]

Lifton points out that Albee was himself an adoptee and perhaps bitter about those adoptive parents who "pretend" that they're the adoptee's "benefactors rather than the benefited"; and that the adoptee's loss of birth parents is not a "psychic trauma" but rather a "felicitous event that has enriched" everyone. [43]

Atwood's handmaids are "breeders"—"two-legged wombs, that's all, sacred vessels, ambulatory chalices"—the reproductive replacements for the sterile, and/or aging wives of wealthy men (known as the "Commanders").

Such a wife sits bolt upright on the marital bed, her legs spread wide, as she cradles the breeder's head in her lap and holds both of the breeder's hands "tightly" (the breeder's red skirt is "hitched up to her waist"), while the Commander "fucks the lower part of the breeder's body."

When a handmaid becomes pregnant, the sterile wife is fêted. Other sterile wives come to "see [the breeder's] belly, feel it perhaps, congratulate the wife." Serena Joy is such a wife. Here is the handmaid-narrator's portrait of her:

> *One day I came upon Serena Joy, kneeling on a cushion in the garden, her cane beside her on the grass. She was snipping off the seedpods with a pair of shears. . . . She was aiming, positioning the blades of the shears, then cutting with a convulsive jerk of the hands. Was it the arthritis, creeping up? Or some blitzkrieg, some kamikaze, committed on the swelling genitalia of the flowers? The fruiting body. To cut off the seedpods is supposed to make the bulb store energy.*
>
> *Saint Serena, on her knees, doing penance.*
>
> *I often amused myself this way, with small mean-minded bitter jokes about her; but not for long. It doesn't do to linger, watching Serena Joy, from behind.* [44]

Albee and Atwood have given us scathing and harrowing portraits of adoptive parents who are (or who feel themselves to be) eunuchs—spiteful and deadly. People rarely venture this far into the realms of the Turkish harem; they are superstitious about the eunuch's legendary potential for revenge. People also feel compassion for someone who is unjustly deprived of something (fertility, a child) that human beings value and cherish.

Most people feel that it's safer to say nothing about the relationship between exploitation, baby stealing, and adoption; safer still to sing the praises of good adoptive parents, and keep quiet about the eunuch parents. Safest of all is to collectively deny that baby stealing has ever occurred; and to insist that even if it has, it was done in the best interests of the child.

Aren't adoptive parents entitled to the same private ownership of their children that birth parents have? If so, then aren't they entitled to want the birth mother and her child to disappear from each other's lives? Isn't it understandable for them to intimidate, deceive, shame, imprison, or exile a particular birth mother in order to accomplish this?

What's wrong if all they do is hold a legal contract over a birth mother's head? The birth mother signed it; she knew what she was doing. Aren't contracts the cornerstone of lawfulness and civilization? Why would anyone consider it "cruel" to enforce a legal contract?

In Shakespeare's uncomfortably anti-Semitic *The Merchant of Venice*, Shylock and the merchant Antonio freely enter into a legal contract. If Antonio cannot repay Shylock's loan, then Shylock will be entitled to a "pound of flesh to be cut off nearest the merchant's heart."

Shylock is considered cruel because he attempts to enforce the agreement. When adoptive parents or surrogacy contract clients exact their pound of flesh from young, distraught birth mothers, I think of Portia's response to the "legalism" of Shylock's demand. The court upholds Shylock's contract as lawful and "just." However, Portia is able to use common sense as well as "legalism" to prevent Antonio's death.

> *This bond doth give thee here no jot of blood;*
> *The words expressly are "a pound of flesh":*
> *Take then thy bond, take thou thy pound of flesh;*
> *But, in the cutting it, if thou dost shed*
> *One drop of Christian blood, thy lands and goods*
> *Are, by the laws of Venice, confiscate . . .*

Shed thou no blood; nor cut thou less, nor more,
But just a pound of flesh: if thou tak'st more,
Or less, . . . Thou diest . . .

American birth mothers have been treated with unimaginable cruelty—even if no one wants to admit this. Many have described their experience of being pregnant out of wedlock in the 1950s and 1960s. They were treated as if they, their swollen bellies, and their attachment to their babies were shameful diseases. At the home for unwed mothers, they were shown no mercy; they were allowed no privacy and yet they felt completely alone. One birth mother says:

I had no preparation for labor, and was totally alone. I was left in a cold, bare room, and I could hear other women screaming as I screamed. I wanted to die, but I wanted my child to live. The nurses were sarcastic and unhelpful. I was finally wheeled into the delivery room and knocked out. I was terrified when I awoke from anesthesia and asked to see my baby. A doctor, who had been informed I was not to see the baby, threatened to have me put into the state mental hospital "if I made any trouble." After that threat I stopped asking for anything. But I was still moved to the mental ward "for observation" twenty-four hours later.*45

Another birth mother described how sadistic a hospital nurse was to her. She says that when her "water broke all over the bed," the nurse screamed at her for making a mess and "told her never to do it again. 'Have no fear lady,' I replied, and I never have. It took me thirteen years to get up enough nerve to go to a gynecologist after [this] . . . I was forced to give birth 'minus anesthesia, so I'd remember the pain.' "46

This cruelty did not end, although now more "foreign" than American birth mothers are on the receiving end of it. However, young, unwed, white mothers in America are still hotly tracked, seduced, and betrayed by private adoption facilitators.

In 1978, in the United States, of 115 pregnant women who went to facilitators, 53 percent felt "anxiety" about surrendering the baby; 20 percent said they felt "pressured" (by the facilitator, by the

---

*Many married mothers were also treated cruelly in labor and delivery rooms during the 1950s and 1960s. They still are today.

adoptive parents, or both) to give up the baby; eight mothers were apparently lied to outright about their legal rights. Approximately half these birth mothers were told (either truthfully or not) who would be adopting the baby, which seemed to comfort them.[47]

In 1985, one East Coast facilitator complained about certain hospitals, which, in order to protect themselves from liability suits, insisted that birth mothers carry their babies off the premises by themselves. His point was that this was a dangerous time to allow a birth mother to hold her baby. What if she likes it so much that she changes her mind? Another facilitator told me about a hospital that has a policy of removing birth mothers from the delivery floor altogether; according to him, the nurses at this hospital were so sympathetic (to adoption) that they would "dope them up so much . . . they'd be totally spaced out. You'd get a girl who could barely walk sometimes."

Is sealed-record adoption primarily the way to punish women for getting pregnant outside of marriage? Is this how adoption has always been practiced in the United States?

Historically, adoption took place informally within the extended family or community; the state also placed young orphans into almshouses and bonded older orphans out as servants or apprentices. When someone with money and land wanted to adopt an heir, it could be dealt with through individualized pieces of legislation. Not until 1851 did the first state pass a law establishing a procedure for adoption; its rationale was to secure the right of inheritance for informally adopted children.[48]

In the nineteenth century, mass European immigration coupled with a high rate of maternal mortality in childbirth and parental mortality from infectious diseases led to a huge urban population of orphans and abandoned children. They swamped the streets and the poorhouses of the eastern United States. Child-welfare organizations began to encourage unregulated foster care and adoption. In the years between 1853 and 1929, ninety thousand East Coast orphans were sent on "orphan trains" to the Midwest, where they were publicly displayed for selection by farm householders.[49] According to Betty Jean Lifton, it was "Not until after the turn of the century, when it was found to be cheaper to maintain surplus children in foster homes rather than in large orphanages, that adoption, as we know it, was on its way."[50]

Health care improved; the supply of orphans gradually diminished.[51] Gradually, groups that had traditionally placed orphans and abused children now began to "save" other kinds of children too—by separating them from their families in general and from their mothers in particular. The children of unwashed immigrants, of a conquered Indian race, of immorally unwed mothers, were so "saved."

Homes for unwed mothers were created—places where women could secretly surrender their "children of shame." Now, adoption began to change from placing a child *who had no mother to separating a child from her birth mother* in order to place her elsewhere. This was a way to manufacture orphans. Says one adoptee: "I felt I was an orphan even though I had two sets of parents."[52]

Long before there was an increase in infertility, a shortage of adoptable white babies, or a surrogacy industry, unwed mothers were summarily separated from their children. The reason usually advanced for such cruelty toward birth mothers was that it was done "in the child's best interests."

But was it? Was anyone ever sure—are we even reasonably sure today, that a particular child is better off with adoptive parents because they have longed for a child; or because they can offer more money, education, or material possessions than the child's own unwed, impoverished, or Third World birth mother can?

Germaine Greer has written an impassioned account of child-rearing among the world's hard-core poor. She describes her eight-year-old Calabrian "companion" named Mariuzz, as "one of the most sensitive, wise, and light-hearted individuals [she has] ever met."

> He knew how to listen and he knew how to discuss, and yet he was a child, not a small grown-up. He was always busy, never bored or fractious. He never asked for anything, but was delighted with every small thing he got; a pen, a notepad, and finally, as a going-away present, a goat. It was typical of him to want something that would be of benefit to his whole family.[53]

Greer attributes the boy's behavior to the fact that in his family and in his small village, infants were breast-fed and "held" almost constantly; that there were "always many arms all anxious" to do the holding; that children were always with the adults; and that instead of toys ("hideous things, decoys we use to deflect children from their natural love-objects"), every Calabrian peasant child had "dozens of people to play with."

> *Ever since I met those children, I have been conscious of children as members (or otherwise) of a community, and have formed an unconscious habit of judging lifestyles by their integration of children. . . . I have seen children closing the eyes of their dead parents in Ethiopia, children supporting their families by fishing or begging or wheeling and dealing in Brazil and India, children fighting a war in Southeast Asia, children embedded in a collectivity, children with old people who always have time for them, with young uncles and aunts to induct them into their own youth culture.*
>
> *And I have watched those same children being shipped out of their communities, rescued from hunger, disease, illiteracy, and the threat of early death. [I have seen those children being turned] into self-absorbed consumer[s].* [54]

Greer says she was misunderstood when she wrote in *The Female Eunuch* that she would want "any child she bore to be brought up in Calabria." What she meant was that if she:

> *brought up any child of mine as most of the people I knew brought up theirs, I should end up liking it as little as they liked theirs, which would be, for me, the worst catastrophe, for the more I see of human beings the more I believe that* for most human females, their greatest love affair is with their children. *In our society this is not so, and in our monstrous arrogance we believe that it ought not to be so in other societies.* [55]

What Greer is saying is true for most modern middle- and upper-class children—whether or not they're adopted. Everyone is both beneficiary and victim to those forces that have destroyed our traditional relationship to nature, biology, families, and community.

However, to the extent to which most human beings prefer blood-related families to any other alternative—to that extent adopted children are in the minority and at a perceived disadvantage. Forced, sealed-record adoption, fraught with shame, secrecy, and the exile of birth mothers, doesn't help the situation.

The state tells birth mothers that surrendering a child to adoption must be done swiftly and irrevocably; that this is in an infant's best interests. There can be no "leeway" in the law. (Read: the birth mother cannot have her baby back.)*

How can we take this seriously when the same state keeps infants and children in foster care for years without having them permanently adopted and allows babies to languish in hospitals for months and children to spend the night in city offices—because the state refuses to allocate more than a pittance for their (foster) care?†[56]

Is this entirely accidental—or due perhaps to bureaucratic inertia? How accidental is it, given that "special needs" children in foster care can command a larger federal stipend than "normal" children can, just as children in foster care can command a larger and longer-lasting federal stipend than does the one-time adoption payment the government allows? If the state believes its own rhetoric, how can it excuse the fact that in New York City alone, the mainly nonwhite and "special needs" children spend an average of seven years in foster care without being permanently adopted?[57]

How can the state allow itself seven years to make up its mind when it doesn't allow a birth mother more than thirty to sixty days to change hers; even then, as we have seen, the birth mother often has to fight a custody battle for her own child—even though she may have decided to keep her baby within twenty-four hours of delivery.

Let's assume that the state does sacrifice a birth mother's needs to those of a sperm donor or an adoptive couple. Can this still be said to be in the child's best interests?

What do we know about how adopted children feel about growing up away from and/or without any knowledge of their birth mothers?

Fairy tales tell us (and teach each new generation of children) that children have always idealized their missing mothers—whether their

---

*This same argument has never been advanced or accepted as a reason to prevent constant custodial challenges to mothers who have been their children's sole primary caretakers. The insecurity those children and mothers endure is seen as a very beneficial insecurity.

†The state still pays more for foster care than it does to birth mothers on Aid to Dependent Children.

mothers died in childbirth or surrendered them for adoption; and that children have also tended to transform their missing birth mothers into powerful fairy godmothers. Fairy tales tell us (and teach each new generation of children) that, like Cinderella, everyone can and has blamed, hated, and scapegoated their stepmothers (or the mother of one's own female adolescence) as "evil."*

We know that children's fairy-tale fathers are often seen as the innocent dupes of such "evil" stepmothers. Fathers also tend to be missing. They are men who are kept in the dark, deliberately misinformed, and who, in any event, never do their own dirty work. Some fathers sell their daughters in order to save their own lives, or because their new wives have convinced them to do so.

Snow White was poisoned by the reluctantly aging queen, *her* stepmother; her father the king was too busy to notice. Hansel and Gretel were first victimized—not by the witch, but by their own starving stepmother, who, in order to survive, convinced her husband to sacrifice his children.

Rapunzel's mother so longed for rampion (an herb) that she persuaded her husband to steal some for her. He did so—from a witch's garden. To save his own life, he agreed to surrender his firstborn. Rapunzel's stepmother, the witch, apparently loved her well enough until she turned fertile at age twelve. Then she imprisoned her in a tower—perhaps to prevent her from getting pregnant.

One day a prince rides by, climbs up Rapunzel's long, golden hair, and falls in love with her. When her evil witch of a stepmother finds out about him, she cuts off Rapunzel's hair and banishes her to a desert, saying "I thought I had hidden thee from all the world, but thou hast betrayed me."

In a sense, many of the evil stepmothers are Mother Goddess figures who, like the Greek goddess Demeter, are essentially protesting the loss of their own Persephone-like daughters to patriarchal marriage and motherhood. Such goddesses equate their daughters with themselves as virgin adolescents. They protest mortal woman's fate (death in childbirth, being replaced by a younger woman, aging,

---

*Psychoanalytically, we know that children compartmentalize their one mother into a "good mother" and a "bad mother." This is done to one's primary maternal caretaker, whether she is a birth mother or an adoptive mother.

menopause, etc.). Perhaps the goddess-stepmothers are protesting the loss of their virgin priestesses to patriarchal monotheism.

Rumpelstiltskin is a fairy tale about a pre-conception contract. A miller "boasts" that his daughter can spin gold out of straw. The king immediately locks the girl into a straw-filled room and threatens to kill her if she doesn't spin the straw into gold by morning.

Mysteriously, a "little man" appears and offers to do it for her— first in exchange for her necklace, and then for her ring. By the third night, the miller's daughter has nothing left to barter. She agrees to give the "little man" her not-as-yet-conceived firstborn child. The avaricious king marries this golden goose of a girl. Within a year she gives birth to a "fine child."

She does not want to honor her contract with the strange little man. She offers him all the riches of the kingdom; but no, he would "rather have something living than all the treasures of the world." Strangely, the man takes pity on her; he gives her three days to "discover" his name. If she can't, then she must surrender her child.

Unlike most birth mothers, this miller's daughter is a queen—and she is not being custodially challenged by her husband, the king. She has an entire kingdom to mobilize on her own behalf. She successfully names the man: "Rumpelstiltskin"—and that is the end of him.

These fairy tales are also reminding us or warning us that adoptive mothers or stepmothers can and do neglect, enslave, banish, poison, or sell their stepchildren; that even if this is not true, it's how children remember it; and that genetic fathers rarely rescue their children (especially not their daughters) from servitude, drudgery, suffering, and death.

What do the experts tell us about adoption? For years, the mental-health experts behaved like the worst kind of adoptive parents: they refused to talk about "it." They attacked anyone, even one of their own, for suggesting that adoption should at least be studied. They defended their silence as morally and psychiatrically "in the best interests" of the child and of society.

For example, in 1960, a child psychiatrist, Marshall Schechter, observed that "there was a disproportionate number of adolescent adoptees in his clinic, and they seemed more prone to emotional difficulties than nonadopted children."[58] Mental-health experts met his revelation with outrage and fury. Schechter was overwhelmed by how "emotional" his critics were on a subject they insisted not be studied *because there was no problem!* They accused him of wanting to "sabotage" adoption—as if examining an institution that was truly *beneficial* could lead to its ultimate downfall! Schechter says: "If I wasn't baldheaded by the time I went into one meeting with them, I would have been scalped totally. . . . At least 75 [social workers] shook their fists at me for daring to suggest their practice needed looking into. 'Adoptees do not have special problems!' they shouted at me. 'You are wrong.' "*[59]

Since the beginning of the twentieth century, mental-health experts had been trying to convince women that in order to be normal they must marry and become mothers; and that, as mothers, they must devote themselves to their children full time. If not, they would fail to bond with their children perfectly enough to suit the experts; their children would be "maternally deprived" and would therefore develop neuroses and psychoses.

These same experts were now refusing to consider that perhaps, just maybe, sealed-record adoption was the most severe maternal deprivation of all. Why? Had they all been emotionally crippled by their mothers? Did they now want to save other children from bad birth mothers? Or to punish other birth mothers for the sins of their own mothers?

Were the experts convinced that it was scientifically justified to mistrust women in general and mothers in particular? Were they perhaps unable to deal with their own shortcomings or dissatisfactions as *parents*? Or as *adoptive* parents? Were they punishing biological mothers for being fertile? It's possible; experts are also human.

As early as 1943, at least one American psychiatrist, Florence Clothier, had asked: if the "blood tie" to the "primitive mother" is important to a child's "fundamental security," then wouldn't adoptees tend to be insecure people?[60] In 1952, another psychiatrist, E. Wellisch, wrote that:

---

*Twenty-six years later, ironically, instructively, this same Marshall ("she dyed her hair") Schechter recommended the adoption of Baby M.

Lack of knowledge of their real parents and ancestors can be a cause of maladjustment in children. . . . Persons outside ourselves, (most importantly) our real parents, are essential for the development of our complete body-image . . . the loss of this . . . is a deprivation which may result in the stunting of emotional development. [61]

Wellisch predicted that such "deprivation" could in the future result in an "irrational rebellion against their adoptive parents." Like Schechter, he also suggested that this "deserved to be studied."[62]

In 1964, another psychiatrist, H. J. Sants, distinguished between what he called "genealogical bewilderment" and "adoption stress." He concluded that "transplanting" children from their native soil was a "graft" that could not succeed, that "roots in the natural family can never be severed without a trace," and that children needed to know their natural origins.[63]

In 1986, Dr. Steven Nickman succinctly summarized twenty years of research about the effect of adoption on "adoptees":

Adoptees not related to their parents constitute about 1.5% of the child population; step-parent and [blood-] relative adoptions constitute a similar number. Studies have shown that 13 to 14% of children and adolescents in private psychotherapy are adopted. Psychiatric inpatient units have shown figures of 20 to 30%, and some residential schools for disturbed children have 30 to 40% adopted students. [64]

From the mid-1960s on, research has documented that adoptees characteristically have low levels of self-esteem; learning and school difficulties; and a high incidence of teenage unwed pregnancies, drug addiction, and negative encounters with the law. In addition, they've shown an adult tendency to roam and to gravitate to one's socioeconomic inferiors (presumably in search of one's taboo mother); and a tendency to have children out of wedlock and to surrender them to adoption.[65] Nickman points out that this "psychiatric risk" is just as great among adoptees with wealthy parents; and that while the risk may be diminished by ongoing dialogue about adoption, it cannot be eliminated. Nickman reminds his colleagues that: "When adopted adolescents and adults are interviewed they generally express more pain about having been abandoned by their mothers than about having been abandoned by their fathers. This pain is experienced as a lack of personal worth. . . . Such a conviction of worthlessness is notably resistant to attempts at logical argument."[66]

The same mental-health experts who once minimized the negative effects of adoption may now be exaggerating them. It's also possible that they're not interpreting the statistics adequately. For example, perhaps adoptees are psychiatrically overrepresented because adoptive parents tend to avail themselves of mental-health services more often than do other parents.

Perhaps the same genetic narcissism that accounts for the primacy of the biological family and that leads to an exclusive ownership model of family relations is what drives the (excluded) infertile into adoption in the first place—and then impedes their ability to carry out the family-building task. Perhaps adoptees are actually more stressed by the secretive, closed nature of adoption than they are by the literal physical removal of their birth mothers and genetic fathers. Perhaps what is maddening is the refusal to acknowledge what has happened, or to allow an adoptee access to her birth mother or to her extended blood family.

W hat do adoptees tell us about the adoption experience? According to Betty Jean Lifton, to be adopted is to feel like a "displaced person," a "survivor of a holocaust of one kind or another," an "orphan," an "impostor," "second best" as well as "obligated" because one is "chosen" rather than "born." An adoptee is "haunted" by all her "doubles":

—*even the double has a double. There is the other possible self one might have been had one been kept by one's birth-parents. There is the self one might have been had one been chosen by a different couple. There is the child one's adoptive parents might have had, had they been fertile, or the child they did have who died.*[67]

According to playwright Gary Aylesworth in his play *The Doom Folk*, if you go through life without knowing your birth parents, you're "missing something."

> *It's like a handicap. You adapt to the handicap like you would if you were missing a hand or your sight. But you're still missing something! But, just as I was about to make contact with my birth-mother for the first time I became afraid that if she's no longer missing, that I won't know what to do.* [68]

Novelist Gregory Armstrong describes his parents, both of whom were adopted, as "apologetic and deferential. . . . Both of them lived as if they believed that other people were always better. People with parents. They took so little for themselves. The little they did take they took so apologetically. So deferentially."[69]

According to Lifton, adoptees are (at least unconsciously) all involved in a "search" for the "missing part of themselves"; "reunion" with one's birth mother always gives an adoptee a "feeling of being grounded in the human condition." Aylesworth describes hearing his birth mother's voice, for the first time in thirty-four years, in this way: "Wow! The voice! Just the tone of the voice! Not the words but just the tone! For a split second it goes right into my ear, and down into an inner recess in my heart, and I can almost see . . . Tibet!"[70]

Some adoptees do not want to search for their birth mothers. They are "loyal" to their adoptive parents and feel that to search is to "betray" them. Betty Jean Lifton calls them "militant nonsearchers" who "seem to accept that they don't have a right to their own heritage" and who have a "will not to know."

Apparently the majority of searchers have been women. According to Lifton, this is because women are "closer to their feelings than men," and because, as potential mothers themselves, they "yearn for some knowledge of that woman who went before them into the rites of childbirth—an experience they cannot share with their adoptive mothers."[71]

Lies, secrets, half truths—silence—can never help a child. Every adoptee who is lied to about his birth mother ("she died in childbirth" or "in a car crash") suffers unnecessarily because of that lie. Every adoptive parent who refuses to help his (adult) child find her birth mother is causing unnecessary suffering.

Why not stop coercing poor or unwed birth mothers into giving up their newborn children? Why not open adoption altogether? According to Lifton, the already existing adoption bond may be much "stronger than it seems in time of crisis."

According to social worker James Gritter, an advocate of open adoption, the "beginning goal" of any "pregnancy worker" should be "to keep the family intact." Gritter views the pregnant woman and her fetus and/or the birth mother and her newborn as "the family." As such, he believes that a birth mother has a natural, moral right to change her mind; and also to establish some kind of cooperative, noncustodial relationship with her child.[72]

About 10 percent of the pregnant women who contemplate open adoption *do* decide to keep their babies. Advocates of open adoption believe that this is a risk that adoptive parents should be willing to assume.[73]

There are always risks involved in having a baby. Couples routinely assume such risks when they have a biological child. Women assume enormous risks each time they get pregnant and give birth. Only the advocates of sealed-record adoption—and of surrogacy— seem to feel that people can become parents without having to assume any risk at all.

Is the need to return to the birth mother a biological drive, an instinctive or evolutionary force? Is it possible, "all other things being equal," that most human beings need their birth mothers, that a surrogate will not do as well?*

When Aylesworth found his birth mother he discovered some coincidences. His birth mother's birthday (May 10) was the same as his girlfriend's of eleven years, his birth mother and his girlfriend are both five feet two inches tall, and they both attended a Sacred Heart high school. His girlfriend's name is Jeanette—which is his mother's middle name.[74]

Is it possible that a child's own birth mother is meant for that child; that premature physical separation from that mother—even by the

---

*"All other things being equal" is a legal expression that essentially means that if the birth mother is not unfit and hasn't abandoned the child, and can also provide the child with food and shelter and some family life, then there are no overriding factors that compel us to remove the child from her custody.

child's genetic father—will cause trauma and injury that should be avoided?

In 1981, a white, middle-class, high-school student surrendered her out-of-wedlock child. The biological grandmother offered the lawyer money to ensure that the baby girl would be placed in a good Catholic home.

The girl grew up in New York with a father who was described by neighbors, friends, and even business associates as enormously devoted to her. It was her father, not her mother, who was seen pushing her on the swings in the park, carrying her proudly on his shoulders, showing her off, beaming with love and paternal devotion.

However, on Halloween 1987, a photograph taken of the girl in school revealed a slight, sensitive six-year-old with a haunted, fearful look in her eyes. Several days later she was dead from a beating.

Her birth mother came forward to claim her body for burial. This was the unwed mother who had been told that she could not provide her newborn with a good home; that others could.

Is it thoroughly unreasonable to think that Lisa Steinberg (for that was her name) would have been better off with her birth mother, Michelle Launders, perhaps on welfare, on Medicaid, wearing a thrift-shop Halloween costume on October 30, 1987, than she was in the home of adoption lawyer Joel Steinberg and his common-law wife, Hedda Nussbaum?*

Are we unwilling to even consider the possibility that the birth bond, for a woman, and the genetic bond, for a man, exist in both cases, in the best interests of our species, and therefore in the best interests of each individual child?

Not always; but often enough?

Is it thoroughly unreasonable to think that unless something is drastically, incurably, dangerously wrong with a birth mother, she should be entitled to keep her child; in fact she should be strongly

---

*Lisa Steinberg was never legally adopted; Joel Steinberg apparently never completed and filed the appropriate paperwork. However, he was an adoption lawyer, and had he prepared and filed the documents, nothing would have prevented this de facto adoption from becoming a legal, private adoption in New York. Of course, an adoption through appropriate agency channels would have taken place much differently. But there is no evidence that private adoptions are any less risky than was the Launders/Steinberg child transfer.

encouraged and generously helped to do so, *in the best interests of her child?*

Is it unreasonable to consider that the acquisition of a child by the process of pregnancy and birth is more compelling, and more inalienable, than the acquisition of a child by surrogacy, marriage, or social contract? (In my opinion, a child belongs to no one; but the right to mother the child belongs to his birth mother.) If so, do we need a constitutional amendment that guarantees birth mothers and their children unbroken access to each other?

CHAPTER 6

THE VERDICT, 1988

FEBRUARY 2

It's one year later now. We held our first press conference on February 18, 1987; tomorrow at 10 A.M. the New Jersey supreme court will hand down its decision.

Harold will hold a press conference at 2 P.M. in Red Bank, New Jersey. I—and about ten others, mainly lawyers—will each have two minutes to comment on the decision.

I'm taping a TV show today with Roxanne Pulitzer. She did not sign a surrogacy contract but she still lost custody of her children to their father. The judge viewed him as the more "stable" of the two parents. The judge viewed Roxanne as the less fit of the two parents because, among other reasons, she engaged in extramarital sex after childbirth.

The studio audience consists mainly of middle-aged women who are accustomed to seeing women who look like Roxanne—young, blond, thin, and tall—on their TV screens all the time. On TV or in life, the audience women do not have the power to either approve or disapprove of men's preference for young, blond, thin, and tall women. In Roxanne's case, however, they seem satisfied that she got what she deserved: she lost custody.

The next guest is a sixteen-year-old girl who says she was, as a child, "brutalized" by her father in a custody war. However, her mother's second husband has been a "wonderful father" to her; he also adopted her. As long as there's a good father floating around somewhere, such an audience can tolerate a low level of tension. But they're not happy. They're a little restless. After all, this is the second woman who's said or implied that not all men are good fathers.

The third guest is a fathers' rights activist. He's audience relief. Much of what he says gets applause from this audience. (Do they see him as a savior?) He seems to think that all fathers love their children. He seems to believe that wives more often batter their husbands than the other way around. He seems to believe that all fathers are fit parents, that no father ever abandons his children. Rather, vicious, unfit mothers and terrible judges try to squeeze fathers out of their children's lives. He says that every study has demonstrated that joint custody is *the* solution.

This man seems to me to be misrepresenting facts with a boyishly disarming smile. The more he misrepresents, the more he smiles and the more he is applauded. I am the fourth guest. He interrupts me as I start to answer my first question. He challenges my statistics. Whenever I start to respond, he interrupts again—talks right over me. Instead of having a chance to express my views, I'm being asked to compete for airtime, to see who can talk loudest and fastest.

No one says to him: "It's *her* turn to speak, you had a chance." The host wants to please the audience—and the audience is excited by the prospect of some verbal mud wrestling. They want us to slug it out. Only unarmed Christians versus hungry lions can make them feel alive. That's why so many people, *especially* women, enjoyed seeing Roxanne Pulitzer and Mary Beth Whitehead lose bloody and sensational battles that were stacked against them from the start. Women who have never been allowed to talk back eventually identify with the aggressor and have no pity for a victim who reminds them of themselves.

So. I'm supposed to engage in hand-to-hand verbal combat with this young bully. Verbally, I feel I can take him easily, but I'll lose if I do it. The women in the audience will see me as too combative, too unladylike. I'll also lose if I refuse to talk over him, if I let him silence me.

I'm shaken by the audience's mother hatred and father worship. Suddenly I have terrible forebodings about tomorrow. What if the New Jersey supreme court decides that women are only surrogate uteruses after all? Or that men and money are custodially better for children than women and mother love?

FEBRUARY 3

D Day. I've invited two women to join me: Joan Wile, who helped organize the demonstrations in Hackensack; and Sim Ariel, who's forming an organization to educate people about what happens to women and children involved in custody battles. She's calling it M.O.M.S.—Mothers Opposing Misogynist Systems. ("You don't have to be a mother to join," she says. "It's like M.A.D.D., Mothers Against Drunk Driving.")

What are Mary Beth and the Sterns feeling right now? Where's Baby M—that little shadow figure whom we've never seen in Betsy's or in Mary Beth's arms, but only in her father's arms as he carries her to and from visits with Mary Beth?

Right now, the Sterns are more emotionally at risk than Mary Beth. It's nearly two years since the king's men came on horses in the night and took Mary Beth's baby from her. She's survived that—and the long and terrible public ordeal afterward. As she says, "there'll always be scars," but she's fallen in love, gotten divorced, remarried, and is soon to give birth to her fourth child.

During the years of struggle, the Sterns have had both the baby and immense public sympathy. For them, legal decision days have never meant losing anything.

To me, the Sterns appear brittle and rigid. Might they break if things don't go their way?

Might a decision against them slowly and inexorably kill their love for the baby or their love for each other?

At 10:15 A.M., the radio says that Mary Beth Whitehead Gould lost her bid for custody but that her parental rights have been restored.

Interesting! If her parental rights have been restored, that means that Mary Beth is the baby's only legal mother, that the adoption has been overturned, that *legally* Betsy Stern is only her husband's wife: nothing more, nothing less.

This means that Mary Beth can now do a lot more than apply for visitation. She can apply for custody at any time until Sara is eighteen years old. Baby M's name is Sara: that is her name on the only legal birth certificate. Legally, there is no Melissa, the name the Sterns gave the child.

Curious that the radio should present this victory as a *loss* for Mary Beth. How many more radio or television stations will accidentally or purposely mislead us about what the decision says or what it means?

We drive out to Red Bank for Harold Cassidy's press conference. Spur of the moment, I decide to buy red roses for Harold, to thank him for what he did. We're early—but at least 150 members of the press are already here. I take my place at the table next to the lawyers who assisted Harold directly or who submitted amicus briefs, and next to the representatives of birth mothers who've lost their children to adoption.

Harold walks in with Mary Beth. Incredibly, there is no applause. The same media who gave Gary Skoloff and the Sterns a standing ovation on March 31, 1987, remain seated and silent. The victory—which the radio stations have so far minimized or misunderstood—is not popular. How can the media not be a *little* thrilled that a state supreme court has decreed that baby selling, baby stealing, and baby buying and the exploitation of women as surrogate uteruses are immoral and illegal? That there are some things that money can't buy? That a contract is not always legal or enforceable?

I wonder: Where are those people who thought that a deal is a deal? If slavery isn't legal, are they going to secede from New Jersey and form a patriarchal confederacy?

Harold, poker-faced and bushy-mustached, speaks: "Today's decision of the New Jersey supreme court is a major triumph for human decency. It is a blow to the experimentation with children that has been conducted by a handful of organizations across the country. Paying a woman to give away her baby is not a medical solution to infertility. Instead, it is a commercialization of conception, pregnancy, and childbirth that is contrary to public policy and unquestionably harmful."

Rick Whitehead speaks: "I'm here today simply to say that I'm happy for Mary and for Sara. I was with Mary when Sara was born; I helped Mary when she decided that she could not go through with the surrogacy agreement; I was involved throughout the trial. I'm happy that the courts of New Jersey have recognized that Mary had a right to reject the surrogacy agreement. I'm especially happy that, as Sara grows up, Mary will be a part of her life. I truly believe that Sara will be the better for it."

Then Mary Beth speaks: "I did not begin this as a public crusade, but I am gratified to see that surrogacy has been discredited and delighted to know that my relationship with my daughter will continue for the rest of our lives. As I told you at our press conference almost a year ago, there can never be a court-appointed termination of my love for my daughter."

Mary Beth is extraordinarily well-spoken. She is not a gloating victor. She says that she will not do what the Sterns and Judge Sorkow did when they forcibly removed the baby from Mary Beth's breast; that she will not seek custody, only visitation. The press does not applaud her.

This group applauds when I give Harold his roses—but only after I explain why they should. I say: "Here is a man—and a lawyer!—who took an unknown woman's case *for no fee,* laid out approximately half a million dollars of his own money and time for the sake of certain principles that he holds dear: that all men and all women are created equal; that women are not surrogate uteruses; that birth mothers and their children have a right to each other; that children are at risk when they're adopted away from their birth mothers; and therefore that surrogacy is harmful to children and birth mothers, and therefore to society."

I say: "If every lawyer did what Harold has done—*just once in his or her career,* imagine how different the lives of custodially embattled birth mothers might be. Imagine if impoverished women thought they could actually appeal to a state supreme court, that a lawyer like Harold Cassidy might be willing to absorb a financial body blow for the sake of justice."

Ordinarily, in a custody battle, if a mother opposes visitation, she is condemned as uncooperative, perhaps unfit. If she doesn't accommodate the father's right-to-visit, she may lose custody. Today, the press does not criticize Bill or Betsy for not wanting to share. No one criticizes them for having refused to work it out with Mary Beth in the beginning, when she was only asking for alternate-weekend visitation. No one feels anything but sympathy for them when they say that they will vigorously oppose Mary Beth's right-to-visit.

By the time I get home it's 7 P.M. From now until midnight I'm glued to my TV set. Every program I see reports the decision as a "win" for Bill and a "loss" for Mary Beth. Every newscaster is infuriatingly careful to point out that while paid surrogacy is illegal in New Jersey, it is still legal in other states. Every network has interviewed the one-and-only Betsy Aigen, surrogacy clinic owner and adoptive mother of a child by surrogacy. No network, as far as I can see, has an interview with an unhappy or custodially embattled birth mother.

FEBRUARY 4

The New York newspaper headlines are in. They are more accurate, less biased, than yesterday's TV coverage. *The New York Times* is essentially pleased with the decision: A. M. Rosenthal wants to write a "poem" to the seven judges of the New Jersey supreme court. The *Daily News* thinks it's a bad decision. The *Post* is confused. Its headlines read that BABY M HAS TWO MOMS, but they now refer to the baby as "Sara," not "Melissa." *New York Newsday* calls it a "split decision." They quote the court on the front page: "This is the sale of a child, or, at the very least, the sale of a mother's right to her child . . . Almost every evil that prompted the prohibition of the payment of money in connection with adoptions exists here."

I have many reasons to applaud the decision. How many judges in a capitalist country affirm that "in a civilized society, [there are] some things that money cannot buy"? They write:

> *Employers can no longer buy labor at the lowest price they can bargain for, even though that labor is "voluntary," or buy women's labor for less money than paid to men for the same job, or purchase the agreement of children to perform oppressive labor, or purchase the agreement of workers to subject themselves to unsafe or unhealthful working conditions. There are, in short, values that society deems more important than granting to wealth whatever it can buy, be it labor, love, or life.* [1]

More important: This court does not think that men have a more sacred claim to their children than women do. If anything, they believe that a birth mother may have the more sacred claim—at least when the child involved is still an infant and the mother is perfectly fit.

The judges are not saying that all women must immediately become biological mothers, or that biological mothers are "better" than nonmothers. Nor are they saying that fathers cannot bond with infants or shouldn't relate to them until they're much older.

The court employs feminist language and feminist concepts with both eloquence and rigor. The court is sensitive to the *ideal* of gender neutrality and to the *reality* of gender differences. How many people, including feminists, share the court's common-sense perception that surrogate uteruses and sperm donors are not identical; that the time it takes to provide a sperm donation and nine months of pregnancy are not the same? In terms of "the human stakes involved," the court wonders,

> *how much weight should be given to her nine months of pregnancy, the labor of childbirth, the risk to her life, compared to the payment of money, the anticipation of a child and the donation of sperm?*[2]

The court views both parents as equally entitled to their child. However,

> *this does not mean that a mother who has had custody of her child for three, four or five months does not have a particularly strong claim arising out of the unquestionable bond that exists at that point between the child and its mother; in other words, equality does not mean that all of the considerations underlying the "tender years" doctrine have been abolished.*[3]

Most people, including many lawyers and judges, erroneously believe that women were or still are automatically entitled to custody because of a maternal presumption, and that a maternal presumption is sexist and, like alimony and "fault" divorce, should be abolished.*

---

*The New Jersey supreme court understands that a maternal presumption is not (and never has been) a woman's legal right. The "tender years" doctrine, which is the maternal presumption, was never meant to assist or empower women; it was developed in the best interests of the child. Even so, this presumption was operative in New Jersey for only eleven years—from 1860 to 1871. After that, it was abolished as unfair.

The court is saying that men and women are and must be treated equally, that custody decisions must still be made in the child's best interests—but that a natural bond exists between a birth mother and her infant that does not exist between a father and his infant. They write:

> *The probable bond between mother and child, and the child's need, not just the mother's, to strengthen that bond, along with the likelihood, in most cases, of a significantly lesser, if any, bond with the father—all counsel against temporary custody in the father.* [4]

And then they proceed to affirm father Bill Stern's right to custody in the best interests of the child.

Why? Because they view *parental* rights (which they have restored to Mary Beth Whitehead) essentially as *paternal* rights. Men and women are equal as long as women are identical to men, and/or can be treated as if they were men. The judicial model for a human being—rational, parental, or otherwise—is still a man and not a woman.

But what about the mother-infant bond? Hasn't this court just described it as a unique and beneficial bond that exists only between a birth mother and her infant child? Haven't they emphasized that, contrary to what people who read newspapers thought, the trial experts never proved that Mary Beth Whitehead was maternally unfit? Haven't they written that:

> *It seems to us that given her predicament, Mrs. Whitehead was rather harshly judged—both by the trial court and by some of the experts. She was guilty of a breach of contract, and indeed, she did break a very important promise, but we think it is expecting something well beyond normal human capabilities to suggest that this mother should have parted with her newly born infant without a struggle. Other than survival, what stronger force is there? We do not know of, and cannot conceive of, any other case where a perfectly fit mother was expected to surrender her newly born infant, perhaps forever, and was then told she was a bad mother because she did not.* [5]

What remedy do they propose? How will they restore Mary Beth and Sara to each other? How will they repair the damaged mother-infant bond? Why, with visitation, of course! Like any other non-custodial parent, Mary Beth Whitehead can now apply to a lower court for visitation. Her application must be heard and acted upon within ninety days. Judge Sorkow can never sit on her case again.

FEBRUARY 5

So why hasn't the court given Mary Beth Whitehead custody as the way for her to reconnect with her daughter?

Because, as they note, a child's "best interests" must determine custody; and no one has proven that Mary Beth Whitehead is the "better" parent just because she is maternally bonded to the baby. Granted: her *parental rights* should not have been terminated; but no mother has an automatic right-to-mother or to custody of her infant— not when a father wants custody or the right-to-mother for himself or for his wife.

The court judged the surrogacy contract to be immoral and illegal. When sexual or reproductive wrongdoing occurs, it is the woman, not the man, who will be punished. Prostitutes, not "johns," are arrested, jailed and fined. For example, both Roxanne and Peter Pulitzer engaged in extramarital sex; only Roxanne was custodially punished. Or, for example, both Bill Stern and Mary Beth Whitehead signed an immoral and illegal contract; only Mary Beth is being custodially punished. The court "disagrees with the premise" that

> *in determining custody a court should decide what the child's best interests would be if some hypothetical state of facts had existed. Rather, we must look to what those best interests* are, *today, even if some of the facts may have resulted in part from legal error. The child's best interests come first: we will not punish it for judicial errors, assuming any were made.* [6]

The "child's best interests come first. . . ." Admirably, the court won't sacrifice the child to a *theory* of maternal-infant bonding or to its own *judgment* about Sorkow's "legal error." But it will custodially sacrifice Mary Beth, the mother (but not Bill, the father) in the best interests of this one real child.

However, the court will not sacrifice any other mother but Mary Beth. In the future, no father, no judge, no policeman in the state of New Jersey will be able to separate an infant from her birth mother simply because a surrogacy arrangement may be involved.

> *Any application by the natural father in a surrogacy dispute for custody pending the outcome of the litigation will henceforth require proof of unfitness, of danger to the child, or the like, of so high a quality and persuasiveness as to make it unlikely that such application will succeed. . . . The erroneous transfer of custody, as we view it, represents a greater risk to the child than removal to a foreign jurisdiction, unless parental unfitness is clearly proven.* [7]

How is sacrificing Mary Beth Whitehead's right-to-mother in the child's best interests? Here the court defers to the trial experts. They say,

> *Our custody conclusion is based on strongly persuasive testimony contrasting both the family life of the Whiteheads and the Sterns and the personalities and characters of the individuals. The stability of the Whitehead family life was doubtful at the time of trial. Their finances were in serious trouble (foreclosure by Mrs. Whitehead's sister on a second mortgage was in process). Mr. Whitehead's employment, though relatively steady, was always at risk because of his alcoholism, a condition that he seems not to have been able to confront effectively. Mrs. Whitehead had not worked for quite some time, her last two employments having been part-time.* [8]

They judge the financial instability of the Whiteheads to be not in the best interests of the child. They also accept the expert testimony that Mary Beth was "too controlling," that she had "contempt for professional counselors," and that the child's "prospects for wholesome independent psychological growth and development would be at serious risk."

This is shocking. However, they are on good legal ground. Unfortunately Mary Beth's experts did not argue that she was the "better" of the two parents. As the decision says:

> *Six experts testified for Mrs. Whitehead: one favored joint custody, clearly unwarranted in this case; one simply rebutted an opposing expert's claim that Mary Beth Whitehead had a recognized personality disorder; one testified to the adverse impact of separation on* Mrs. Whitehead; *one testified about the evils of adoption and, to him, the probably analogous evils of surrogacy; one spoke only on the question of whether Mrs. Whitehead's consent in the surrogacy agreement was "informed consent"; and one spelled out the strong bond between mother and child. None of them unequivocally stated, or even necessarily implied, an opinion that custody in the Whiteheads' was in the best interests of Melissa—the ultimate issue.* [9]

FEBRUARY 6

I must agree that Mary Beth's experts do not address the question of whether the child would be better off in Mary Beth's custody. However, I still find it shocking, disappointing, that such good jurists can describe the experts chosen by the court-appointed guardian ad litem as "each clearly free of all bias and interest."[10]

In his report, Dr. Marshall Schechter describes how he and the other experts met with Lorraine Abraham for eight hours *before* they observed the baby with either Mary Beth or Bill, and how they met together again at the end of their observation period.*

At the end of its ninety-five-page opinion, the court says:

> *While probably unlikely, we do not deem it unthinkable that, the major issues having been resolved, the parties' undoubted love for this child might result in a good faith attempt to work out the visitation themselves, in the best interests of their child.* [11]

*See Appendix C.

FEBRUARY 8

The court does not leave visitation to "good faith." It advises the trial court to

> *recall the touchstones of visitation: that it is desirable for the child to have contact with both parents; that besides the child's interests, the parents' interests also must be considered; but that when all is said and done, the best interests of the child are paramount. . . . We have decided that Mrs. Whitehead is entitled to visitation at some point, and that question is not open to the trial court on this remand.* *12

With this decision, the New Jersey supreme court has decided that the surrogacy contract is invalid and that *paid* surrogacy does violate the baby-selling statutes and is illegal in New Jersey. However, de facto surrogacy remains as legal as ever. All a man has to do is convince a woman to marry him; all a couple have to do is convince a love-starved and self-destructive woman to be their surrogate uterus for *free*.

Traditionally, women are supposed to have a child for *someone else:* for the greater glory of God, country, family, and man. Secretly, women may have a baby for their own pleasure or for the real or imagined power it may give them. However, women are not supposed to admit this and are not respected for saying so. Women are not supposed to profit from their own pleasure; only men are.

So: women have babies for *someone else*, and give them up to *someone else*, in the hope that this life-offering will command male love, affection, attention, and protection for both mother and child. And half the time, it may do just that.

But what about when it doesn't? What about those sperm donors, unwed fathers, and legal husbands who abandon their families entirely, abuse rather than cherish them—or who challenge good enough mothers for custody? What legal rights do women have to defend themselves against being abandoned, abused, or custodially challenged?

---

*As of the week of February 11, 1988, the Sterns agreed to negotiate visitation out of court.

What rights do legal or common-law wives have? A man may tell a woman he loves her; he may marry her; he may live with and support her for a period of time. He may impregnate her. Then, if the baby is to his liking, and the mother is not, he can abandon her and then challenge her for custody of their child.

Chances are, and statistics bear this out, that the birth mother, whether she is legally wed or not, will be seen as less fit than the father, both financially and psychologically. If the father, perhaps along with his new wife, does not want the birth mother to exercise her parental right-to-visit, he can physically harass or verbally humiliate her out of visiting. If this doesn't work, he can attempt to brainwash the child against her birth mother; he can move far away (either with or without court approval); he can also legally harass the birth mother with an endless series of actions to prove that maternal visitation is not in the child's best interests.

What rights do surrogate-contract mothers have? All the New Jersey supreme court has said is, in effect, that a man can't call a woman a surrogate uterus and pay her to be one.

Bill Stern did not pay Mary Beth Whitehead the ten-thousand-dollar fee (she refused to accept it). He has custody of the child anyway. In fact, a sperm donor and/or contract father can even *refuse* to pay the money once his surrogate gives birth, and then attempt to secure custody of the child.

The surrogate has several choices: She can give the child up to the father and slink away. She can refuse to give the child to the father and can face a custody trial—which she will probably lose. (The father might use that ten thousand dollars to hire, say, Lee Salk and other experts who can prove she is the less fit of the two parents.)

The surrogate may try to sue the father for the money he specifically promised her for the child. She probably will not do well financially; she may even be prosecuted because, according to family lawyer and antisurrogacy advocate Bob Arenstein, payment (at least in New Jersey, Louisiana, Nebraska, Kentucky, and Michigan) is, as of February 1988, illegal.* The surrogate can also flee with the child as Mary Beth Whitehead did, and be declared a kidnapper, lose her child, and be imprisoned. She can . . . well, that's about it.

*Strictly speaking, under the adoption and baby-selling statutes, commercial surrogacy may be illegal in every American state.

Now the father's forfeit of money probably won't be enforced; it's illegal and he won't pay it. But in the best interests of the child, the state will enforce the mother's custodial loss. As it did in the Baby M case.

The New Jersey supreme court notes that if it were true that 10 to 15 percent of all married couples wanted children but were infertile, the state might then have a compelling interest in legalizing and enforcing surrogacy.

> *If the Legislature were to enact a statute providing for enforcement of surrogacy agreements, the validity of such a statute might depend on the strength of the state interest in making it more likely that infertile couples will be able to adopt children. As a value, it is obvious that the interest is strong; but if, as plaintiffs assert, ten to fifteen percent of all couples are infertile, the interest is of enormous strength. This figure is given both by counsel for the Sterns and by the trial court. We have been unable to find reliable confirmation of this statistic, however, and we are not confident of its accuracy. We note that at least one source asserts that in 1982, the rate of married couples who were both childless and infertile was only 5.8%.*
>
> *On such quantitative differences, constitutional validity can depend, where the statute in question is justified as serving a compelling state interest. The quality of the interference with the parents' right of companionship bears on these issues.* [13]

Is the court arguing that the state might, in the future, be willing to enforce surrogacy contracts if a sufficient number of married couples who wanted children were infertile? Is the court saying that the state may one day have to assist the infertile in the best interests of society? How vigorously? And at whose expense?

Should woman's natural ability to reproduce the species be subjected to compelling state interest? Should it be harnessed or colonized in the service of somebody else's need or right to have children? If women as a caste don't want to become biological mothers, can men use a "compelling state interest" argument to force them into pregnancy and motherhood against their will or against their best interests?

Are women still denied our civil and reproductive rights in the best interests of the patriarchal state? Are women still enslaved because men want, but can't have, children? Is this a compelling enough reason to justify our exclusion from the Constitution?

How can we be fair to men, when they want children but they cannot have children? How can we be fair to anyone who wants children and cannot have them?

Does the constitutional right to procreate give a sterile man the right to sue the state because another man is fertile? Does equality under law make the state responsible for rendering men equal in experience?

Does the Constitution, which protects our parental rights, also make the state responsible for rendering a man (who has not borne a child) and a woman (who has) equal in how they experience that child?

Can a man and a woman be in equal positions with respect to a child whom she bore, she birthed, she breast-fed, she raised, and of whom she is the primary caretaker and psychological parent, while he never changed a diaper?

Are the same man and woman in equal positions with respect to an engineering job if he studied for seven years, got four patents, and worked in the field for fourteen years, while she never cracked a book?

Can she take his job?

Can he take her motherhood?

What would be fair to birth mothers? What would be fair to children? What would be fair to people who have no uterus, or no functioning uterus, or no sperm? Is it fair to say to them, simply and brutally: "People cannot always have what they want"?

Is it fair to let birth mothers lord it over the infertile because of mere biology? Is it fair that some children are born strong and healthy and others are born with lifelong physical problems?

What to do?

Is the profather and antimother bias in our society so deep and so powerful that we can do nothing? When we try to do something, how can we avoid making a bad situation worse? For example, in the spirit of gender equality, prime-time TV has given us career women and divorced mothers; it has also given us the motherless child. Punky Brewster's mother abandoned her in a shopping mall, but it's okay because a wonderful old man adopted her! The kid on "Silver Spoons" seems to have been cheerfully hatched from a silver egg; on "Different Strokes," an admirable rich white man adopted two black brothers, and they never even missed their mother!

The intact families are "Father Knows Best" remakes, led by Bill Cosby, whose family is, like the show, his. (A fit mother is present but does not threaten Dad for the limelight.) The mothers are fading, being killed off, running away, being canceled out . . .

I don't oppose the idea that fathers should be responsible for half the "grunt work" of childcare, but I'm frightened when TV fathers are turned into heroes for doing the very same thing that devalues mothers. I'm frightened by the way in which some fathers feel that even in order to do a minimal amount of childcare, they must first "beat out" a child's mother to win the "best parent of the year award."

I don't oppose fathers caring for a child—as long as it's done in a spirit of cooperation; and as long as it doesn't threaten a birth mother's ongoing relationship with her child. Unless he's altruistically motivated, a father who has done some childcare some of the time may feel more entitled to banish his child's birth mother from the family than he would if he were a traditional, absent, and authoritarian father. According to Dr. Judith Herman,

> [T]he idea of integrating men into the world of children, simple as it sounds, is profoundly radical. . . . Many of the causes that women have supported most passionately in the last century—temperance, animal rescue, the suppression of vice—can best be understood as attempts to get men out of the barroom, the game pit, the whore house, and into the home. Only in the last decade have feminists dared to suggest, not only that men come home, but that they engage in the work that is done there: housework and childcare.
>
> Unfortunately, the new male interest in fatherhood often tends to focus more on paternal rights than on paternal obligations. The integration of fathers into families cannot be carried out under the banner of "father power." . . . As long as fathers retain their authoritarian role, they can never know

*what it means to share a work of love on the basis of equality,
or what it means to nurture the life of a new generation. When
men no longer rule their families, they may learn for the first
time what it means to belong to one.*[14]

Many fathers view maternal custody as an encroachment on their
rights. The custodial assault is often a father's assertion of his right
to rule and own the family. A Colorado mother was jailed for kidnapping her two sons after her ex-husband took her to court sixteen times
to argue custody. She ran away with her children once it became clear
that these courtroom assaults would never end. In her impassioned
letter to me, she wrote:

> *I was accused, but not convicted, of sleeping with men, sleep-
> ing with women, going back to school ("more important to her
> than her child"), not going back to school ("doesn't do any-
> thing to improve herself"), going on welfare ("lazy"), going
> to work full time ("a career monster"), being too dependent
> ("overconnected to her children, smothering"), being too inde-
> pendent ("not devoted to mothering"). I was tried and I "won"
> again and again.*
> AND I NEVER SIGNED A SURROGACY CON-
> TRACT!
> *But the battle to be a mother was never over. My mother-
> hood was made into a trial and my children's childhood was
> laid waste and then I ran away. Now I have something to say.*
> *I say that being a surrogate uterus is the ultimate taxation
> without representation.*
> *I say that being pregnant with somebody else's baby is
> oppression. Will you say that what is in me is not me, and
> what I create is not mine? Must I labor in the service of others,
> and never for myself? Do you mean to turn my body and my
> womb into somebody else's private property? Do you mean to
> nationalize my womb? Do you call this freedom?*
> *So, Phyllis Chesler, it isn't the surrogacy* contract *that is
> immoral; it is* surrogacy *that is immoral. If I bear a child,
> am I not his mother? Am I not then entitled to mother him?
> Am I not entitled to continue to mother him, tomorrow and*

*always? Otherwise am I not made into a surrogate uterus,
even though . . .*
     I NEVER SIGNED A SURROGACY CONTRACT.

In 1988, the New Jersey supreme court said that it is illegal to pay
a woman to be a surrogate mother, that babies can't be sold, that in
the future no one can use police or contractual force against a birth
mother if she tries to keep her baby.

But if a court can't legally terminate a mother's love for her child,
how can it legislate the hatred of women out of existence? What can
any court do about the ways in which people—and the media—
continue to blame women for their own victimization? Writing on
February 6, 1988, journalist Michele Landsberg says:

> *Just one year ago, the media were in full cry after Ms.
> Whitehead. It was like a wholesale retreat to the double
> standards of the 1950's: clean-cut, middle-class boy versus
> tainted "bad girl" of the underclass. William Stern, the sperm
> donor, was "the natural father." She, the birth mother, was
> "the surrogate." He was controlled; she was distraught. She
> was "contemptible" for agreeing to have a baby-for-sale, and
> then "irresponsible" for turning down the money and trying
> to keep the baby.*
>
> *"A deal's a deal!" everyone said. "She signed the contract,
> didn't she? She knew what she was doing." There was an
> almost unanimous public sentiment that "breaking the con-
> tract" was a crime against society.* [15]

Now it is done. A widely respected state supreme court has, in my
lifetime, spoken in the language of feminists. My involvement as an
organizer in the campaign against surrogacy is over. The larger
campaign for women's reproductive and custodial rights must continue.

EPILOGUE

I n Harold J. Cassidy's supplemental brief to the New Jersey supreme court, he addressed the question of Baby M's future education. He wrote:

The most important education she will receive will not come from Bill Stern or Mary Beth Whitehead. It will more likely come from the court's determination of who her parents in life will be and under what arrangement she will get to know them. She will know that her father tried to pay her mother. She will know that her mother loved her and wanted to be part of her life. The outcome of this case will teach her about values in a greater measure than perhaps any other source.

Will she be taught that money can buy anything, or will she be taught that there are relationships which are too important to be influenced by money?

Will she be taught that in life it is not what you know but who you know, or will she be taught that justice is available to all people?

Will she be taught that if you gain an unfair advantage

it will pay off, or will she be taught that unfair advantages should be treated in life for what they are—unfair?

Will she be taught that you may satisfy your own needs in life even at the expense of others around you, or will she be taught that you must be sensitive to the harm that your conduct imposes upon others?

Baby M will learn what we will learn.

On April 6, 1988, Judge Birger M. Sween ordered liberal, unsupervised visitation to begin immediately between Mary Beth Whitehead-Gould and Baby M, her daughter.

APPENDICES

Appendix A

Text of the Surrogate Parenting Agreement signed by William Stern, Mary Beth Whitehead, and Richard Whitehead on February 6, 1985.

Surrogate Parenting Agreement

This AGREEMENT is made with reference to the following facts:

(1) WILLIAM STERN, Natural Father, is an individual over the age of eighteen (18) years who is desirous of entering into this Agreement.

(2) The sole purpose of this Agreement is to enable WILLIAM STERN and his infertile wife to have a child which is biologically related to WILLIAM STERN.

(3) MARY BETH WHITEHEAD, Surrogate, and RICHARD WHITEHEAD, her husband, are over the age of eighteen (18) years and desirous of entering into this Agreement in consideration of the following:

Now THEREFORE, in consideration of the mutual promises contained herein and the intentions of being legally bound hereby, the parties agree as follows:

1. MARY BETH WHITEHEAD, Surrogate, represents that she is capable of conceiving children. MARY BETH WHITEHEAD understands and agrees that in the best interest of the child, she will not form or attempt to form a parent-child relationship with any child or children she may conceive, carry to term and give birth to, pursuant to the provisions of this Agreement, and shall freely surrender custody to WILLIAM STERN, Natural Father, immediately upon birth of the child; and terminate all parental rights to said child pursuant to this Agreement.

2. MARY BETH WHITEHEAD, Surrogate, and RICHARD WHITEHEAD, her husband, have been married since 12/2/73, and RICHARD WHITEHEAD is in agreement with the purposes, intents and provisions of this Agreement and acknowledges that his wife, MARY BETH WHITEHEAD, Surrogate, shall be artificially inseminated pursuant to the provisions of this Agreement. RICHARD WHITEHEAD agrees that in the best interest of the child, he will not form or attempt to form a parent-child relationship with any child or children MARY BETH WHITEHEAD, Surrogate, may conceive by artificial insemination as described herein, and agrees to freely and readily surrender immediate custody of the child to WILLIAM STERN, Natural Father; and terminate his parental rights; RICHARD WHITEHEAD further acknowledges he will do all

acts necessary to rebut the presumption of paternity of any offspring conceived and born pursuant to aforementioned agreement as provided by law, including blood testing and/or HLA testing.

3. WILLIAM STERN, Natural Father, does hereby enter into this written contractual Agreement with MARY BETH WHITEHEAD, Surrogate, where MARY BETH WHITEHEAD shall be artificially inseminated with the semen of WILLIAM STERN by a physician. MARY BETH WHITEHEAD, Surrogate, upon becoming pregnant, acknowledges that she will carry said embryo/fetus(s) until delivery. MARY BETH WHITEHEAD, Surrogate, and RICHARD WHITEHEAD, her husband, agree that they will cooperate with any background investigation into the Surrogate's medical, family and personal history and warrants the information to be accurate to the best of their knowledge. MARY BETH WHITEHEAD, Surrogate, and RICHARD WHITEHEAD, her husband, agree to surrender custody of the child to WILLIAM STERN, Natural Father, immediately upon birth, acknowledging that it is the intent of this Agreement in the best interests of the child to do so; as well as institute and cooperate in proceedings to terminate their respective parental rights to said child, and sign any and all necessary affidavits, documents, and the like, in order to further the intent and purposes of this Agreement. It is understood by MARY BETH WHITEHEAD, and RICHARD WHITEHEAD, that the child to be conceived is being done so for the sole purpose of giving said child to WILLIAM STERN, its natural and biological father. MARY BETH WHITEHEAD and RICHARD WHITEHEAD agree to sign all necessary affidavits prior to and after the birth of the child and voluntarily participate in any paternity proceedings necessary to have WILLIAM STERN'S name entered on said child's birth certificate as the natural or biological father.

4. That the consideration for this Agreement, which is compensation for services and expenses, and in no way is to be construed as a fee for termination of parental rights or a payment in exchange for a consent to surrender the child for adoption, in addition to other provisions contained herein, shall be as follows:

(A) $10,000 shall be paid to MARY BETH WHITEHEAD, Surrogate, upon surrender of custody to WILLIAM STERN, the natural and biological father of the child born pursuant to the provisions of this Agreement for surrogate services and expenses in carrying out her obligations under this Agreement;

(B) The consideration to be paid to MARY BETH WHITEHEAD, Surrogate, shall be deposited with the Infertility Center of New York (hereinafter ICNY), the representative of WILLIAM STERN, at the time of the signing of this Agreement, and held in escrow until completion of the duties and obligations of MARY BETH WHITEHEAD, Surrogate, as herein described.

(C) WILLIAM STERN, Natural Father, shall pay the expenses incurred by MARY BETH WHITEHEAD, Surrogate, pursuant to her pregnancy, more specifically defined as follows:

(1) All medical, hospitalization, and pharmaceutical, laboratory and therapy expenses incurred as a result of MARY BETH WHITEHEAD'S pregnancy, not covered or allowed by her present health and major medical insurance, including all extraordinary medical expenses and all reasonable expenses for treatment of any emotional or mental conditions or problems related to said pregnancy, but in no case shall any such expenses be paid or reimbursed after a period of six (6) months have elapsed since the date of the termination of the pregnancy, and this Agreement specifically excludes any expenses for lost wages or other non-itemized incidentals related to said pregnancy.

(2) WILLIAM STERN, Natural Father, shall not be responsible for any latent medical expenses occurring six (6) weeks subsequent to the birth of the child, unless the medical problem or abnormality incident thereto was known and treated by a physician prior to the expiration of said six (6) week period and in written notice of the same sent to ICNY, as representative of WILLIAM STERN by certified mail, return receipt requested, advising of this treatment.

(3) WILLIAM STERN, Natural Father, shall be responsible for the total costs of all paternity testing. Such paternity testing may, at the option of WILLIAM STERN, Natural Father, be required prior to release of the surrogate fee from escrow. In the event WILLIAM STERN, Natural Father, is conclusively determined not to be the biological father of the child as a result of an HLA test, this Agreement will be deemed breached and MARY BETH WHITEHEAD, Surrogate, shall not be entitled to any fee. WILLIAM STERN, Natural Father, shall be entitled to reimbursement of all medical and related expenses from MARY BETH WHITEHEAD, Surrogate, and RICHARD WHITEHEAD, her husband.

(4) MARY BETH WHITEHEAD'S reasonable travel expenses incurred at the request of WILLIAM STERN, pursuant to this Agreement.

5. MARY BETH WHITEHEAD, Surrogate, and RICHARD WHITEHEAD, her husband, understand and agree to assume all risks, including the risk of death, which are incidental to conception, pregnancy, childbirth, including but not limited to, postpartum complications. A copy of said possible risks and/or complications is attached hereto and made a part hereof.

6. MARY BETH WHITEHEAD, Surrogate, and RICHARD WHITEHEAD, her husband, hereby agree to undergo psychiatric evaluation by JOAN EINWOHNER, a psychiatrist as designated by WILLIAM STERN or an agent thereof. WILLIAM STERN shall pay for the cost of said psychiatric evaluation. MARY

BETH WHITEHEAD and RICHARD WHITEHEAD shall sign, prior to their evaluations, a medical release permitting dissemination of the report prepared as a result of said psychiatric evaluations to ICNY or WILLIAM STERN and his wife.

7. MARY BETH WHITEHEAD, Surrogate, and RICHARD WHITEHEAD, her husband, hereby agree that it is the exclusive and sole right of WILLIAM STERN, Natural Father, to name said child.

8. "Child" as referred to in this Agreement shall include all children born simultaneously pursuant to the inseminations contemplated herein.

9. In the event of the death of WILLIAM STERN, prior or subsequent to the birth of said child, it is hereby understood and agreed by MARY BETH WHITEHEAD, Surrogate, and RICHARD WHITEHEAD, her husband, that the child will be placed in the custody of WILLIAM STERN'S wife.

10. In the event that the child is miscarried prior to the fifth (5th) month of pregnancy, no compensation, as enumerated in paragraph 4(A), shall be paid to MARY BETH WHITEHEAD, Surrogate. However, the expenses enumerated in paragraph 4(C) shall be paid or reimbursed to MARY BETH WHITEHEAD, Surrogate. In the event the child is miscarried, dies or is stillborn subsequent to the fourth (4th) month of pregnancy and said child does not survive, the Surrogate shall receive $1,000.00 in lieu of the compensation enumerated in paragraph 4(A). In the event of a miscarriage or stillbirth as described above, this Agreement shall terminate and neither MARY BETH WHITEHEAD, Surrogate, nor WILLIAM STERN, Natural Father, shall be under any further obligation under this Agreement.

11. MARY BETH WHITEHEAD, Surrogate, and WILLIAM STERN, Natural Father, shall have undergone complete physical and genetic evaluation, under the direction and supervision of a licensed physician, to determine whether the physical health and well-being of each is satisfactory. Said physical examination shall include testing for venereal diseases, specifically including but not limited to, syphilis, herpes and gonorrhea. Said venereal disease testing shall be done prior to, but not limited to, each series of inseminations.

12. In the event that pregnancy has not occurred within a reasonable time, in the opinion of WILLIAM STERN, Natural Father, this Agreement shall terminate by written notice to MARY BETH WHITEHEAD, Surrogate, at the residence provided to the ICNY by the Surrogate, from ICNY, as representative of WILLIAM STERN, Natural Father.

13. MARY BETH WHITEHEAD, Surrogate, agrees that she will not abort the child once conceived except, if in the professional medical opinion of the inseminating physician, such action is necessary for the physical health of MARY BETH WHITEHEAD or the child has been determined by said physician to be physiologically abnormal. MARY BETH WHITEHEAD further agrees,

upon the request of said physician to undergo amniocentesis or similar tests to detect genetic and congenital defects. In the event said test reveals that the fetus is genetically or congenitally abnormal, MARY BETH WHITEHEAD, Surrogate, agrees to abort the fetus upon demand of WILLIAM STERN, Natural Father, in which event, the fee paid to the Surrogate will be in accordance to Paragraph 10. If MARY BETH WHITEHEAD refuses to abort the fetus upon demand of WILLIAM STERN, his obligations as stated in this Agreement shall cease forthwith, except as to obligations of paternity imposed by statute.

14. Despite the provisions of Paragraph 13, WILLIAM STERN, Natural Father, recognizes that some genetic and congenital abnormalities may not be detected by amniocentesis or other tests, and therefore, if proven to be the biological father of the child, assumes the legal responsibility for any child who may possess genetic or congenital abnormalities.

15. MARY BETH WHITEHEAD, Surrogate, further agrees to adhere to all medical instructions given to her by the inseminating physician as well as her independent obstetrician. MARY BETH WHITEHEAD also agrees not to smoke cigarettes, drink alcoholic beverages, use illegal drugs, or take non-prescription medications or prescribed medications without written consent from her physician. MARY BETH WHITEHEAD agrees to follow a prenatal medical examination schedule to consist of no fewer visits than: one visit per month during the first seven (7) months of pregnancy, two visits (each to occur at two-week intervals) during the eighth and ninth month of pregnancy.

16. MARY BETH WHITEHEAD, Surrogate, agrees to cause RICHARD WHITEHEAD, her husband, to execute a refusal of consent form.

17. Each party acknowledges that he or she fully understands this Agreement and its legal effect, and that they are signing the same freely and voluntarily and that neither party has any reason to believe that the other(s) did not freely and voluntarily execute said Agreement.

18. In the event any of the provisions of this Agreement are deemed to be invalid or unenforceable, the same shall be deemed severable from the remainder of this Agreement and shall not cause the invalidity or unenforceability of the remainder of this Agreement. If such provision shall be deemed invalid due to its scope or breadth, then said provision shall be deemed valid to the extent of the scope or breadth permitted by law.

The Bergen County Probation Department Custody Investigation Report, made by probation officer Charles Bene in October 1986 after he interviewed both William and Elizabeth Stern and Richard and Mary Beth Whitehead. The following is the report's summary and recommendation.

This Officer has had the opportunity of interviewing both of the families in this matter and has been able to observe, at least to some extent, the existing family interaction.

While at the home of the STERNS, and during the interview, I observed MR. STERN to be a doting father who looked after the baby most of the time while I was there during the three and one-half hour interview. On a subsequent visit to the STERN home while MR. STERN was at work, I observed MRS. STERN caring for the baby in what appeared to be a loving manner. As of October 15, 1986, the baby appears to be well-nourished, neatly dressed, and well-cared for in general. The baby smiles easily and is able to crawl.

I have found no reason to conclude that the STERNS are doing anything other than a good job in raising the child while they have temporary custody.

The baby has not been observed in the custody of the WHITEHEADS; however, from what is seen of their home environment and from neighbors' accounts of how their children have been raised thus far, there are certainly no negative aspects of their family interaction. This Officer was impressed by the most favorable comments given to the WHITEHEAD children in terms of their courtesy and behavior.

The WHITEHEAD home, quite like the STERNS' home, is neat and clean and adequately furnished and makes a most favorable physical environment for any child.

While there have been some personal problems that the WHITEHEADS have experienced in terms of finances and alcohol abuse in particular, this Officer comes away with the impression that these problems should not be held against the WHITEHEADS at this time.

Neither MR. nor MRS. WHITEHEAD have had the benefit of a higher education, and while their judgement in the past could have been better, this amounts to second guessing.

It appears to this Officer that MRS. WHITEHEAD has suffered a great deal of postpartum emotional stress which may have contributed to her lack of proper judgement. The couple appears to be a typical, lower middle-class type family, who possess no pretenses as to who they are and what they should be. They have been candid with this Officer, and MRS. WHITEHEAD strikes me as being the type of person who will follow through on this issue or any other cause for the principle of it. Of course, this particular issue is of an importance that probably cannot be measured.

This Officer has investigated this matter and considered the issue from the point of view that any legal contract ever existed. I have disregarded the legality of any such contract and, rather, considered the primary interests of what is best for the child. The issue is no longer which of the parents has a greater love or need for the child.

It appears that in terms of providing material belongings, the STERNS are in a better position to provide for the baby considering their degree of affluence and earning potential.

The WHITEHEADS, on the other hand, are a close-knit family who have obviously done a fine job in raising their two children thus far. Although their neighbors have turned against them, they are still complimentary toward the WHITEHEADS, particularly MARY BETH WHITEHEAD's helping personality.

Based upon information gathered during our investigation, this Officer could find no reason why either of the families party to this action would not make more than adequate parents.

Texts of a selection of the mental health reports made on the psychological conditions of the parties involved in the Baby M case.

The psychological report of Joan Einwohner, the clinical psychologist hired in April, 1984, by the Infertility Center of New York to evaluate Mary Beth Whitehead as a candidate for surrogacy.

Ms. Whitehead arrived punctually accompanied by her sister-in-law. They had traveled two and a half hours to make an early morning appointment. Ms. Whitehead is a very verbal person, readily friendly and readily expressive of feelings. She articulates clearly and expresses her ideas well. She describes herself as often dominant in the relationship with her husband. She was able to be open about not liking to be interviewed and was sure all the preliminaries would be more of a problem to her than being pregnant. The desire to participate in the surrogate program was her own and she has prepared her husband, children and parents to accept her plan. She does not want to rear more children now that her own are in school and no longer as demanding, though she expects to have strong feelings about giving up the baby at the end. The Rorschach also indicates that she greatly enjoys the playfulness and games she experiences in caring for children. She says she wants to have the experience of pregnancy again now she is older since her first two were born when she was a teenager. She also feels it is a good thing for her children to have the experience of seeing her pregnant. These motives seem stronger than the monetary recompense although she feels she will be able to provide extras for her children with the money and also set aside money for their education.

Ms. Whitehead is in the average range of intelligence. Her ability to assess reality and respond in ways characteristic of most people is well developed. The MMPI indicates she is able to handle work and personal responsibilities without undue worry. In fact, she has a marked tendency to deny problems and present herself as well adjusted and adequate. She tends to be optimistic and hope for the best. It would seem that her husband is emotionally distant and does not provide the vital human interaction she needs for a sense of well being. Ms. Whitehead has a need to be noticed and be significant to others. Although she tends to deny her emotional needs initially, she does respond with pleasant, warm affect with the passage of time. Some indication that she perceives her role as one of serving others may be influencing her to help another woman in this way. She seems to have genuine social concern. It would be very important to her to have the emotional support of the adoptive parents during pregnancy and birth and a friendly relationship with them.

It is the examiner's impression that Ms. Whitehead is sincere in her plan to become a surrogate mother and that she has thought extensively about the plan. However, I do have some concern about her tendency to deny feelings and think it would be important to explore with her in somewhat more depth whether she will be able to relinquish the child at the end. She mentioned that her husband has had a vasectomy and it might be informative to find out why he did so and what her feelings have been about no longer being able to conceive in their relationship. In spite of much talk about how wearying she finds pre-school children, she does care for her sister-in-law's two year old during the day and one wonders about her underlying needs to have a child at home. She describes herself as having been deeply involved with her own two in earlier years and knows she should be encouraging more independence on their part. She may have more needs to have another child than she is admitting.

Except for the above reservations, Ms. Whitehead is recommended as an appropriate candidate for being a surrogate volunteer.

The Child Custody Evaluation Report written by psychologist David Brodzinsky, an expert witness hired by Lorraine Abraham, the guardian ad litem, based on psychological testing of both the Sterns and the Whiteheads, as well as on interviews and observations of both families. The following excerpts were chosen to reflect aspects of the Sterns' characters that the media did not to cover.

On Bill Stern:

Mr. Stern displays some difficulty in handling emotions. In fact, he does not have good access to his inner, emotional life. Rather, he protects himself from this potentially threatening area through such defenses as denial, distancing, intellectualization, and rationalization. The conflict in this area appears to reflect an underlying vulnerability to feelings of abandonment and loss. The extermination of his extended family in the concentration camps, the loss of his father—his confidant and protector—at 12 years of age, the ambivalent relationship with his mother through his formative years, and the absence of a strong supportive network of friends have left their mark on Mr. Stern. . . . Mr. Stern was presented a picture of a small boy sitting by himself in the doorway of a log cabin. His task was to make up a story about the boy—to describe who he was, what he was thinking and feeling, and what would happen to him. Mr. Stern began his story by stating, "It's the depression. This poor boy is sitting there." At that point, he started to cry and stated that the picture was too painful and he could not continue. Such a response is unusual and reflects a loss of distance between the stimulus and personal needs and conflicts. Furthermore, in discussing his desire for a child and his fear of losing Sara Melissa in the custody dispute, Mr. Stern often was overcome by his emotions. . . .

Another personality characteristic noted in Mr. Stern is a tendency toward suppression of hostile-aggressive impulses. . . .

Given Mr. Stern's strong need for a child, his vulnerability regarding loss, and his self-proclaimed tendency toward over-protection, one might question whether he is likely to "smother" his daughter—that is, to foster an over-dependent and enmeshed relationship between Sara Melissa and himself. Although this is a possibility in a person who has the character structure described above, my impression is that it is unlikely in the present case. . . .

One area in which Mr. Stern has been unsuccessful in differentiating Sara Melissa's needs from those of his own is with regard to her future need for contact with both biological parents. Research and clinical experience suggests that children who are adopted or experience divorce often suffer from lack of knowledge and/or contact with biological parents. Mr. Stern has indicated that should he not get custody, he believes that it is in Sara Melissa's interests for her not to have contact with him. He worries that such contact will only cause her confusion. . . . What he is denying is the pain and anguish he (and Betsy) will suffer should the Whiteheads get custody. Instead of focusing on their own pain, he has projected it on to his daughter. . . . Mr. Stern's position neglects the sense of loss that children in Sara Melissa's situation often feel. Contact with the noncustodial parent (in Mr. Stern's scenario, himself) would undoubtedly reduce the child's sense of loss. Thus, Mr. Stern's position regarding visitation is not as clearly thought out as he believes; nor does it solely represent the needs of the child.

On Betsy Stern:

Like her husband, Betsy Stern shows some conflict in handling instinctual drives. When hostile-aggressive and sexual urges are stimulated, she defends against the ensuing anxiety by a well developed system of defenses including denial, undoing, regression, sublimation, displacement, and obsessive-compulsive patterns. These defenses are generally quite successful in binding the anxiety associated with these conflict areas. . . .

Mrs. Stern has strong nurturance needs. This part of her personality emerged quite often in the projective test material. Some evidence of unresolved dependencey conflicts also was noted.

... Like her husband, the only area in which she has difficulty separating her needs from those of the baby is with regard to the value of contact with the noncustodial family (whoever it may be).

The psychological evaluation of the primary individuals in the Baby M case by psychiatrist Marshall Schechter, an expert witness hired by Lorraine Abraham, the guardian ad litem. This evaluation was based on other mental health reports, interviews with the Sterns and Whiteheads, and psychological tests, specifically the Cattell Personality Inventory. The following excerpt of this evaluation reflects the findings of the Cattell test as well as Dr. Schechter's recommendations regarding the custody of Baby M.

The Cattell done on Mrs. Whitehead (this being a personality inventory) suggested a detachment and an uninvolvement and somewhat of an impulsivity on her test responses. Her Thematic Apperception Test revealed sparse answers and the inkblot test also had relatively few disorders.

Mrs. Stern on the Cattell scored high on being a fake good, high on submissiveness, high on self-assuredness and high on expediency with the inkblot test indicating an openness to self awareness and a capacity to sublimate instinctual drive. The Thematic Apperception Test demonstrated a richness of fantasy and the stories more suggestive of capacity to think but not to act on impulse.

Mr. Stern demonstrated a wide variation of various segments of the intellectual tests with a diminution of scores that are most sensitive to anxiety. He demonstrated a good grasp or reality, was self sufficient and open to new ideas. He tends to protect himself by denial and intellectualization. There is some concern about loss and abandonment. When these themes are touched on, a depressed affect is evident, but it is interesting that he is able to recover relatively easily from these overwhelming emotions. Generally he represents a person who is usually optimistic. The testing and certainly the observations confirmed this, indicate a much greater capacity to meet the needs of the baby than he himself gives himself credit for.

Mr. Whitehead demonstrates some compulsive tendencies which makes him able at analyzing certain life situations. He is somewhat emotionally reserved and controlled and he binds anxiety by being controlled. He is also practical, somewhat submissive, and bound by rules and moralistic rationalization. He pretty much is what he presents himself as being although he does attempt to present himself at times in a socially good light. There are some evidences on the projective tests of suppressed anger which are generally under control.

Tuesday, as mentioned above, is a bright, involved, steady and stable child who follows her mother's moods and suggestions carefully. She seems to be, of the two older children, the more favored, and she certainly has worked in her friendships, sports activities and academically to constantly win praise for her performances. There are some suggestions that at age 10 she is noting some rebelliousness toward her mother, but this certainly is well within the norm for a child at this stage of development. (See sealed portion of the report).

In the adults, Mr. and Mrs. Stern and Mr. Whitehead I can find no diagnosable condition other than that which relates to the pressures and stresses of the current circumstances.

It is, however, in Mrs. Whitehead that I believe there is an appropriate codifiable diagnosis which is that of a Mixed Personality Disorder.

The Diagnostic and Statistical Manual of Mental Disorders states, *"Personality traits* are enduring patterns of perceiving, relating to, and thinking about the environment and oneself, and are exhibited in a wide range of important social and personal contexts. It is only when personality traits are inflexible and maladaptive and cause either significant impairment in social or occupational functioning or subjective distress that they constitute *Personality Disorders.* The manifestations of Personality Disorders are generally recognizable by adolescence or earlier and continue throughout most of adult life though they often become less obvious in middle or old age."

Under the term Borderline Personality Disorder, one of the elements required is impulsivity or unpredictability some of which may potentially be self-damaging. As a series of events and behaviors dealing with this symptom in Mrs. Whitehead, I would submit that taking Ryan out of his class in second grade was an impulsive act; her suicidal and homicidal threat contained in the tape was also a potential self-damaging act; taking her children to the Infertility Clinic was also a potentially self-damaging act to the children; not reading the application from the Infertility Clinic so that she didn't know what she was getting herself into was also an impulsive self-damaging act; and lastly the handing of Baby M out the window to Mr. Whitehead and then going down to Florida was also an unpredictable, impulsive act. Still under Borderline Personality Disorder is a pattern of unstable and intense personal relationship in which manipulation is a significant behavior. Mr. Whitehead indicated that he did not want her to go through with the surrogate pregnancy plus telling her that the pregnancy could cause personality change. It was observed not only by myself and the other members of the child advocate team but also reported by Mr. and Mrs. Messer that Mrs. Whitehead dominated her husband. Mrs. Whitehead indicated that she felt that she was adopted because she looked different from the other girls in the family. Despite the fact that she indicated that

she resembled her father, she did not feel as if she, too, belonged within
that family unit. She also stated in one of the depositions that Ryan felt
the same kind of pain that she was feeling in this entire circumstance of
the current trial, as if she and he were fused and he felt the pain that she
was experiencing to the same extent that she did which helped account for
some of the poor school grades he was obtaining. Also under Borderline
Personality Disorder speaks of physically self-damaging acts and suicidal
gestures, and under this, one could note not only the suicidal threat and
homicidal threat contained in the tape, but the fact that she didn't read the
surrogate agreement to understand fully about what its meaning was to her
and to her family; that there might be included in this agreement a requirement that the child be aborted or amniocentesis be undertaken if the donor
wished. If amniocentesis revealed a potential inborn error of metabolism
or a genetic abnormality and the donor refused to accept responsibility then
the responsibility for rearing this child would fall on Mr. and Mrs. Whitehead.

Under Narcissistic Personality Disorders there is noted a sense of self
importance and a sense of specialness to the various life problems encoun-
tered. Mrs. Whitehead makes an assumption that because she is the mother
that the child, Baby M, belongs to her. This gives no credence to or value
to the genetic contribution of the birth father. Mrs. Whitehead also saw
herself as a possible surrogate for her sister and if she, Mrs. Whitehead,
became pregnant, then God would see that her sister got pregnant also.
Under Narcissistic Personality Disorder there is also the need for exhibi-
tionism and constant attention which seems present with Mrs. Whitehead
appearing on magazine covers and allowing Tuesday to go on TV "when
she wants to do it." Under Narcissistic Personality Disorder there is noted
a condition of entitlement where surprise and anger occur if others don't
do what she wants. This element can be seen not only on the tape with the
suicidal and homicidal threats, but also the threat to drag the Sterns
through the mud by charging Mr. Stern with sexually molesting her daughter, Tuesday. Also under Narcissistic Personality Disorder is interpersonal
exploitativeness and disregard of others. Regarding this, Mrs. Whitehead
. . . (See sealed portion of the report); her husband said no to the surrogate
parenthood which she ignored; . . . and finally the cost of their mortgage
foreclosed and possibly all of the monies from the jobs done by Mr.
Whitehead tied up in repayment of the attorneys and others to whom they
are indebted. Under Narcissistic Personality Disorder there is a lack of
empathy indicated. This was very clear in her treatment of the children in
the observation that we had at the Whitehead home. Little question has
come up in her mind about what will happen to Ryan and Tuesday, their
feelings about the mother's actions in undertaking the surrogate parent

role, and also the way they will feel concerning their loss of contact with their half sibling, Baby M. Besides this, there is little thought about what the remarks of other people will do in the present as well as in the future regarding Tuesday's and Ryan's personality development. According to one of the transcripts, Mrs. Whitehead does not recall what questions the children asked about the pregnancy or what her answers were to them. Also under Narcissistic Personality Disorder we find a depressed mood which certainly was present on that first occasion and then subsequently noted on the tape with the amount of crying and unhappiness and threatening suicide as she did. Also under Narcissistic Personality Disorder it indicates a preoccupation with grooming and remaining youthful. It was accidentally discovered that Mrs. Whitehead's hair is totally white and has been for a number of years. Since this makes her feel old, she feels, she dyes her hair very frequently in order to remain youthful appearing. Under Narcississtic Personality Disorders it notes "these peopple justify their deficits by rationalization or by prevarication." Throughout all of her depositions to direct questions by all of the attorneys involved, Mrs. Whitehead continued to state that she didn't know and in this fashion prevented any information about her being on the record. She stated to me that the Sterns were lying regarding the suicide tape and the tape on sexual abuse of Tuesday, whereas a few days later she stated that when her attorney reminded her of the contents she did recall what they were.

Under the Histrionic Personality Disorder, it indicates the role of the victim. She directly stated to me that she was being victimized. There is the report of a hypertension of 180/90 which was then said to be 140/90 and a report also of her being in intensive care in Florida near death with a temperature of 106 degrees which actually was recorded in the hospital records at 103–4 degrees. This was all done to her because the Sterns were pursuing getting Baby M. The Histrionic Personality Disorder also craves novelty. Where else in the life events that are under her control could she have anything better than being a surrogate parent to enhance a feeling of being novel and unique. Also under Histrionic Personality Disorder it notes that these people are quick to form friendships but then can become demanding, manipulative with suicidal threats. In the deposition, it becomes evident that she felt very close and friendly to the Sterns who then turned against her with subsequent anger and suicidal and homicidal threats as well as threats to "drag them through the mud." Under Histrionic Personality Disorder it noted in the original psychological testing as well as the interaction that I observed and that Mr. and Mrs. Messer, Mrs. Whitehead's parents, also indicated, namely, that she was the dominant one in the marriage. She also told Mr. Whitehead after she took Baby M from the Sterns in a few minutes' time all of the emotions she went through but at the time that she described this to him, literally a few minutes after she had taken the child, her husband stated that her mood was good; she also did not discuss having Tuesday on a TV program with her husband; when the name Melisa came up Mrs. Whitehead began to cry as did Mr. Whitehead. Under Histrionic Personality Disorder being egocentric is also listed. Throughout the interview with Baby M, Mrs. Whitehead continued to indicate that the child always wanted what the mother had with there being no evidence whatsoever of any interest on the baby's part with what the mother was doing or in the way that she was using anything in that setting.

Under the term Schizotypal Personality Disorder, they list magical thinking, which I believe is inherent in the concept that if she became pregnant God would give her sister a child. Besides this there is a note of unreality as Mrs. Whitehead talks about the extent of their debts and that they will be paying it off the rest of their life without recognizing the extraordinary nature of the expenses and the relatively difficult time that they would have with their present vocational and educational training to pay any of the outstanding debts. Under Schizotypal Personality Disorder it is also noted having ideas of reference. Her statements about the Sterns as causing all the difficulties to her and that they found out all of her weak and sensitive points during the pregnancy itself so that then they could use these pieces of information to make her life miserable subsequently; she also noted that the attorneys (albeit not her counsel), the judge, and the Sterns are controlled by the power of the press; and the Sterns will be pretending to have given birth to Baby M.

Under Paranoid Personality Disorder, it is listed that there is an expectation of trickery or harm. Mrs. Whitehead stated that she expects the Sterns are going to run away and change their name and won't tell Baby M who her family is. Number 2 under Paranoid Personality Disorder is hypervigilence which seems to be an ever present state with Mrs. Whitehead at this time. Number 3 under Paranoid Personality Disorder is a guardedness or secretiveness. It isn't Mrs. Whitehead who is interested in the press, it is the others, but on the advice of counsel she is appearing in the various news media. Number 4 under Paranoid Personality Disorder is an avoidance of accepting blame even when warranted. The contract and then the subsequent pregnancy she does not see as her fault. This becomes particularly evident when she indicates that she has not read the contract. Five under Paranoid Personality Disorder is the readiness to counterattack with the most blatant threat to kill Baby M as heard on the tape.

There could be other elements that would be discovered over time and with more thorough detailed history from other individuals who knew her when she was younger. There does seem to me to be sufficient evidence from the results of my observation that she does suffer from a Mixed Personality

Disorder which does not yield readily to any form of medical treatment. In order for any treatment process to have any hope of success there is a requirement that there be an awareness of some disorder which causes discomfort. In Mrs. Whitehead, unfortunately, we see an individual who is unable to accept responsibility for any of her actions and therefore blames the rest of the world in making her a victim for behaviors which she initiated. The painful thing to observe is the direct and also potential harm that will accrue to Ryan and Tuesday who deserve to know something about their half sister. I believe that Mr. Whitehead will as he always has done be supportive and be capable of tolerating the extremes of distress that may beset his wife if the court should decide that they should not get custody of the baby. Since the behaviors related to the Mixed Personality Disorders emphasize impulsivity, any visitation that the court would consider should be continued under strict supervision.

My recommendations, however, at this particular point in time and because of the developmental principles of personality development with which we deal in a child of Baby M's age, is basically to recommend custody of Baby M to Mr. and Mrs. Stern. The recommendation also is that there be no contact between the Whitehead family and Baby M for at least a five-year period of time during which consolidation of some of the early personality developments are expected to take place. I would hope that the court would maintain jurisdiction and see that a review by a competent team (similar to those under the auspices of the child advocate) be regathered for a reevaluation of Baby M's emotional, cognitive, and behavioral development. Based on that evaluation, as well as possibly subsequent ones, the court would be in a much better position to judge whether the child could withstand the undercutting of trust which Mrs. Whitehead and through her Tuesday and Ryan and Mr. Whitehead as well, might make Baby M extremely uncomfortable and place her in a vulnerable position. From my clinical experience I believe that there is clear and convincing proof that the mental disability which I have described in Mrs. Whitehead is established and will continue indefinitely regardless of medical treatment. I also, unfortunately, believe that immediate severance of the relationship is the least detrimental alternative for the child.

Appendix D

The "We Are All Unfit" letter, released to the public on March 12, 1987.

BY THESE STANDARDS, WE ARE ALL UNFIT MOTHERS

"Mrs. Whitehead had difficulty accurately reading her daughter's behavior signals as well as separating her own needs from those of her daughter."

David Brodzinsky, Ph.D.

"Mrs. Whitehead feels that Sara/Melissa belongs with her because she is the mother. . . . She is almost myopic in her view that her role as a biological mother enables her to understand her children better than anyone else."

Judith Brown Greif, Ph.D.

"Mrs. Whitehead has a Narcissistic Personality Disorder. . . . [A] Narcissistic Personality Disorder [includes] a preoccupation with grooming and remaining youthful. It was accidentally discovered that Mrs. Whitehead's hair is totally white and has been for a number of years. Since this makes her feel old, she dyes her hair very frequently in order to remain youthful-appearing. . . . Under Histrionic Personality Disorder, it indicates the role of a victim. . . . Mrs. Whitehead stated that she felt that she was a victim and became very emotional as she described the fact that the child was ripped away from her, the mother, who was breast-feeding her. . . ."

Marshall D. Schechter, M.D.

"Dr. Schechter faulted Mrs. Whitehead for saying 'Hurray!' when the baby played Patty Cake by clapping her hands together. The more appropriate response for Mrs. Whitehead, he said, was to imitate the child by clapping her hands together and saying 'Patty Cake' to reinforce the child's behavior. He also criticized Mrs. Whitehead for having four pandas of various size available for Baby M to play with. Dr. Schechter said pots, pans and spoons would have been more suitable."

The New York Times 2/24/87

There are increasingly complex questions of custody today—both in cases involving surrogate parents and those involving divorce—and we strongly urge the legislators and jurists who will deal with these matters to recognize that a mother need not be perfect to "deserve" her child.

185

(signed)

Jennifer Allen, Judith Arcana, Alice Arlen, Margaret Atwood, Ann Banks, Irene Barbaro, Pauline Bart, Robin Becker, Janet Benshof, Louise Bernikow, Kathleen Betsko, Jane Bevans, Anne Bowen, Pamela Brandt, Marie Brenner, Nina Feinberg Brickman, E.M. Broner, Joyce Burland, Susan Chace, Susan Cheever, Phyllis Chesler, Camilla Clay, Jan Cleary, Sheryl Connelly, Blanche Wiesen Cook, Gena Corea, Judy Corman, Gretchen Cryer, Betsy Damon, Donna DeMatteo, Andrea Dworkin, Barbara Ehrenreich, Ronnie Eldridge, Delia Ephron, Nora Ephron, Barbara Epstein, Marilyn French, Betty Friedan, Linda Gordon, Cecilia Greene, Lois Gould, Nancy Haberman, Jean Halberstam, Elizabeth Hardwick, Susan Harman, Bertha Harris, Brett Harvey, Molly Haskell, Carolyn Heilbrun, Judith Hennessee, Merle Hoffman, Bell Hooks, Jane Isay, Elizabeth Janeway, Sandy Johnson, Ann Jones, Erica Jong, Ethel Kahn, Susan Kander, Adrienne Kennedy, Florynce Kennedy, Ynestra King, Rachel Koenig, Eva Kollish, Bea Kreloff, Jill Krementz, Maxine Kumin, Kathleen Lahey, Jackie Leo, Mary Lumet, Harriet Lyons, Karen Malpede, Jane Mansbridge, Elaine Markson, Valerie Martin, Eve Merriam, Sue Miller, Kate Millett, Nancy Milford, Susannah Moore, Anne Navasky, Lynn Nesbit, Janet Neipris, Susan Newcomer, Leslie Newman, Annabel Nichols, Lisa Oppenheim, Grace Paley, Jan Peterson, Letty Cottin Pogrebin, Sally Quinn, Kit Reed, Carol E. Rinzler, Sonia Jaffe Robbins, Marisa Robles, Ruby Rohrlicht, Selina Romany, Phyllis Rose, Judith Rossner, Barbara Katz Rothman, Florence Rush, Sara Salter, Leah Schaefer, Lynn Sharon Schwartz, Lauren Scott, Barbara Seaman, Sybil Shainwald, Donna Shalala, Myra Shapiro, Nancy Shaw, Charlotte Sheedy, Gail Sheehy, Alix Kates Shulman, Carly Simon, Roberta Sklar, Ann Snitow, Diane Sokolow, Rosalind Solomon, Susan Sontag, Dawn Steel, Gloria Steinem, Catherine R. Stimpson, Meryl Streep, Nadine Taub, Alice Trillin, Maria Tucci, Ana Varona, Lindsy Van Gelder, Sharon Weizenbaum, Kate White, Joan Wile, Ellen Willis, Vera B. Williams, Barbara Winslow, Elizabeth Wood

AMICUS CURIAE BRIEFS

On March 31, 1987, Judge Harvey Sorkow upheld the surrogate-parenting contract and severed Mary Beth Whitehead's parental rights.

Lawyer Harold J. Cassidy filed notice that he would appeal this decision; the New Jersey supreme court agreed to hear his appeal.

On August 21, 1987, Cassidy filed a two-hundred-page appeal brief. Seventeen organizations also filed amicus curiae ("friend of the court") briefs.*

Fourteen of the Amici urged the Supreme Court to strike the surrogacy contract, restore Mary Beth Whitehead's parental rights and nullify the adoption of Baby M. One of the briefs, that of RESOLVE, was filed to educate the court about infertility, and took no position on the ruling; two briefs, filed by a surrogacy clinic owner and by the National Association of Surrogate Mothers, asked the supreme court to uphold Judge Sorkow's ruling.

The amicus curiae briefs filed were as follows:

(1) Amicus curiae brief filed by Dr. Betsy P. Aigen, director of a surrogacy clinic.

(2) Amicus curiae brief filed by the American Adoption Congress written by attorney George B. Gelman:

> *The American Adoption Congress is an organization of those involved in adoption, which is dedicated to promoting openness and honesty in adoption. In its brief, it argued that New Jersey's adoption law does apply to surrogacy and that its standards must be met before a [parental] termination can be entered. Otherwise, the court is not acting in the child's best interests, since "not being unnecessarily separated from a natural parent is fundamental to a child's best interests." In support it reviewed the scientific research which demonstrates that adoptees are more prone to psychopathology. Applying the adoption standards leads to one conclusion: that there be no termination of Mary Beth Whitehead's [parental] rights.†*

---

*An amicus curiae brief is one in which parties who have an interest in the outcome of a case may offer the court information they consider important even if they are not parties to the case.

†This description, and those that follow for certain other amici, was made available at the February 3, 1988, press conference coordinated by Harold Cassidy.

(3) Amicus curiae brief filed by the Catholic League for Religious and Civil Rights (the "Catholic League"), written by attorneys Steven N. Taleb and Steven F. McDowell:

> *The Catholic League for Religious and Civil Rights is a national organization which seeks to combat religious prejudice and discrimination and to preserve religious freedom rights and to preserve parental rights in the context of the traditional family. In its brief, it argued that surrogacy must be evaluated under adoption law principles and that it is contrary to those principles, which prohibit baby selling and permit a mother to change her mind about relinquishment. Enforcement of a surrogacy arrangement would violate the constitutional rights of the mother. Recognition of surrogacy would create far more problems than it solves, including legal and functional, economic, cultural and social (particularly in terms of the concept of family units) and psychological problems.*

(4) Amicus curiae brief submitted by Communications Workers of America, AFL-CIO, written by attorney Steven P. Weissman:

> *The Communications Workers of America is a union representing 500,000 workers both in the private and public sectors. In its brief, it focused on that part of Judge Sorkow's decision which dealt with the Constitutional right to procreate and specifically on that part which cited to a United States Supreme Court opinion from 1905, Lochner v. New York. That opinion, the brief argues, has long since been abandoned and discredited by the Supreme Court and is no longer good law. That opinion reflected a belief that legislation could not protect workers in the workplace, a belief that has long since been rejected. Any reliance on it could seriously jeopardize workers' rights.*

(5) Amicus curiae brief submitted by Concerned United Birthparents, Inc. (referred to below as "CUB"), written by attorneys John R. Holsinger, Merrill O'Brien, Mary Sue Henifin, John H. Hall, and Terry E. Thornton:

> *Concerned United Birth Parents is an organization whose members include birth parents, adoptees, and others involved in adoption, which seeks to educate the public with respect to adoption from the perspective of birth parents and adoptees. In its brief, it reviewed the studies which show that women who relinquish children for adoption have social and psychological problems, and concluded that surrogacy arrangements will lead to the same kind of problems*

for the birth mother, especially where the relinquishment is forced against her will. Moreover, it reviewed the law regarding the relative constitutional rights of the litigants in this case, and concluded that while the couple do not have a constitutional right to terminate, the birth mother does have constitutional rights which must be protected. It argued that New Jersey's adoption law does apply to surrogacy and its standards must be satisfied before a termination can be entered, contrary to Judge Sorkow's approach. Finally, it argued that it was inappropriate to consider wealth-based and gender-based criteria in determining best interests.

(6) Amicus curiae brief filed by Concerned Women for America, Eagle Forum, National Legal Foundation, Family Research Council of America, United Families Foundation, and Judicial Reform Project ("Eagle Forum"), written by David H. Dugan, III, and Joy R. Jowdy:

The Concerned Women for America Educational and Legal Defense Foundation is an organization which seeks to promote liberty and traditional moral values; it appeared in this action jointly with the Eagle Forum, the National Legal Foundation, the Family Research Council of America, the Judicial Reform Project of the Institute for Government and Politics of the Free Congress Foundation and the United Families Foundation. In their brief, they argued that surrogacy arrangements are void against public policy, because they are contrary to adoption law principles, including the statutes against baby selling and the policies against unconsidered decisions to surrender. They reviewed the law in a wide variety of fields and argued that in all cases its policies were inconsistent with surrogacy. They argued that enforcement would create problems for the child, including legal, psychological, physical and other problems, for the adult participants, for the siblings and for society.

(7) Amicus curiae brief submitted by the Foundation on Economic Trends, Jeremy Rifkin, Betty Friedan, Gloria Steinem, Gena Corea, Barbara Katz-Rothman, Lois Gould, Marilyn French, Hazel Henderson, Grace Paley, Evelyn Fox Keller, Shelly Mindin, Rita Arditti, Dr. Janice Raymond, Dr. Michelle Harrison, Dr. W. D. White, Sybil Shainwald, Mary Daly, Kathleen Lahey, Karen Malpede, Phyllis Chesler, Kristen Golden, Letty Cottin Pogrebin, and Ynestra King (the "Foundation"), written by attorneys Alfred F. Russo, Andrew C. Kimbrell, and Edward Lee Rogers:

The Foundation on Economic Trends has devoted itself to attempting to ensure the proper regulation of biotechnology; it ap-

peared in this action jointly with a group of 22 prominent writers, scholars, public health workers, sociologists, doctors and feminist activists. In their brief, they argued that in evaluating surrogacy, the commercial aspects and its implications for society cannot be ignored. Surrogacy exploits the women involved, by ignoring their rights as parents and by victimizing them physically, economically and emotionally. Moreover, surrogacy is a form of baby trafficking, which is prohibited. They suggest that if the commercialization of surrogacy is accepted, the door to eugenics will be reopened. As well, they contend that surrogacy is contrary to the policies of law, which are an attempt to protect the mother-child relationship. Finally, they contend that the mother's relationship with her child must be afforded protection by the state unless a compelling reason exists to the contrary.

(8) Amicus curiae brief filed by the Gruter Institute for Law and Behavioral Research, Inc. ("Gruter"), written by Louis E. Della Torre, Jr.:

The Gruter Institute is a non-profit California organization which brings together distinguished scholars from various academic disciplines to study the relationship of law and behavioral sciences. In its brief, it reviewed the scientific research available on the mother-child relationship, particularly on bonding, and reported that this research leads to the conclusion that "it is questionable whether any woman can fully appreciate in advance the emotional consequences of separation from an infant to whom she has just given birth." As a result, they argue, the law must hold that the surrogate parenting agreement is voidable at the option of the birth mother, or in the alternate that it cannot be the subject of an award of specific performance.

(9) Amicus curiae brief submitted by the Hudson County Legal Services Corporation and National Center on Women and Family Law, Inc. ("Hudson County"), written by attorneys Kathleen E. Kitson, Sharon F. Liebhaber, and Myra Sun:

The Hudson County Legal Services Corp. provides legal services for low-income individuals in civil actions, including family matters; the National Center on Women and Family Law advises and assists advocates for low-income women and children in custody litigation. In their brief, they contend that Judge Sorkow relied in his opinion below on differences in the parties' economic and educa-

tional circumstances, and that this reliance was improper and against public policy.

(10) Amicus curiae brief filed by the Committee on Mother and Child Rights, Inc. and Origins ("Mother and Child") written by Attorney Priscilla Read Chenoweth:

The Committee on Mother and Child Rights is a national organization which seeks to ensure that child custody decisions do not turn on financial considerations, but rather take into account the mother's biological and nurturing contributions; Origins is a New Jersey organization of women who have lost children to adoption, which seeks to improve the adoption process. In their brief, they argue that the ex parte order entered by Judge Sorkow on May 5, 1986, removing the child from the Whiteheads and giving the child to the Sterns was improper, since there was neither a legal nor a factual basis for it. Moreover, the surrogacy arrangement is unenforceable since it is contrary to the statute prohibiting baby selling and the policies in favor of maintaining ties between parents and their children. In addition, they take issue with the best-interest hearing conducted by Judge Sorkow, contending that he failed to give proper consideration to the nature of the relationship between mother and child and that the improper ex parte order and his resolution of the surrogacy issue in effect created a presumption in favor of the Sterns. Finally, there is no basis for a termination of parental rights in this case.

(11) Amicus curiae brief filed by the National Association of Surrogate Mothers, written by Herbert D. Hinkle.

(12) Amicus curiae brief submitted by the National Committee for Adoption, Inc., written by Joseph M. Nardi, Jr., and Edward F. Canfield:

The National Committee for Adoption is an organization whose members include adoption agencies, which seek to upgrade adoption practices. It argued that it is inappropriate to apply contract law principles to a surrogacy arrangement, because it involves a child and intangible emotional factors are therefore implied, and because enforcement of surrogacy is contrary to our historical, ethical and religious traditions; instead, adoption law principles must be applied. Applying these principles leads to the conclusion that surrogate parenting agreements are invalid. Finally, it contends that any other conclusions would lead to chaos in the adoption field,

*since there would be no difference between approved agency and
private placement adoptions and since the profit motive would become a factor in adoptions, thereby shifting the focus of the process
from the child to others.*

(13) Amicus curiae brief filed by the New Jersey Catholic Conference,
written by attorney William F. Bolan, Jr.:

*The New Jersey Catholic Conference is composed of the Bishops
who head the Archdioceses and Dioceses in the State of New Jersey,
and provides a means by which they may speak on matters of public
policy. In its brief, it argues that surrogacy is not consistent with
the statutes prohibiting baby selling and that therefore, surrogacy
agreements are void as against public policy. It states that in this
situation the court should defer to the legislature. Moreover, it
argues that, contrary to the conclusion of Judge Sorkow, there is no
Constitutional right to engage in a surrogacy arrangement, and
that therefore there is no basis for declaring the statutes unconstitutional as applied to surrogacy. To the contrary, there are compelling reasons for finding the statutes constitutional, including the
need to protect the human dignity of the child, the need to prevent
exploitation of women, and the need to protect the stability of
marriage and the family as institutions in our society.*

(14) Amicus curiae brief filed by Odyssey Institute International, Inc.;
Odyssey Institute of Connecticut, Inc.; Florence Fisher; Judianne Densen-
Gerber; Senator Connie Binsfeld; and Angela Holder; written by Paul J.
McCurrie and Cyril C. Means, Jr.:

*Odyssey Institute is an organization which seeks to help drug-
dependent children and adults; it has appeared together with various individuals who have an interest in the surrogacy issue. In their
brief, they argued that surrogacy is contrary to the Thirteenth
Amendment and the federal statutes such as the Anti-Peonage Act,
which were adopted under that Amendment, since it is an arrangement for sale of a child for money. Moreover, the Constitutional
right to procreate is not a justification for enforcing the arrangement. Finally, the brief reviews the English law regarding surrogacy, which has held that surrogacy arrangements are void.*

(15) Amicus curiae brief submitted by RESOLVE, Inc., written by
Jerrold N. Kaminsky.

(16) Amicus curiae brief filed by the Rutherford Institute ("Rutherford") written by attorneys Richard J. Traynor, John W. Whitehead, and David A. French:

> *The Rutherford Institute is an organization that has been active in cases relating to religious freedoms including cases concerning family and marriage issues. In its brief, it argued that there is significant harm to the child born of a surrogacy arrangement, because the transfer of the child is a form of prohibited commercialism. Moreover, surrogacy depersonalizes the mother, treating her as a commodity, is a threat to the integrity of marriage and the family unity, and denegrates human dignity by changing the focus of why children would be procreated, and has the potential to be an exploitation of the poor by the elite. Finally, it argues that surrogacy violates the adoption laws, in particular the statutes against baby selling.*

(17) Amicus curiae brief submitted by the Women's Rights Litigation Clinic at Rutgers Law School, the New York State Coalition on Women's Legislative Issues, and the National Emergency Civil Liberties Committee ("Rutgers"), written by attorney Nadine Taub:

> *The Women's Rights Litigation Clinic is an educational project at Rutgers Law School whereby students work on ongoing litigation and other legal projects concerning discrimination law and women's rights, including reproductive issues. The New York State Coalition on Women's Legislative Issues seeks to deal with issues of gender bias; the National Emergency Civil Liberties Committee addresses issues of reproductive freedom and gender. In their brief, they argue that there was no legal basis to terminate Mary Beth Whitehead's parental rights, and that Judge Sorkow's decision that he could terminate based on generalized principles without regard to statutory criteria was in error and is dangerous precedent. Moreover, they argue that Judge Sorkow impermissibly used sex-based and class-based stereotypes in evaluating the conduct of the parties.*

Points and Conclusion of Harold Cassidy's main appeal brief to the New Jersey supreme court, filed August 21, 1987.

POINT I

Scientific research and the expert testimony introduced at trial demonstrate that there will be harm to the participants in surrogacy arrangements, including the children born of such arrangements, the birth mother, and the siblings.

POINT II

Defendant Mary Beth Whitehead has a constitutional right to the continued companionship of her child which is protected under both the federal and the state constitutions. The trial court failed to recognize this right, and impermissibly terminated the relationship.

POINT III

The surrogate parenting agreement is unenforceable, since it is contrary to the public policies that the state of New Jersey considers worthy of protection. The court below therefore committed reversible error by enforcing the agreement.

POINT IV

Enforcement of the surrogate parenting agreement is not required because of Plaintiffs' constitutional right to procreate; the trial court's conclusion to the contrary is reversible error.

POINT V

The surrogate parenting agreement is invalid and/or unenforceable, applying traditional principles of contract law and remedies law.

POINT VI

Once the conclusion is reached that the surrogate parenting agreement cannot be enforced, then this court must not permit a de facto enforcement of the agreement under some other guise. The only proper resolution is to place the child with the mother unless she is found to be unfit. Since no such finding can be made here, the child must be returned to her mother, Mary Beth Whitehead.

POINT VII

The Einwohner report shows that Mrs. Whitehead was not recommended or approved as being capable of surrendering her baby following birth. Fairness and justice require that she not be compelled to surrender her baby because of a failure of an implied condition precedent that she had to have been determined to be psychologically capable of giving up her baby; Mr. Stern is estopped from relying on the promise to surrender, and there was no duty to surrender the baby as a result of mutual mistake, breach of contract and equitable fraud.

POINT VIII

The agreement between Mary Beth Whitehead and William and Elizabeth Stern is invalid and should not be enforced as it was procured by fraudulent representations on the part of William and Elizabeth Stern.

POINT IX

Plaintiffs William and Elizabeth Stern are not entitled to specific performance of the surrogate parenting agreement, because their conduct throughout was not fair, just and equitable, but rather was sharp and aimed at an unfair advantage and their conduct when they came to court constituted unclean hands. The trial court committed reversible error by granting the remedy nonetheless.

POINT X

The trial court prejudged the case, demonstrated a lack of objectivity and bias against the defendant. His findings of fact are not entitled to deference.

POINT XI

In his review of the propriety of specific enforcement of the contract, the court failed to employ the proper standard for the interests of the child. Under any standard the child's interests are best served by being placed with her mother. The court ignored factors which should have been considered, employed factors which should not have been considered, and improperly applied and incorrectly analyzed other factors. The judgment must be vacated and an order entered directing that the child be placed in the care and custody of her mother.

POINT XII

There is no basis in law for a termination of Mary Beth Whitehead's parental rights. The court cannot deny her and her family, at the minimum, the right to reasonable visitation.

POINT XIII

In connection with the testimony by the expert witnesses the trial court made numerous rulings that were erroneous. The trial court barred expert testimony on the effects of surrogacy; the trial court barred Marshall Klaus, M.D., and Reuben Pannor, M.S.W., from testifying; he consistently ruled that Defendants' experts' testimony was set forth within the four corners of their report; and he consistently permitted Plaintiffs' and the guardian's experts to testify even though their testimony did not meet legal standards these rulings were prejudicial to Defendants. Therefore, a new trial must be granted.

POINT XIV

The trial court committed reversible error by refusing to consider the rights of the Whitehead children and by refusing to permit them to testify.

CONCLUSION

For reasons set forth above, this court must reverse the trial court, vacate the Order of Judgment, enter an Order awarding permanent custody to Mary Beth Whitehead, and further order a remand for a trial court to hold a hearing to determine reasonable and appropriate visitation for Mr. Stern.

APPENDIX G

Excerpts from the New Jersey supreme court decision "In the Matter of Baby M," handed down on February 2, 1988.

ON SURROGACY CONTRACTS

We invalidate the surrogacy contract because it conflicts with the law and public policy of this State. While we recognize the depth of the yearning of infertile couples to have their own children, we find the payment of money to a "surrogate" mother illegal, perhaps criminal, and potentially degrading to women. Although in this case we grant custody to the natural father, the evidence having clearly proved such custody to be in the best interests of the infant, we void both the termination of the surrogate mother's parental rights and the adoption of the child by the wife/stepparent. We thus restore the "surrogate" as the mother of the child. . . .

We find no offense to our present laws where a woman voluntarily and without payment agrees to act as a "surrogate" mother, provided that she is not subject to a binding agreement to surrender her child. Moreover, our holding today does not preclude the Legislature from altering the current statutory scheme, within constitutional limits, so as to permit surrogacy contracts. Under current law, however, the surrogacy agreement before us is illegal and invalid. . . .

One of the surrogacy contract's basic purposes, to achieve the adoption of a child through private placement, though permitted in New Jersey "is very much disfavored." . . . Its use of money for this purpose—and we have no doubt whatsoever that the money is being paid to obtain an adoption and not, as the Sterns argue, for the personal services of Mary Beth Whitehead—is illegal and perhaps criminal. . . . In addition to the inducement of money, there is the coercion of contract: the natural mother's irrevocable agreement, prior to birth, even prior to conception, to surrender the child to the adoptive couple. Such an agreement is totally unenforceable in private placement adoption. . . . Integral to these invalid provisions of the surrogacy contract is the related agreement, equally invalid, on the part of the natural mother to cooperate with, and not to contest, proceedings to terminate her parental rights, as well as her contractual concession, in aid of the adoption, that the child's best interests would be served by awarding custody to the natural father and his wife—all of this before she has even conceived, and, in some cases, before she has the slightest idea of what the natural father and adoptive mother are like. . . .

In this case a termination of parental rights was obtained not by proving the statutory prerequisites but by claiming the benefit of contractual provisions. From all that has been stated above, it is clear that a contractual agreement to abandon one's parental rights, or not to contest a termination action, will not be enforced in our courts. The Legislature would not have so carefully, so consistently, and so substantially restricted termination of parental rights if it had intended to allow termination to be achieved by one short sentence in a contract.

Since the termination was invalid, it follows, as noted above, the adoption of Melissa by Mrs. Stern could not properly be granted. . . .

The surrogacy contract's invalidity, resulting from its direct conflict with the above statutory provisions, is further underlined when its goals and means are measured against New Jersey's public policy. The contract's basic premise, that the natural parents can decide in advance of birth which one is to have custody of the child, bears no relationship to the settled law that the child's best interests shall determine custody. . . .

The surrogacy contract guarantees permanent separation of the child from one of its natural parents. Our policy, however, has long been that to the extent possible, children should remain with and be brought up by both of their natural parents. That was the first stated purpose of the previous adoption act. . . . While not so stated in the present adoption law, this purpose remains part of the public policy of this State. . . . This is not simply some theoretical ideal that in practice has no meaning. The impact of failure to follow that policy is nowhere better shown than in the results of this surrogacy contract. A child, instead of starting off its life with as much peace and security as possible, finds itself immediately in a tug-of-war. . . .

The surrogacy contract violates the policy of this State that the rights of natural parents are equal concerning their child, the father's right no greater than the mother's. "The parent and child relationship extends equally to every child and to every parent, regardless of the marital status of the parents." . . . The whole purpose and effect of the surrogacy contract was to give the father the exclusive right to the child by destroying the rights of the mother. . . .

Under the contract, the natural mother is irrevocably committed before she knows the strength of her bond with her child. She never makes a totally voluntary, informed decision, for quite clearly any decision prior to the baby's birth is, in the most important sense, uninformed, and any decision after that, compelled by a pre-existing contractual commitment, the threat of a lawsuit, and the inducement of a $10,000 payment, is less than totally voluntary. Her interests are of little concern to those who controlled this transaction. . . .

Worst of all, however, is the contract's total disregard of the best interests of the child. There is not the slightest suggestion that any inquiry will be made at any time to determine the fitness of the Sterns as custodial parents, of Mrs. Stern as an adoptive parent, their superiority to Mrs. Whitehead, or the effect on the child of not living with her natural mother.

This is the sale of a child, or, at the very least, the sale of a mother's right to her child, the only mitigating factor being that one of the purchasers is the father. Almost every evil that prompted the prohibition of the payment of money in connection with adoptions exists here. . . .

The long-term effects of surrogacy contracts are not known, but feared—the impact on the child who learns her life was bought, that she is the offspring of someone who gave birth to her only to obtain money; the impact on the natural mother as the full weight of her isolation is felt along with the full reality of the sale of her body and her child; the impact on the natural father and adoptive mother once they realize the consequences of their conduct.

ON CONSTITUTIONAL ISSUES

Both parties argue that the Constitutions—state and federal—mandate approval of their basic claims. The source of their constitutional arguments is essentially the same: the right of privacy, the right to procreate, the right to the companionship of one's child, those rights flowing either directly from the fourteenth amendment or by its incorporation of the Bill of Rights, or from the ninth amendment, or through the penumbra surrounding all of the Bill of Rights. They are the rights of personal intimacy, of marriage, of sex, of family, of procreation. Whatever their source, it is clear that they are fundamental rights protected by both the federal and state Constitutions. . . .

The right asserted by the Sterns is the right of procreation; that asserted by Mary Beth Whitehead is the right to the companionship of her child. We find that the right of procreation does not extend as far as claimed by the Sterns. . . .

The right to procreate, as protected by the Constitution, . . . very simply is the right to have natural children, whether through sexual intercourse or artificial insemination. It is no more than that. Mr. Stern has not been deprived of that right. Through artificial insemination of Mrs. Whitehead, Baby M is his child. The custody, care, companionship, and nurturing that follow birth are not parts of the right to procreation; they are rights that may also be constitutionally protected, but that involve many considerations other than the right of procreation. To assert that Mr. Stern's right of procreation gives him the right to the custody of Baby M would be to assert that Mrs. Whitehead's right of procreation does *not* give her the right to the custody of Baby M. . . .

ON CUSTODY

With the surrogacy contract disposed of, the legal framework becomes a dispute between two couples over the custody of a child produced by the artificial insemination of one couple's wife by the other's husband. Under the Parentage Act the claims of the natural father and the natural mother are entitled to equal weight, *i.e.*, one is not preferred over the other solely because it is the father or the mother. The applicable rule given these circumstances is clear: the child's best interests determine custody. . . .

Our custody conclusion is based on strongly persuasive testimony contrasting both the family life of the Whiteheads and the Sterns and the personalities and characters of the individuals. The stability of the Whitehead family life was doubtful at the time of trial. Their finances were in serious trouble. . . . Mr. Whitehead's employment, though relatively steady, was always at risk because of his alcoholism, a condition that he seems not to have been able to confront effectively. Mrs. Whitehead had not worked for quite some time, her last two employments having been part-time. One of the Whiteheads' positive attributes was their ability to bring up two children, and apparently well, even in so vulnerable a household. Yet substantial question was raised even about that aspect of their home life. The expert testimony contained criticism of Mrs. Whitehead's handling of her son's educational difficulties. Certain of the experts noted that Mrs. Whitehead perceived herself as omnipotent and omniscient concerning her children. She knew what they were thinking, what they wanted, and she spoke for them. As to Melissa, Mrs. Whitehead expressed the view that she alone knew what that child's cries and sounds meant. Her inconsistent stories about various things engendered grave doubts about her ability to explain honestly and sensitively to Baby M—and at the right time—the nature of her origin. Although faith in professional counseling is not a *sine qua non* of parenting, several experts believed that Mrs. Whitehead's contempt for professional help, especially professional psychological help, coincided with her feelings of omnipotence in a way that could be devastating to a child who most likely will need such help. In short, while love and affection there would be, Baby M's life with the Whiteheads promised to be too closely controlled by Mrs. Whitehead. The prospects for a wholesome independent psychological growth and development would be at serious risk.

It seems to us that given her predicament, Mrs. Whitehead was rather harshly judged—both by the trial court and by some of the experts. She was guilty of a breach of contract, and indeed, she did break a very important promise, but we think it is expecting something well beyond normal human capabilities to suggest that this mother should have parted with her newly born infant without a struggle. Other than survival, what stronger force is there? We do not know of, and cannot conceive of, any other case where a perfectly fit mother was expected to surrender her newly born infant, perhaps forever, and was then told she was a bad mother because she did not. We know of no authority suggesting that the moral quality of her act in those circumstances should be judged by referring to a contract made before she became pregnant. We do not countenance, and would never countenance, violating a court order as Mrs. Whitehead did, even a court order that is wrong; but her resistance to an order that she surrender her infant, possibly forever, merits a measure of understanding. We do not find it so clear that her efforts to keep her infant, when measured against the Sterns' efforts to take her away, make one, rather than the other, the wrongdoer. The Sterns suffered, but so did she. And if we go beyond suffering to an evaluation of the human stakes involved in the struggle, how much weight should be given to her nine months of pregnancy, the labor of childbirth, the risk to her life, compared to the payment of money, the anticipation of a child and the donation of sperm?

We have a further concern regarding the trial court's emphasis on the Sterns' interest in Melissa's education as compared to the Whiteheads'. That this difference is a legitimate factor to be considered we have no doubt. But it should not be overlooked that a best-interests test is designed to create not a new member of the intelligentsia but rather a well-integrated person who might reasonably be expected to be happy with life. "Best interests" does not contain within it any idealized lifestyle; the question boils down to a judgment, consisting of many factors, about the likely future happiness of a human being. Stability, love, family happiness, tolerance, and, ultimately, support of independence—all rank much higher in predicting future happiness than the likelihood of a college education. . . .

Six experts testified for Mrs. Whitehead: one favored joint custody, clearly unwarranted in this case; one simply rebutted an opposing expert's claim that Mary Beth Whitehead had a recognized personality disorder; one testified to the adverse impact of separation on *Mrs. Whitehead;* one testified about the evils of adoption and, to him, the probable analogous evils of surrogacy; one spoke only on the question of whether Mrs. Whitehead's consent in the surrogacy agreement was "informed consent"; and one spelled out the strong bond between mother and child. None of them unequivocally stated, or even necessarily implied, an opinion that custody in the Whiteheads was in the best interests of Melissa—the ultimate issue. The Sterns' experts, both well qualified—as were the Whiteheads'—concluded that the best interests of Melissa required custody in Mr. Stern. Most convincingly, the three experts chosen by the court-appointed guardian *ad litem* of Baby M, each clearly free of all bias and interest, unanimously and persuasively recommended custody in the Sterns.

ON VISITATION

This is not a divorce case where visitation is almost invariably granted to the non-custodial spouse. . . . In the instant case, Mrs. Whitehead spent the first four months of this child's life as her mother and has regularly visited the child since then. Second, she is not only the natural mother, but also the legal mother, and is not to be penalized one iota because of the surrogacy contract. Mrs. Whitehead, as the mother (indeed, as a mother who nurtured her child for its first four months—unquestionably a relevant consideration), is entitled to have her own interest in visitation considered. Visitation cannot be determined without considering the parents' interests along with those of the child.

In all of this, the trial court should recall the touchstones of visitation: that it is desirable for the child to have contact with both parents; that besides the child's interests, the parents' interests also must be considered; but that when all is said and done, the best interests of the child are paramount.

We have decided that Mrs. Whitehead is entitled to visitation at some point, and that question is not open to the trial court on this remand. The trial court will determine what kind of visitation shall be granted to her, with or without conditions, and when and under what circumstances it should commence. . . .

While probably unlikely, we do not deem it unthinkable that, the major issues having been resolved, the parties undoubted love for this child might result in a good faith attempt to work out the visitation themselves, in the best interests of their child.

ON THE FUTURE OF SURROGACY

This case affords some insight into a new reproductive arrangement: the artificial insemination of a surrogate mother. The unfortunate events that have unfolded illustrate that its unregulated use can bring suffering to all involved. . . .

We have found that our present laws do not permit the surrogacy contract used in this case. Nowhere, however, do we find any legal prohibition against surrogacy when the surrogate mother volunteers, without any payment, to act as a surrogate and is given the right to change her mind and to assert her parental rights. . . .

Legislative consideration of surrogacy may provide the opportunity to begin to focus on the overall implications of the new reproductive biotechnology—*in vitro* fertilization, preservation of sperm and eggs, embryo implantation and the like. . . . The problem can be addressed only when society decides what its values and objectives are in this troubling, yet promising, area.

The judgment is affirmed in part, reversed in part, and remanded for further proceedings consistent with this opinion.

JUSTICES CLIFFORD, HANDLER, POLLOCK, O'HEARN, GARIBALDI, and STEIN join in this opinion. WILENTZ, C.J., writing for a unanimous Court.

NOTES

2: On Civilization and Its Discontents

1. Merle Hoffman, "On the Issues," *The Journal of Substance for Progressive Women*, vol. viii, 1987.

2. Bill's description is contained in his own direct testimony Mary Beth's description of that day is reported in her lawyer Harold Cassidy's appeal brief. Betsy Stern "said that [Mary Beth] might as well take the baby's things as the Sterns would not be needing them."

3. Transcript of Superior Court proceedings, direct examination of Elizabeth Stern by Gary Skoloff.

4. Transcript pages 12, 25, 120, 121, 122, etc., of Bill Stern's and Betsy Stern's testimony on direct examination by their lawyer, Gary Skoloff.

5. The reports by Brodzinsky, Greif, and Schechter.

6. According to the trial transcripts and Harold Cassidy's appeal brief, the Sterns trusted the fact that the previous sperm donor who was "working with" Mary Beth was a *psychologist*. If he was willing to trust her, then so should the Sterns.

7. Meg Lundstrom and Susan Edelman, *The Bergen Record*, January 9, 1987.

8. In 1987, in New Hampshire, Jessie Murabito, a custodially challenged mother, went to jail for a week rather than turn over her two children to their father, who she said was sexually abusing them. Murabito relented and was freed only after the judge stipulated that the children's visits with the father would be supervised. At trial, in response to Jessie Murabito's experts' evidence that the father was sexually abusing the children, two psychologists claimed that no sexual abuse had occurred. The judge concurred.

The court's expert had testified that Jessie had breast-fed her children excessively. According to Sara Dustin, a Murabito supporter and founder of a New Hampshire group, Parents for Justice, Jessie Murabito was being punished for breast-feeding her children. Dustin writes that once the bottle-feeding industry was perfected, mothers were directed to replace themselves with bottles and to strictly distance themselves from their babies. She writes: "Our relationship to our children was to be professional, time-efficient and industrialized so they would become modern, self-disciplined and self-sufficient beings free from neurotic attachments to their parents. . . . No wonder Jessie Murabito stands accused in 1987 of loving her children too much."

9. A number of men and men's groups have legally argued that they should not be obligated to pay child support on the grounds that women have trapped them (and their sperm) by force and against male will.

10. According to Dr. Allwyne J. Levine, "During the course of the pregnancy, Mrs. Whitehead expressed a desire to deal only with Mrs. Stern, and then after the pregnancy she rarely spoke to Dr. Stern even on the telephone. Dr. Stern said that he felt like an intruder, that Mrs. Whitehead was carrying his baby and he felt extremely awkward."

11. Rita Arditti, Renate Duelli Klein, and Shelley Minden, *Test-Tube Women, What Future for Motherhood* (London: Pandora Press, 1984); Dennis L. Breo and Noel Keane, *The Surrogate Mother* (New York: Everest House, 1981); Gene Corea, *The Mother Machine* (New York: Harper & Row, 1985); Philip J. Parker, M.D., "Motivation of Surrogate Mothers: Initial Findings," Clinical and Research Reports, *American Journal of Psychiatry*, 140:1, January 1983 (Parker claims to have interviewed 225 surrogacy applicants. His first study was about 125 such applicants); Ann Rule, *Small Sacrifices: A True Story of Passion and Murder* (New York: New American Library, 1987).

Between 1981 and 1986, stories appeared across the nation about early surrogacy-contract custody battles, including those of Denise Thrane and Judy Stiver, and about then happy surrogacy-contract mothers such as Elizabeth Kane. These articles appeared in publications such as *The New York Times, Newsweek, The New York Daily News, The Washington Post,* and *The San Francisco Chronicle.*

Once the Baby M trial began, in-depth coverage of the trial and the issues it raised appeared across the nation and of course on television. In-depth interviews with other unhappy and with happy surrogacy-contract mothers appeared in various places. Especially useful were the many articles written by: Rochelle Sharpe (Gannett News Service, *New Republic*), Meg Lundstrum and Michael J. Kelly *(The Bergen Record),* Bob Porte *(St. Petersburg Times),* and Ivar Peterson and Robert Hanley *(The New York Times).*

12. Details about the Elizabeth Diane Downs case are drawn from Ann Rule, op. cit.

13. Not all incest victims develop a "multiple personality" nor does everyone afflicted with "multiple personality syndrome" marry, become pregnant, or commit infanticide. Incestuous abuse is only one of at least fourteen demographic variables correlated with the kinds of women who sign surrogacy contracts. Each of these variables (e.g., poverty, religious childhoods, etc.) may be a necessary but not a sufficient predictor of who will become a contract mother.

For example, most sexual prostitutes tend to be economically impoverished or poorly educated women—but not all economically impoverished or poorly educated women are sexual prostitutes. Similarly, sexual prostitutes tend to have a high rate of incestuous-abuse histories—but not all incest victims become sexual prostitutes.

3: INDUSTRIALIZED PREGNANCY

1. Sociologist Barbara Katz Rothman refers to contemporary surrogacy as the "commodification" and "proletarianization" of motherhood. Rothman, "Comment on Harrison: The Commodification of Motherhood," *Gender and Society*, 1:3, September 1987.

2. This case is known as *Scott* v. *Pulley*, 705 SW2d 666 (Tenn. App. 1985).

3. This case is known as *McKinney* v. *Ivey*, 698 SW2d 506 (Ark. 1985).

4. This information is contained in Noel Keane's own book, written with Dennis L. Breo, *The Surrogate Mother* (New York: Everest House, 1981), and in numerous newspaper articles (for example, in *The Detroit News*, May 4, 1978; *The Bergen Record*, August 31, 1986).

5. Elizabeth Kane (a pseudonym) has published a book about her experience entitled *Birth Mother: America's First Legal Surrogate Mother, Her Change of Heart* (New York: Harcourt, Brace, 1988). Susan Edelman, "Surrogates Comfort One Another," *New York Post*, September 8, 1981.

6. Ann Rule, op. cit.

7. Rochelle Sharpe, "Client's Freedom Tops Other Concerns," Gannett News Service (date unknown).

8. Judith Lasker and Susan Borg, *In Search of Parenthood: Coping with Infertility and High Tech Conception* (Boston: Beacon Press, 1988).

9. Anne Taylor Fleming, "Our Fascination with Baby M," *New York Times Magazine*, March 29, 1987.

10. Judith Lasker and Susan Borg, op. cit.

11. These nine threatened or actual lawsuits took place in California (3), Michigan (3), New Jersey (1), Ohio (1), and Wisconsin (1).

12. Rochelle Sharpe, Gannett News Service, March 29, 1987. This case illustrates how similar surrogacy-contract and marriage-contract mothers are. In any custody challenge, the women are disadvantaged. Their bond to the baby, begun in pregnancy, is completely discounted in favor of male advantages.

13. An article in *The Record* (Porter, Texas) on November 12, 1987 (UPI), pointed out that the family of the woman could indeed sue; it was the county that had no legal recourse. The article referred to the event as the "first surrogate death," when in fact it was the death of twenty-four-year-old Denise Mounce, and her uterus, and *her* baby.

14. Journalist Rochelle Sharpe has described most of these lawsuits in *The New Republic* article or in her pieces for the Gannett news chain during the time of the Baby M case.

4: JOURNAL OF A BRIEF CAMPAIGN, 1987

1. I ultimately raised eighteen hundred dollars for Mary Beth's appeal and/or as emergency funds for her personally. Helen Hunt raised some funds in Massachusetts and, as I've noted, so did Cathy Rutler in New Jersey. Harold Cassidy must

have spent approximately half a million dollars in time and expenses, which he'll probably never recoup.

Many feminists donated their time and services: every demonstrator, every lawyer who filed an amicus brief, everyone who attended the meetings at Lois Gould's, etc. In addition, Betty Freidan conducted a workshop in California on the "Baby M case" and was able to interest the Southern California branch of the ACLU in developing a position paper; much later, Michelle Harrison, Alan Karcher and Gena Corea joined Jeremy Rifkin and Andrew Kimbrell (of the Foundation for Economic Trends) in forming the Coalition Against Surrogacy.

The single largest sum of money I received was donated by Joanne Steele, the former owner of *Majority Report*, a feminist newspaper. Gloria Steinem sent a personal check, as did approximately twenty-five to thirty others, including: Roslyn and Daniel Bologh (NY), Paulette and Michael Bowles (MD), Cara F. Burke (MD), Robert and Susan Cecil (MD), Charlotte F. Chapman (VA), Sharon and Joseph DeAngelo (CA), Patricia DeRosa (NY), Melissa Farley (CA), Claudia Flanagan (NY), Harold and Mary Geist (MD), Barbara Goldblatt (NJ), Carolyn and Kenneth Harris (MD), A and G Kassalow (VA), Carolyn F. Lewis (VA), Teresa Montini (CA), Douglas and Carolyn Pierce (MD), Mary and Paul Renald (VA), Florence Rush (NY), Carolyn Sher (MD), Anne Smith (Toronto, Can.), Sybil Shainwald (NY), Stanley and Joan Weiss (MD), Lillian and William Wolf (NY), "Women Gathering," and Elizabeth Yu (VA).

5: A Pound of Flesh

1. B. Bodenheimer, "New Trends and Requirements in Adoption Law Proposals for Legislative Change," 49 *So. Cal. Law Review* 10, 13 (1975).

Gail Davenport, The Birthparent Support Network, White Plains, N.Y., cited by Riben, ch. 3, p. 2.

Paul T. Fullerton, "Independent Adoption: The Inadequacies of State Law," 753 *Washington University Law Quarterly*, winter 1985.

Betty Jean Lifton, *Lost and Found: The Adoption Experience* (New York: The Dial Press, 1979).

William Meezan, Sanford Katz, and Eva Manoff Russo, *Adoption Without Agencies: A Study of Independent Adoptions* (New York Child Welfare League of America, Inc., 1978).

Fred Powledge, *The New Adoption Maze and How to Get Through It* (New York: C. V. Mosby Company, 1985).

Marsha Riben, *Shedding Light*, manuscript, 1987.

2. Leverett Millen and Samuel Roll, "Solomon's Mothers: A Special Case of Pathological Bereavement," *American Journal of Orthopsychiatry*, 55:3 (July 1985).

3. Edward K. Rynearson, M.D., "Relinquishment and Its Maternal Complications: A Preliminary Study," *American Journal of Psychiatry*, 139:3 (March 1982).

4. Winkler and Van Keppel, *Relinquishing Mothers in Adoption*, 1984.

5. Deykin, Campbell and Patti, "The Postadoption Experience of Surrendering Parent," 54 *American Journal of Orthopsychiatry*, 271, 1984.

6. Powledge, op. cit., 54, citing a 1981 study.

7. Phyllis R. Silverman, Ph.D., Professor of Social Work in Health Care Program, Massachusetts General Hospital Institute of Health Professionals, Letter dated November 13, 1986, to Harold J. Cassidy, Esq. re: Baby M case.

8. Powledge, op. cit., p. 5.

9. Silverman, op. cit.

10. Lifton, op. cit., p. 225.

11. Lifton, op. cit., p. 219.

12. Riben, op. cit., p. 19.

13. Millen and Roll, op. cit., p. 22.

14. Shawyer, *Death by Adoption*, cited by Riben, op. cit., at ch. 3, p. 18.

15. Powledge, op. cit., p. 20.

16. Lifton, op. cit., pp. 216–17.

17. Lifton, op. cit., p. 218.

18. Edmond Mech, "Orientation of Pregnancy Counselors Toward Adoption," unpublished, cited by Riben, op. cit., at ch. 3, p. 18.

19. *Landaverde* v. *Howie*, reported in *Family Law Reporter* 8/16/83, 9 FLR 2601. In a sense, Christina was initially impoverished and endangered by the American state. Fleeing for her life, she was then temporarily deprived of her natural son—by that same American state.

20. Fullerton, op. cit.

21. Richard Posner and Elizabeth M. Landes, "Economics of the Baby Shortage, *Journal of Legal Studies*, 1978, cited in Powledge, op. cit. at pp. 267–69.

22. Meezan, Katz, and Russo, op. cit.

23. Meezan, Katz, and Russo, op. cit., p. 53.

24. Meezan, Katz, and Russo, op. cit.

25. Lifton, op. cit., p. 8.

26. Mary Kathleen Benet, *The Politics of Adoption* (New York: The Free Press, 1987), p. 164, citing "Blood, The Family."

This study revealed three major categories of adopters: adoptions by professional men of out-of-wedlock children, adoptions by lower-middle-class stepmothers, and adoptions by the lower class of distant relatives whose parents were unable to care for them. These last two groups were composed of people who knew each other. The first group accounted for half of all adoptions (or over fifty thousand a year in 1960) and was subject to the rule of impersonality and confidentiality. It protected the babies from the shame of "illegitimacy"; it protected the birthmothers from shame; it protected the women's families from social disapproval; most of all it protected the adoptive parents from the birth mother's knock on the door.

27. Powledge, op. cit., p. 225.

28. Riben, op. cit., ch. 3, p. 7.

29. Powledge, op. cit., p. 10.

30. Powledge, op. cit., p. 122.

Also, foster parents, once forbidden to adopt their foster children, now actually have preference in adopting them in forty-three states and the District of Columbia (Powledge, p. 58, citing a 1981 survey).

31. Meezan, Katz, and Russo, op. cit., p. 85.

There actually is a "good" reason for whites not to adopt black children. In 1962, the National Association of Black Social Workers issued a statement declaring that black youth had the right to their own cultural heritage. Black children compose 37 percent of those waiting for adoption, over two and a half times their proportion in the population, and those black children need to be adopted. But putting it on the basis of the child's interest is somewhat dangerous for the adopter's case, because one could argue that the most that good whites can do for black children is not to adopt one but to engage in political struggle against racism and poverty. It's not that the adopter doesn't want to help black (or Korean or Latin) children; it's that he wants to do it *his* way, regardless of whether it is the best way or whether the peoples in question want it done another way.

32. Powledge, op. cit., p. 69.

33. Powledge, op. cit., p. 34.

34. Powledge, op. cit., pp. 31–32.

35. Powledge, op. cit., p. 69.

36. Lifton, op. cit., p. 10.

37. Powledge, op. cit., p. 169.

38. Susan T. Viguers, *With Child: One Couple's Journey to Their Adopted Children* (New York: Harcourt Brace Jovanovich, 1986), pp. 58, 85.

39. Ibid.

40. Ibid., p. 215.

41. Ibid., p. 216.

42. Lifton, op. cit., p. 58.

43. Lifton, op. cit., p. 51.

44. Margaret Atwood, *The Handmaid's Tale* (New York: Houghton Mifflin Co., 1986).

45. Lifton, op. cit., p. 214.

46. Lifton, op. cit., pp. 214–15.

47. Meezan, Katz, and Russo, op. cit., p. 115.

48. Stephen B. Presser, "The Historical Background of the American Law of Adoption," 11 *Journal of Family Law* 443, 1971.

49. Powledge, op. cit., p. 6.

50. Lifton, op. cit., p. 10.

51. Eileen Simpson, "No Euphemisms: Call Them 'Orphans,' " *The New York Times*, May 1, 1987.

52. Lifton, op. cit., p. 44.

53. Germaine Greer, Introduction, *The Madwoman's Underclothes* (New York: Atlantic Monthly Press, 1986).

54. Ibid.

55. Ibid.

56. Powledge, op. cit., p. 169, quoting Betty Laning, adoption activist.

57. Benet, op cit, p. 185.

58. Marshall Schechter, "Observations on Adopted Children," *A.M.A. Archives on General Psychiatry* 3, July 1960; Marshall Schechter, M.D., et al., "Emotional Problems of the Adoptee," *Archives of General Psychiatry* 10, February 1964, cited by Lifton, op. cit., p. 44.

59. Marshall Schechter, talk at Adoption Forum, an Adoptee Group in Philadelphia, 1978, cited by Lifton, op. cit. at 44.

60. Florence Clothier, M.D., "The Psychology of the Adopted Child," *Mental Hygiene* 27, April 1943, cited by Lifton, op. cit., at 17, 44.

61. E. Wellisch, "Children Without Genealogy: A Problem of Adoption," *Mental Health* 13, 1952, cited by Lifton, op. cit., at 47–48.

62. Ibid.

63. H. J. Sants, "Genealogical Bewilderment in Children with Substitute Parents," *British Journal of Medical Psychology* 37, 1964, cited by Lifton, op. cit., at 48–50.

64. Steven Nickman, M.D., Harvard Medical School, Massachusetts General Hospital, letter dated October 19, 1986, to Harold J. Cassidy, Esq. re: Baby M case.

65. Remi J. Cadoret, et al., "Studies of Adoptees from Psychiatrically Disturbed Biological Parents II: Temperament, Hyperactive, Antisocial, and Developmental Variables," *The Journal of Pediatrics* 87, August 1975.

Lynn Cunningham, et al., "Studies of Adoptees from Psychiatrically Disturbed Biological Parents: Psychiatric Conditions in Childhood and Adolescence," *British Journal of Psychiatry* 126, 1975.

Raymond R. Crowe, M.D., "The Adopted Offspring of Women Criminal Offenders: A Study of Their Arrest Records," *Archives of General Psychiatry* 27, November 1972.

Barney Greenspan and Elizabeth J. Fleming, "The Effect of Adoption on Adolescent Development," paper delivered at American Orthopsychiatric Association, March 1975.

James J. Lawton, Jr., M.D., and Seymour Z. Gross, "Review of Psychiatric Literature on Adopted Children," *Archives of General Psychiatry* 11, December 1964.

Alexina M. McWhinnie, "The Adopted Child in Adolescence," in *Adolescence: Psychological Perspectives*, eds. Gerald Caplan and Serge Lebovici (New York: Basic Books, 1969).

Meezan, Katz, and Russo, op. cit.

Nickman, op. cit.

D. R. Offord, M.D., et al., "Presenting Symptomatology in Adopted Children," *Archives of General Psychiatry* 20, January 1969.

Powledge, op. cit.

N. M. Simon and A. G. Senturia, "Adoption and Psychiatric Illness," *American Journal of Psychiatry* 122, February 1966.

A. D. Sorosky, A. Baran, and R. Pannor, "Adoption and the Adolescent: An Overview," in *Adolescent Psychiatry*, eds. S. C. Feinstein and P. Giovacchini, vol. 5, J. Jason Aaronson, 1977.

J. Triseliotis, *In Search of Origins: The Experiences of Adopted People* (London: Routledge and Kegan Paul, 1973).

66. Nickman, op. cit.

67. Lifton, op. cit., pp. 34–35.

68. Gary Aylesworth, "The Doom Folk: Millions Now Living Will Never Die," San Francisco, 1987.

69. Gregory Armstrong, *Wanderers All*, cited by Lifton, op. cit., at 66.

70. Aylesworth, op. cit., p. 7.

71. Lifton, op. cit., p. 75.

72. Powledge, op. cit., p. 227.

73. Powledge, op. cit., pp. 255–58.

74. Aylesworth writes: "When I joined ALMA (Adoptees' Liberty Movement Association), I met a woman who, upon being reunited with her birth mother, discovered that they had both been looking for each other at the very same time and in the very same towns. When both birth mother and daughter were 'hearing voices,' the mother entered a church and saw a statue of the Virgin Mary. The Virgin Mary had a face that resembled the mother's face, but was ever so slightly different. After reuniting with her daughter, she realized it was her daughter's face that she saw. This encounter in a church took place at the same time her daughter was having 'Virgin Mary fantasies' in a mental hospital."

6: THE VERDICT, 1988

1. Slip Opinion, pp. 50–51 (citations omitted).

2. Slip Opinion, p. 80.

3. Slip Opinion, pp. 70–71, n. 17.

4. Slip Opinion, p. 84.

5. Slip Opinion, p. 79.

6. Slip Opinion, pp. 74–75.

7. Slip Opinion, p. 85.

8. Slip Opinion, pp. 76–77.

9. Slip Opinion, pp. 82–83.

10. Slip Opinion, p. 83.

11. Slip Opinion, p. 93.

12. Slip Opinion, p. 90.

13. Slip Opinion, p. 68, n. 16.

14. Judith Lewis Herman, *Father-Daughter Incest* (Cambridge, Mass.: Harvard University Press, 1981).

15. Michele Landsberg, *Globe and Mail* (Toronto), February 6, 1988.